Understanding Our Country

Understanding the Social Sciences Program

Frederick M. King

Herbert C. Rudman

LoDoris R. Leavell

Mary H. Butler
Mary Fields-Taylor
Victoria Larsen

Trudy McFarland
Roger Marchese
Jo Ann Ogunbambi

Jeanne N. Peterson
Carolyn Schmitz
Thomas F. Toomey

LAIDLAW BROTHERS • PUBLISHERS
A Division of Doubleday & Company, Inc.
RIVER FOREST, ILLINOIS

Irvine, California   Chamblee, Georgia   Dallas, Texas   Toronto, Canada

UNDERSTANDING THE SOCIAL SCIENCES PROGRAM	Understanding People Understanding Families Understanding Communities	Understanding Regions of the Earth Understanding Our Country Understanding the World

Project Director Wayne H. Talley / *Supervising Editor* Carole E. Murphy / *Staff Editors*
Karen K. Janowicz, Barbara E. Knous, Barbara Joan LeRoy / *Art Director* Gloria J. Muczynski /
Production Director LaVergne G. Niequist / *Photo Researcher* William A. Cassin /
Production Supervisor Kathleen Kasper / *Production Associate* Gary E. Baldwin / *Production Assistant*
Carolyn J. Ply / *Artists* Paul Hazelrigg, Frank Larocco, Donald Meighan, Donald Pitcher /
Cover Design Tak Murakami

PHOTO CREDITS

Abbot Hall, Board of Selectmen, 214. Alfa Studio, 194, 431. Alpha Photo Associates, Inc., 422. The American Museum of Natural History, painting by Arthur A. Jansson, 69. The Art Institute of Chicago, 377 (left). Artstreet, 12, 61, 115, 148 (bottom left), 243, 269, 326, 406. Authenticated News International, 416. D. R. Baston, 54 (left). Bethlehem Steel Company, 347 (right). The Bettmann Archive, 24, 52, 58, 96, 106, 108, 118, 126, 131, 132, 139, 141 (left), 144, 185, 203, 255, 259, 263 (top), 265, 285 (both), 286, 302 (top), 317 (top), 330, 331 (bottom), 335 (bottom), 339, 342, 347 (left), 348, 364, 374 (bottom), 375 (center), 384 (November 9, 1932, and January 24, 1973), 399. Margaret Bourke-White, Life Magazine © 1945 Time, Inc., 412. The British Museum, 85 (left). Brown Brothers, 362, 371, 373, 397 (top), 403. The Butler Institute of American Art, 288. Camerique, 81, 200 (top), 393 (left). The Charleston Library Society, 179. The Chicago Historical Society, 379. Courtesy of Children's Television Workshop, 455 (top). Cincinnati Art Museum, 304. The Cleveland Museum of Art, The Hinman B. Hurlbut Collection, 299. Colonial Williamsburg, 178, 190, 207. Colorado Historical Society, 291 (bottom right), 315. Culver Pictures, Inc., 112, 221 (left), 224, 239, 284, 296 (both), 300, 320, 324, 327, 332, 374 (top), 375 (top and bottom), 380, 386 (left), 391, 395, 398, 400, 410 (right), 413 (bottom). Currier & Ives, 336. Robert Davis, 148 (top right), 153 (top), 167 (top). Robert Davis/J. M. McLean, 111 (top). Dr. E. R. Degginger, 370. The Denver Art Museum, 86 (left). A. Devaney, Inc., 429. De Wys, Inc., 156. De Wys, Inc./Bell, 367. De Wys, Inc./H. Byram, 71. De Wys, Inc./Everett C. Johnson, 151. De Wys, Inc./Wasinski, 457 (top). De Wys, Inc./Rocky Weldon, 457 (bottom). Walt Disney Productions, 455 (bottom). E. I. du Pont de Nemours & Co., Wilmington, Delaware, 421. Editorial Photocolor Archives, Inc., 225 (bottom), 232, 313 (top), 450 (right). Harrison Forman, 77 (bottom), 153 (bottom), 158 (top). Thomas Gilcrease Institute of American History and Art, 68, 317 (bottom), 352. Globe Photos, Inc./Robert Moulton, 148 (top left). The Granger Collection, 258, 386 (right). Group 3 Studios, 162. John Hancock Mutual Life Insurance Company, 158 (bottom). Grant Heilman, 55 (top right), 63. Grant Heilman/Alan Pitcairn, 55 (bottom left and bottom right). Historical Pictures Service, 101, 105, 111 (bottom), 122, 124, 141 (right), 143, 160 (inset), 165, 166, 174, 188, 198, 200 (bottom and bottom inset), 206, 209, 211 (left), 215, 219 (all), 225 (top), 241, 242 (top), 254, 257, 260, 275 (bottom), 277, 278, 279, 291 (top), 295, 301, 302 (bottom), 303 (left and center), 310, 311, 322, 335 (top), 338, 340, 341, 345, 349, 350, 353, 354, 358, 365 (both), 378, 384 (August 18, 1920; October 25, 1929; August 15, 1945; April 12, 1955), 388, 405 (left), 408, 427. Historical Society of Pennsylvania, 273. Ronald Holle, 36. The Image Bank/John Lewis Stage, 168. Imperial War Museum, painting by Sir William Orpen, 372. Hugo Jaeger, Life Magazine © 1938 Time, Inc., 410 (left). Jefferson National Expansion Memorial, 268. Brent Jones, 440 (bottom left). Kennedy Galleries, Inc., New York, 235. 252. M. Knoedler & Co., Inc., 292. Lambert Photos, 136, 170, 196, 221 (right). Robert Larocco, 128. The Library of Congress, 417, 462 (all), 463 (all), 464 (Warren G. Harding through Dwight D. Eisenhower). Tony Linck, 64. Los Angeles County Museum of Art, 357. McCormick Collection, State Historical Society of Wisconsin, 313 (bottom). Franklin McMahon, Jr., 54 (right). Magnum/Burt Glinn, 428. The Mariner's Museum, 152. Maryland Historical Society, 272. Massachusetts Department of Commerce and Development, Division of Tourism, 263 (bottom). Gloria Muczynski, 109, 135, 411. Museum of the American Indian, Heye Foundation, New York, 74, 79, 87 (both). Museum of Art, Rhode Island School of Design, Jesse Metcalf Fund, 298 (right). Museum of the City of New York, 308. Museum of Fine Arts, Boston, Herman and Zoe Oliver Sherman Fund, 167 (bottom, detail from "Pat Lyon at the Forge" by John Neagle). Museum of Fine Arts, Boston, 377 (right). Museum of New Mexico, Chapman Collection, 78. NASA, 92. The National Maritime Museum, London, 154. National Oceanic and Atmospheric Administration, 14. Newfoundland and Labrador Tourist Development Office, St. Johns, 98. The New-York Historical Society, 275 (top), 344. The New York Public Library, 182. New York State Museum, 86 (right). Charles O'Rear, 77 (top). Oregon Historical Society, 318. Peabody Museum, 80 (detail from "Indian Hunters" by Rindesbacher). Peace Corps Photo, 448. Peale Museum,

(Photo Credits continued on page 480)

ISBN-0-8445-6505-9

Copyright © 1979 by Laidlaw Brothers, Publishers
A Division of Doubleday & Company, Inc.

CONTENTS

7

LIST OF MAPS

LIST OF CHARTS AND GRAPHS

Unit 1

The Land and the People

Think of snowy mountain peaks where the air is clear and cold. Picture a hot, dry desert under the blazing sun. Think of rich farm fields at harvest time. Think of roaring ocean tides on rocky shores or of the silence of a deep forest. These things are all part of our country.

Think of our people. There are people with different backgrounds, different ideas, and different ways of life. But they are all Americans. This book will help you understand the story of our country. You will learn about the first people who lived here. And you will study life in the United States today. But in order to understand the story of our country, you must know something about the land and the people.

In this unit you will find out different ways of studying the United States and its people. You will find answers to the following questions:

What can you learn about our country from globes and maps?

How are charts, time lines, and graphs used to present facts about our country and its people?

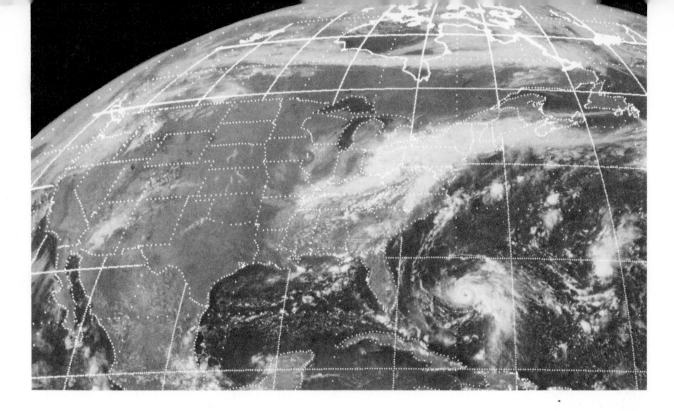

CHAPTER 1

Looking at the United States

1. **Viewing our country on globes**
2. **Viewing our country on maps**
3. **Studying our country with charts**
4. **Interpreting our country through a time line and graphs**

The picture on this page shows one way of looking at the United States. This picture of our country was taken from space. From the picture you can see the shape of our country's land. And you can get some idea of the size of our country. What other things might you want to know about our country that can't be seen in this picture?

Globes and maps are helpful in showing what our country's land looks like. They may also show how the land is used. But some facts about our country can't be presented on globes or maps. What other ways can you think of for presenting facts about our country?

In this chapter you will find out some ways of presenting facts about the United States. And you will learn some skills that will help you find out more about our country.

1

Viewing our country on globes

Parallels of latitude The east-west lines on a globe are called **lines of latitude.** Each line forms a circle. These lines are called **parallels** [PAR-uh-LEHLZ] because they run in the same direction, but they never meet.

Each of these lines has a number. The number tells how far north or south of the equator a place is. Look at the picture on this page. How far north is A? How far south is B?

Meridians of longitude The north-south lines on a globe are called **lines of longitude.** Each line forms a half circle from the North Pole to the South Pole. These lines are called **meridians** [muh-RIHD-ee-uhnz].

Each of these lines has a number. The number tells how far east or west of the prime meridian a place is. Look again at the picture on this page. What number does the prime meridian have?

Locating places on a globe Lines of latitude and lines of longitude cross one another. This makes it easy to find places on a globe. Use the picture on this page to find the letter at 30° N, 30° W. What letter is at 60° S, 60° E?

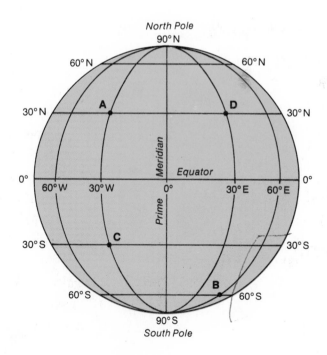

Northern Hemisphere

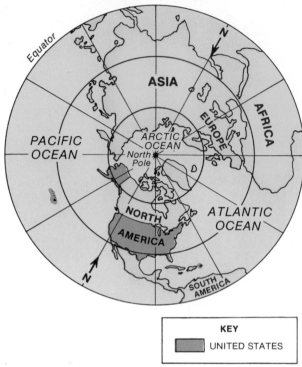

KEY
UNITED STATES

Southern Hemisphere

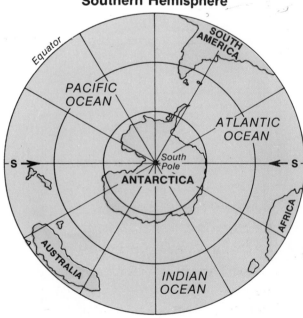

Lines of latitude and lines of longitude are not really on the earth. But they are put on globes to help people find places. To find places in your neighborhood, you might use a street address. A street address is generally made up of a house or apartment number and a street name. To find places on a globe, you can use an "earth address." An "earth address" is made up of two numbers. The first number stands for a line of latitude. The second number stands for a line of longitude. The "earth address" is the point at which the two lines cross. Do you think all places on the earth have an "earth address?" Why or why not?

The four hemispheres of the earth The equator is halfway between the North Pole and the South Pole. This line divides the earth into a northern half and a southern half. Each half of the earth is called a **hemisphere.** The land and water between the equator and the North Pole are in the Northern Hemisphere. What land and water are in the Southern Hemisphere? Look at the pictures on this page. Is our country in the Northern Hemisphere or the Southern Hemisphere?

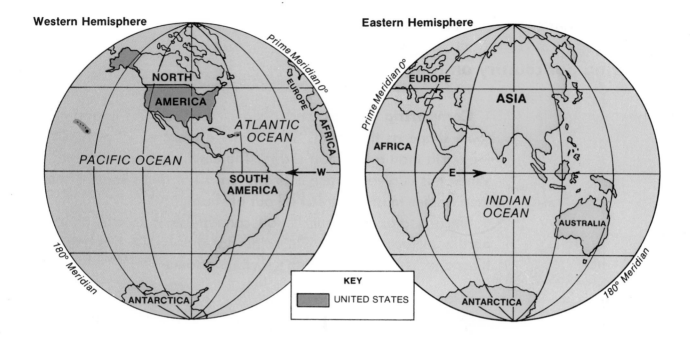

Western Hemisphere

NORTH
AMERICA

ATLANTIC
OCEAN

PACIFIC OCEAN

SOUTH
AMERICA

Prime Meridian 0°

EUROPE

AFRICA

W

180° Meridian

ANTARCTICA

Eastern Hemisphere

Prime Meridian 0°

EUROPE

ASIA

AFRICA

E

INDIAN
OCEAN

AUSTRALIA

180° Meridian

ANTARCTICA

KEY

UNITED STATES

The earth can also be divided in half another way. The prime meridian and the 180° line divide the earth into a western half and an eastern half. The land and water from 0° *west* to 180° are in the Western Hemisphere. The land and water from 0° *east* to 180° are in the Eastern Hemisphere. Look at the pictures on this page. Is our country in the Western Hemisphere or the Eastern Hemisphere?

wrap ·up

- How are lines of latitude and lines of longitude used to locate places on a globe?
- How is the earth divided into hemispheres?
- Between what lines of latitude and longitude would you find the "earth address" of the place where you live?

2

Viewing our country on maps

Comparing globes and maps A globe has almost the same shape as the earth. So it shows a more exact picture of the earth than a flat map shows. The earth's surface is curved. When this curved surface is drawn on a flat map, some of the land bodies must be stretched out of shape.

Since a globe is round, you cannot use it to see all the earth's surface at once. But some flat maps, like the one on this page, show all the earth's surface at once.

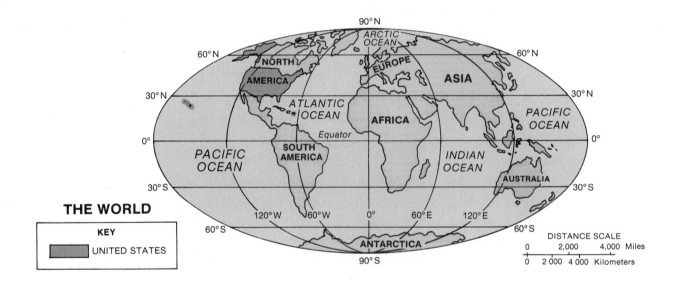

THE WORLD

KEY
UNITED STATES

Using map symbols Things that stand for other things are called **symbols.** Mapmakers use symbols to stand for the things they want to show on maps. Sometimes color is used as a symbol. Lines, dots, stars, and squares are also used on maps to stand for different things.

A symbol may stand for different things on different maps. So you must look at a **map key** to find out what a symbol means. Find the map key for the map on this page. What do the circled stars stand for? Why do you think it is important to look at the map key before you use a map?

Using map scale   Mapmakers draw maps to **scale**. This means that a small measure on a map stands for a larger measure on the earth. You can use the **distance scale** on a map to find out what measure the mapmaker used.

The scale for the map of North America on this page is 1 inch = about 1,000 miles. Using this same scale, 1 centimeter = about 630 kilometers. Compare the scale on this map with the scale for the world map on page 18. An inch (centimeter) stands for a shorter distance on the map of North America than on the world map. So the map of North America is drawn to a larger scale than the world map is.

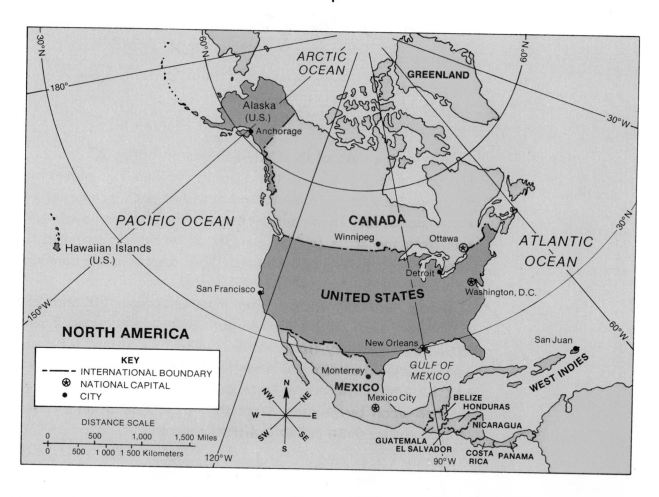

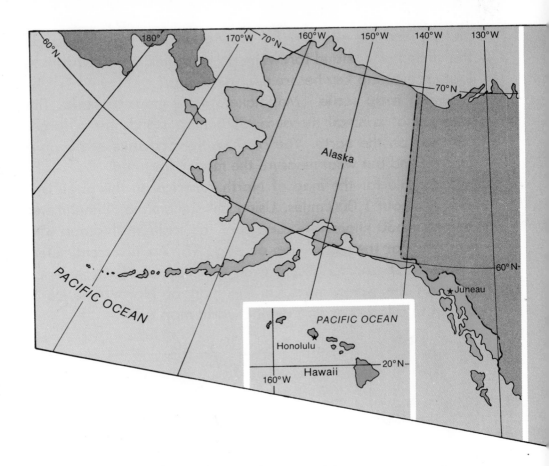

Look at the map of the United States on pages 20 and 21. Use your ruler to measure the distance between two places on the map. Look at the scale to find out what each inch or centimeter stands for. Then multiply the number of miles or kilometers from the scale by the number of inches or centimeters between the places you measured. Your answer is the number of miles or kilometers between the places.

Using political maps The map on pages 20 and 21 shows how people have divided our country into states. Each state has **boundary lines,** or lines where the state begins or ends. Notice that some of these lines follow something physical, such as a river or a lake. But most of these lines were decided upon by people. Maps that show how people have divided the land are called **political maps.**

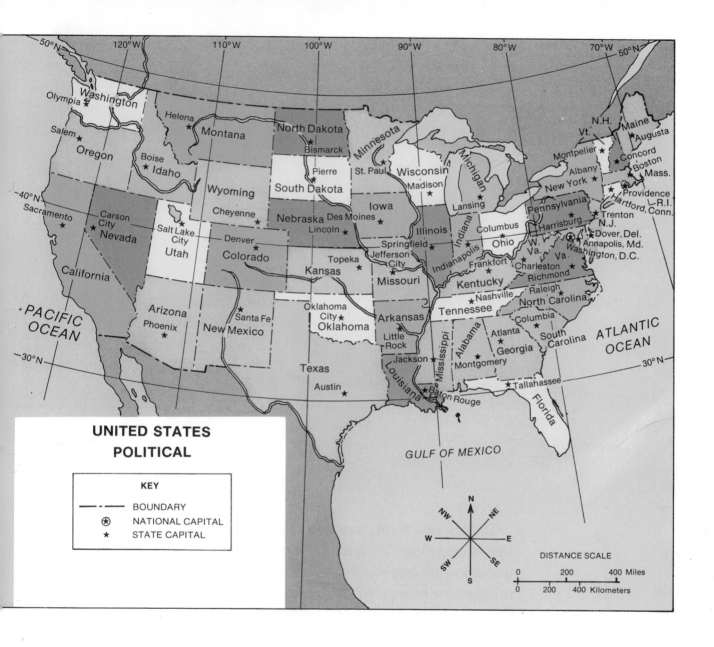

UNITED STATES POLITICAL

KEY
- — · — · — BOUNDARY
- ⊛ NATIONAL CAPITAL
- ★ STATE CAPITAL

DISTANCE SCALE

| 0 | 200 | 400 Miles |

| 0 | 200 | 400 Kilometers |

This map also shows where people have built some cities. It shows the **capital,** or seat of government, for each state. And it shows the capital for our whole country. The map key helps you know which cities are state capitals and which city is our country's capital.

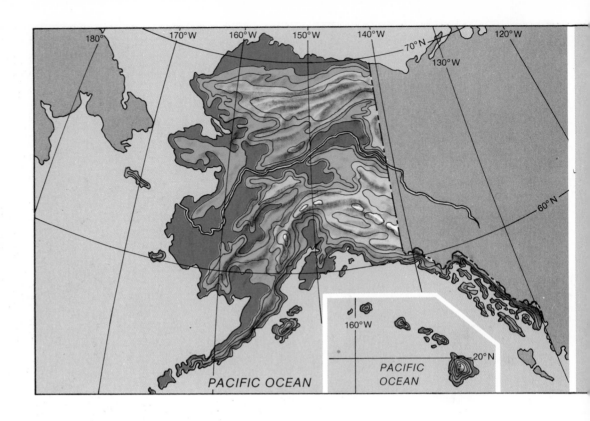

Using physical maps   Look at the map of the United States on pages 22 and 23. This map shows the major rivers and lakes of our country. It also shows some of the mountains of our country. What lakes form part of the northern boundary of our country? What mountains are found in the eastern part of our country? Maps that show how the land looks are called **physical maps.** How might such maps be useful to you?

Color is used on this map to show the height of the land. The map key helps you find out what each color stands for. What color on this map stands for land that is at sea level? What color stands for the highest land?

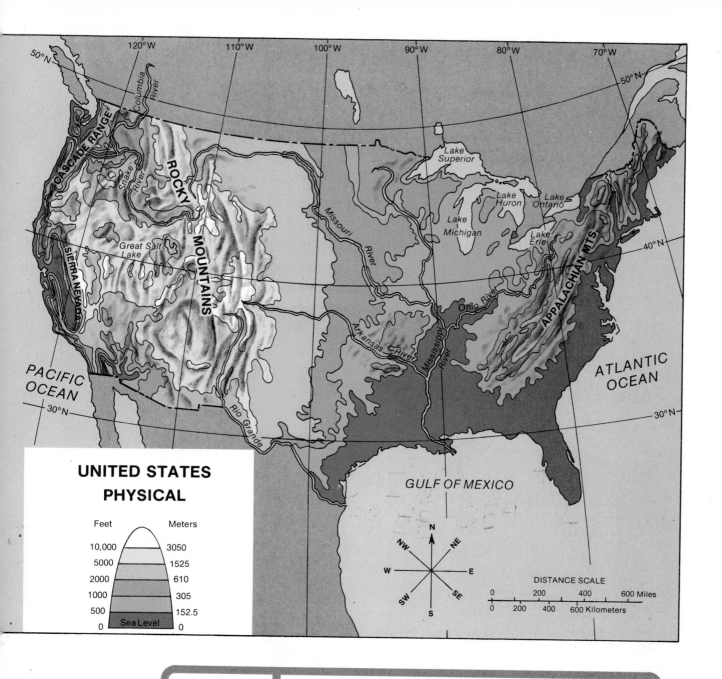

UNITED STATES PHYSICAL

Feet		Meters
10,000		3050
5000		1525
2000		610
1000		305
500		152.5
0	Sea Level	0

DISTANCE SCALE

wrap
•up

- How are maps more useful than globes?
- How are map keys and distance scales used?
- Why might you use a political map of our country?

A Biographical Sketch

Mapping a nation

Major John Wesley Powell took part in the great task of mapping America's West. He led a group of explorers down the canyons of the Colorado River. On that journey Powell and his group mapped the last unknown part of our country.

Major Powell used his map to fight for better land use in the West. The

western part of our country receives little rainfall. But Powell had a plan for dividing the land so that farmers could get an equal share of the water supply.

In 1881 Major Powell was made director of the U.S. Geological Survey. He was put in charge of our country's map work. Powell saw the need for a detailed map of our country. So he asked the government for money to carry out his plan of making a set of maps. Each map would show a small part of our country. Powell wanted to make the maps easy to understand so that everyone could use them.

Under Major Powell's direction several groups began the task of mapping our country. Powell helped prepare a set of map symbols to be used by each group. Why do you think Powell wanted all the groups to use the same map symbols?

John Wesley Powell's ideas are still being used today. And the task of making detailed maps of all parts of our country is not yet finished. But the maps are being prepared. And they are being drawn according to the plan that Major Powell began nearly one hundred years ago.

3

Studying our country
with charts

Using charts   People use a **chart** to find facts quickly. A chart is made up of columns and rows. The columns go up and down the page, and the rows go across the page.

People put many different kinds of facts on charts. Look at the charts in this lesson. Each chart shows facts about our country. Which chart would you use to find out who was President from 1901 to 1909? Which chart would you use to find out the name of the largest city in Idaho? Which chart would you use to find out how far Seattle, Washington, is from Miami, Florida?

Finding facts on charts   Look at Chart 1. The first column lists the name of each state. The second column tells the date that each place became a state and the order in which the states entered the Union. The third column tells the **population,** or about how many people live in each state. What do the fourth and fifth columns of this chart show?

CHART 1
SOME FACTS ABOUT THE STATES

State	Entered Union	Population (1975 Figures)	Natural Resources	Largest City
Alabama	1819 22nd state	3,614,000	Coal, iron, petroleum, forests	Birmingham
Alaska	1959 49th state	352,000	Petroleum, gold, natural gas, fish, forests	Anchorage
Arizona	1912 48th state	2,224,000	Copper, sand, gravel, silver	Phoenix

State	Entered Union	Population (1975 Figures)	Natural Resources	Largest City
Arkansas	1836 25th state	2,116,000	Bauxite, petroleum, forests	Little Rock
California	1850 31st state	21,185,000	Petroleum, natural gas, tungsten, forests	Los Angeles
Colorado	1876 38th state	2,534,000	Coal, natural gas, petroleum, uranium	Denver
Connecticut	1788 5th state	3,095,000	Stone, sand, gravel	Bridgeport
Delaware	1787 1st state	579,000	Sand, gravel, stone, fish	Wilmington
Florida	1845 27th state	8,357,000	Phosphate, limestone, fish	Jacksonville
Georgia	1788 4th state	4,926,000	Marble, clay, forests	Atlanta
Hawaii	1959 50th state	865,000	Bauxite, stone	Honolulu
Idaho	1890 43rd state	820,000	Silver, lead, zinc, forests	Boise
Illinois	1818 21st state	11,145,000	Coal, petroleum, clay, stone	Chicago
Indiana	1816 19th state	5,311,000	Limestone, coal, clay, petroleum	Indianapolis
Iowa	1846 29th state	2,870,000	Coal, limestone, sand, gravel	Des Moines
Kansas	1861 34th state	2,267,000	Petroleum, natural gas, forests	Wichita
Kentucky	1792 15th state	3,396,000	Coal, petroleum, natural gas, forests	Louisville
Louisiana	1812 18th state	3,791,000	Natural gas, salt, petroleum, sulfur	New Orleans
Maine	1820 23rd state	1,059,000	Granite, forests, fish	Portland
Maryland	1788 7th state	4,098,000	Stone, forests, fish	Baltimore

State	Entered Union	Population (1975 Figures)	Natural Resources	Largest City
Massachusetts	1788 6th state	5,828,000	Stone, sand, gravel, fish	Boston
Michigan	1837 26th state	9,157,000	Iron, copper, salt, forests	Detroit
Minnesota	1858 32nd state	3,926,000	Iron, granite, forests	Minneapolis
Mississippi	1817 20th state	2,346,000	Petroleum, clay, natural gas, forests	Jackson
Missouri	1821 24th state	4,763,000	Lead, limestone, coal, clay	St. Louis
Montana	1889 41st state	748,000	Petroleum, copper, coal	Billings
Nebraska	1867 37th state	1,546,000	Petroleum, natural gas, sand, gravel	Omaha
Nevada	1864 36th state	592,000	Copper, gold, tungsten, silver	Las Vegas
New Hampshire	1788 9th state	818,000	Granite, gravel, forests	Manchester
New Jersey	1787 3rd state	7,316,000	Stone, sand, gravel, fish	Newark
New Mexico	1912 47th state	1,147,000	Uranium, coal, petroleum, natural gas, copper	Albuquerque
New York	1788 11th state	18,120,000	Talc, salt, zinc, lead, clay	New York City
North Carolina	1789 12th state	5,451,000	Feldspar, phosphate, sand, gravel, forests	Charlotte
North Dakota	1889 39th state	635,000	Petroleum, coal, clay	Fargo
Ohio	1803 17th state	10,759,000	Petroleum, coal, salt, natural gas	Cleveland
Oklahoma	1907 46th state	2,712,000	Petroleum, coal, natural gas, stone	Oklahoma City
Oregon	1859 33rd state	2,288,000	Stone, nickel, forests, fish	Portland

State	Entered Union	Population (1975 Figures)	Natural Resources	Largest City
Pennsylvania	1787 2nd state	11,827,000	Coal, limestone, petroleum, natural gas	Philadelphia
Rhode Island	1790 13th state	927,000	Granite, forests, fish	Providence
South Carolina	1788 8th state	2,818,000	Kaolin, granite, limestone, sand, forests	Columbia
South Dakota	1889 40th state	683,000	Gold, copper, iron, lead, silver, uranium	Sioux Falls
Tennessee	1796 16th state	4,188,000	Zinc, marble, coal, phosphate, forests	Memphis
Texas	1845 28th state	12,237,000	Petroleum, natural gas, salt, sulfur	Houston
Utah	1896 45th state	1,206,000	Copper, gold, silver, lead, coal, petroleum	Salt Lake City
Vermont	1791 14th state	471,000	Marble, granite, talc, forests	Burlington
Virginia	1788 10th state	4,967,000	Coal, clay, stone, fish	Norfolk
Washington	1889 42nd state	3,544,000	Coal, gold, lead, forests, fish	Seattle
West Virginia	1863 35th state	1,803,000	Coal, natural gas, petroleum, limestone, forests	Huntington
Wisconsin	1848 30th state	4,607,000	Sand, gravel, iron, stone, forests, fish	Milwaukee
Wyoming	1890 44th state	374,000	Coal, petroleum, uranium, iron	Cheyenne

Chart 2 shows some facts about the Presidents of our country. The third column of the chart tells the state in which each person lived when that person became President. When was Franklin D. Roosevelt the head of our government? What was the home state of Dwight D. Eisenhower? Which leaders came from the state of Illinois?

CHART 2
PRESIDENTS OF THE UNITED STATES

President	Years in Office	Home State*
George Washington	1789–1797	Virginia
John Adams	1797–1801	Massachusetts
Thomas Jefferson	1801–1809	Virginia
James Madison	1809–1817	Virginia
James Monroe	1817–1825	Virginia
John Quincy Adams	1825–1829	Massachusetts
Andrew Jackson	1829–1837	Tennessee
Martin Van Buren	1837–1841	New York
William Henry Harrison	1841–1841	Ohio
John Tyler	1841–1845	Virginia
James K. Polk	1845–1849	Tennessee
Zachary Taylor	1849–1850	Louisiana
Millard Fillmore	1850–1853	New York
Franklin Pierce	1853–1857	New Hampshire
James Buchanan	1857–1861	Pennsylvania
Abraham Lincoln	1861–1865	Illinois
Andrew Johnson	1865–1869	Tennessee
Ulysses S. Grant	1869–1877	Illinois
Rutherford B. Hayes	1877–1881	Ohio
James A. Garfield	1881–1881	Ohio
Chester A. Arthur	1881–1885	New York
Grover Cleveland	1885–1889	New York
Benjamin Harrison	1889–1893	Ohio
Grover Cleveland	1893–1897	New York
William McKinley	1897–1901	Ohio
Theodore Roosevelt	1901–1909	New York
William Howard Taft	1909–1913	Ohio
Woodrow Wilson	1913–1921	New Jersey
Warren G. Harding	1921–1923	Ohio
Calvin Coolidge	1923–1929	Massachusetts
Herbert C. Hoover	1929–1933	California
Franklin D. Roosevelt	1933–1945	New York
Harry S Truman	1945–1953	Missouri
Dwight D. Eisenhower	1953–1961	New York
John F. Kennedy	1961–1963	Massachusetts
Lyndon B. Johnson	1963–1969	Texas
Richard M. Nixon	1969–1974	New York
Gerald R. Ford	1974–1977	Michigan
James E. Carter	1977–	Georgia

*State in which the person was living when elected

CHART 3
HIGHWAY DISTANCE BETWEEN SELECTED CITIES

	Bismarck, North Dakota	Chicago, Illinois	Miami, Florida	Phoenix, Arizona	Portland, Maine	Seattle, Washington	
Bismarck, North Dakota		831 1 330	2,150 3 440	1,463 2 341	1,873 2 997	1,195 1 912	Miles Kilometers
Chicago, Illinois	831 1 330		1,377 2 203	1,713 2 741	1,042 1 667	2,031 3 250	Miles Kilometers
Miami, Florida	2,150 3 440	1,377 2 203		2,298 3 677	1,606 2 570	3,273 5 237	Miles Kilometers
Phoenix, Arizona	1,463 2 341	1,713 2 741	2,298 3 677		2,699 4 318	1,437 2 299	Miles Kilometers
Portland, Maine	1,873 2 997	1,042 1 667	1,606 2 570	2,699 4 318		3,055 4 888	Miles Kilometers
Seattle, Washington	1,195 1 912	2,031 3 250	3,273 5 237	1,437 2 299	3,055 4 888		Miles Kilometers

Chart 3 shows the highway distance between some cities in our country. You will notice that each city is listed at the left side *and* at the top of the chart. Find Chicago, Illinois, at the left side of the chart. Now find Portland, Maine, at the top of the chart. What is the highway distance between these cities? Now find Portland, Maine, at the left side of the chart, and find Chicago, Illinois, at the top of the chart. Is the highway distance between these two cities the same as before? Why is this so? Why do you think there are blank spaces on the chart?

wrap ·up

- What kind of information is shown on charts?
- How are facts arranged on charts?
- Why might you use a chart?

4

Interpreting our country
through a time line and graphs

Using a time line   People use a **time line** to show dates in our country's history. A time line stands for a certain length of time. The marks on a time line show dates on which important things happened. The distance between the marks stands for the length of time between the dates.

Look at the time line on this page. It shows the dates of some of our country's spaceflights. When was the first United States spaceflight? How many years after the first United States spaceflight was the first moon landing?

SOME UNITED STATES SPACEFLIGHTS, 1961–1977

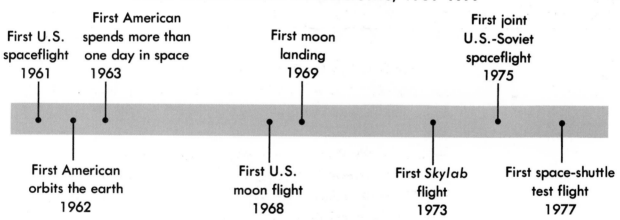

First U.S.
spaceflight
1961

First American
spends more than
one day in space
1963

First moon
landing
1969

First joint
U.S.-Soviet
spaceflight
1975

First American
orbits the earth
1962

First U.S.
moon flight
1968

First *Skylab*
flight
1973

First space-shuttle
test flight
1977

Using graphs   A drawing that shows numbers in a way that is easy to understand is called a **graph.** People use graphs to compare certain kinds of information. Some graphs compare amounts. Others show changes in amounts over a certain length of time.

The title of a graph helps you know what kind of facts are shown on the graph. Look at the titles of the graphs in this

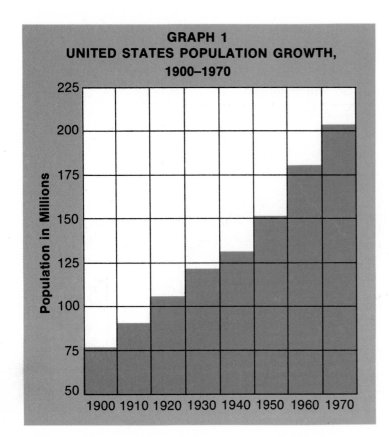

GRAPH 1
UNITED STATES POPULATION GROWTH,
1900–1970

Population in Millions

225
200
175
150
125
100
75
50

1900 1910 1920 1930 1940 1950 1960 1970

lesson. Which graph would you use to compare the growth of Philadelphia and Detroit from 1920 to 1970? What might you learn from Graph 1?

Different kinds of graphs Each graph in this lesson helps you find out something about our country. Look at Graph 1 on this page. It is called a *bar graph*. Each bar stands for the number of people living in the United States at a certain time. You can use this graph to see how the population changed from 1900 to 1970. About how many more people lived in the United States in 1960 than in 1950?

Graph 2 on page 33 is a *pictograph*. You can use it to compare the **urban,** or city, population with the **rural,** or farm and small town, population of the United States. How can you tell what each figure stands for? Some of the figures are not finished. What do you think they stand for?

Look at Graph 3 on page 33. It is called a *line graph*. You can use it to compare the number of people living in five cities of our country. You can also see how the population of each city changed from 1920 to 1970. Which city had the fewest people in 1920? Which city had the fewest people in 1970? About how many more people lived in New York than in Chicago in 1940?

GRAPH 2
URBAN AND RURAL POPULATION OF THE UNITED STATES, 1890–1970

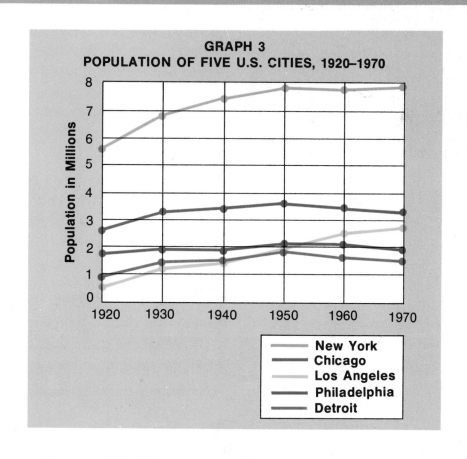

1890	
1910	
1930	
1950	
1970	

Each 👤 = 10 Million People Living in Urban Communities
Each 👤 = 10 Million People Living in Rural Communities

GRAPH 3
POPULATION OF FIVE U.S. CITIES, 1920–1970

Population in Millions

1920 1930 1940 1950 1960 1970

— New York
— Chicago
— Los Angeles
— Philadelphia
— Detroit

GRAPH 4
UNITED STATES USE OF PETROLEUM

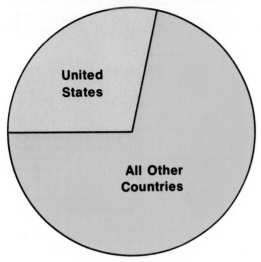

The graphs on this page are *circle graphs*. Graph 4 shows the United States use of **petroleum** [puh-TROH-lee-uhm], or oil. The whole circle stands for all the oil that is used by all the countries of the earth. The blue part of the circle shows how much of the oil is used by the United States. Graph 5 shows how much of the world's oil supply is found in the United States. Is the United States oil supply larger or smaller than the amount of oil used by the United States? How does this fact help explain the need to **conserve**, or save, oil in our country?

GRAPH 5
UNITED STATES PETROLEUM SUPPLY

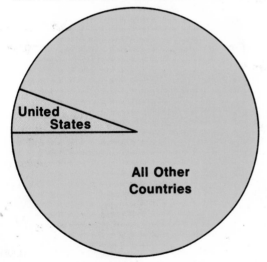

wrap ·up

- What does a time line show?
- What are some uses of graphs?
- Why might you use graphs?

Chapter-End Activities

The chapter-end activities may be done by writing the questions or statements and the answers on a separate sheet of paper or by writing just the answers on a separate sheet of paper, whichever your teacher desires.

Words and Terms

parallels of latitude	chart
meridians of longitude	population
hemisphere	urban
map key	petroleum
physical maps	

1. The _____ of a place is the number of people who live there.
2. East-west lines on a globe are called _____.
3. _____ show how the land looks.
4. Half the earth is called a _____.
5. North-south lines on a globe are called _____.
6. Symbols used on a map are explained in a _____.
7. A _____ shows facts in an organized way.
8. A graph might help you compare the amount of _____, or oil, used by different countries.

Fact Recall

1. A (globe, time line) shows when events in history took place.
2. The number of miles or kilometers between two places is shown on a (distance scale, map key).
3. A (political map, chart) shows how people have divided our country into states.
4. To get an understanding of the shape of the earth, you would use a (graph, globe).
5. A (graph, map key) might show how the population of a city changed over a certain length of time.

Concepts and Understandings

1. What kinds of information about our country can be learned from globes and maps?
2. How are parallels of latitude and meridians of longitude used to locate places in our country?
3. How are time lines useful in the study of our country's history?
4. Why do people use charts and graphs to present facts about our country?

CHAPTER 2

Our Country's Geography and People

1. Our country's climates
2. Our country's land
3. Our country's people

Look at the picture on this page. How would you describe this part of our country? How is this person using the land? The study of the earth and how people use the earth is called **geography** [jee-AHG-ruh-fee]. In this chapter you will learn about the geography of our country. You will find out what the weather is like in different parts of our country. And you will find out about the water and the land of the United States. Why do you think these things are important? You will also find out some facts about our country's people. You will learn where people live and some reasons why they live there. What other things might you want to know about the people of the United States?

Our country's climates

Describing climate The kind of weather a place has over a long time is called **climate**. Climate depends in part on latitude. Places that are far from the equator generally have a colder climate than places that are near it. The height of the land is also important. Places on highlands are generally cooler than places on lowlands.

The climate of a place is described in terms of **temperature** and **precipitation**. Temperature is how hot or cold a place is. Precipitation is water that falls to the earth, generally as rain or snow.

Many different climates Our country has many different climates. Look at the map on this page. Each color on the map stands for a different kind of climate.

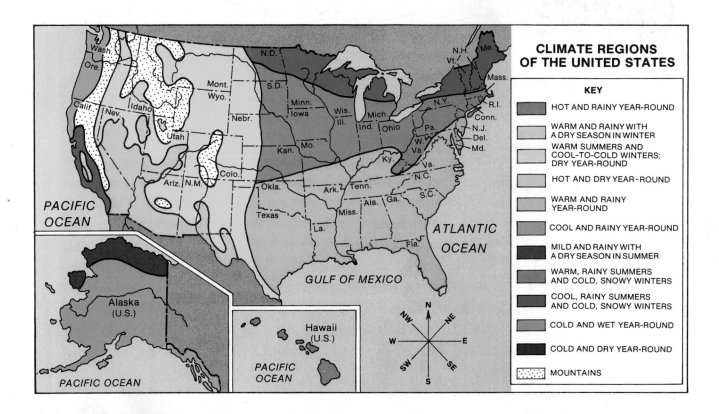

CLIMATE REGIONS OF THE UNITED STATES

KEY

- HOT AND RAINY YEAR-ROUND
- WARM AND RAINY WITH A DRY SEASON IN WINTER
- WARM SUMMERS AND COOL-TO-COLD WINTERS; DRY YEAR-ROUND
- HOT AND DRY YEAR-ROUND
- WARM AND RAINY YEAR-ROUND
- COOL AND RAINY YEAR-ROUND
- MILD AND RAINY WITH A DRY SEASON IN SUMMER
- WARM, RAINY SUMMERS AND COLD, SNOWY WINTERS
- COOL, RAINY SUMMERS AND COLD, SNOWY WINTERS
- COLD AND WET YEAR-ROUND
- COLD AND DRY YEAR-ROUND
- MOUNTAINS

If you live in the northeast United States, you are likely to have cold, snowy winters and cool summers. But if you live in the Southeast, you are likely to have warm weather and plenty of rainfall year-round. People who live in the southwest United States have a warm, dry climate. But people who live in the Northwest are likely to have plenty of rain. People who live in northern Alaska have a cold, dry climate. People who live in Hawaii have a hot, rainy climate. What kind of climate do you live in?

How climate affects people   The way people live often has something to do with the kind of climate in which they live. How do you think climate affects people's needs for clothing and housing? How might climate affect the kinds of things that people can do outdoors?

Climate has a lot to do with what grows in different parts of our country. Most crops depend on a certain amount of precipitation. The eastern half of our country receives more rainfall than the western half. How does this help explain why much of our country's farmland is in the East?

Temperature is also important to the growing of crops. Foods such as potatoes and apples need cool temperatures. But oranges and grapefruits grow best in warm temperatures. Why are such matters important in helping people decide what crops to grow?

Climate and land use   Look at the map on page 39. It shows some ways in which people use our country's land. Notice that much of the land around the Great Lakes is used for industry and trade. This land use does not depend on climate. What other land use on this map does not depend on climate?

Climate does help people decide how to use the land in different parts of our country. How do people use most of the land in the western part of our country? What use do they make of most of the land in Alaska? What two uses do they make of most of the land in Hawaii?

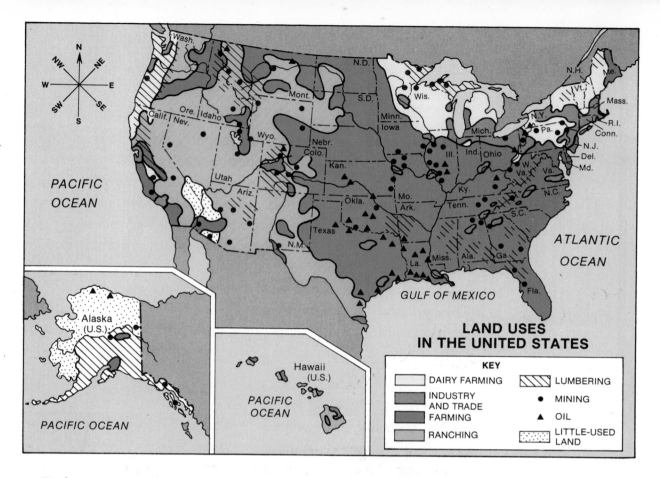

LAND USES IN THE UNITED STATES

KEY

☐ DAIRY FARMING	▨ LUMBERING
▨ INDUSTRY AND TRADE	● MINING
▨ FARMING	▲ OIL
▨ RANCHING	▨ LITTLE-USED LAND

Today people do not depend on climate as much as they did in the past. Today they use **irrigation** [IHR-uh-GAY-shuhn], or the bringing of water to farm fields, in dry parts of our country. How might this make it possible to grow crops in the western part of the United States? What other changes in our way of life have made it easier for people to live and work in different climates?

wrap·up

- What is climate?
- How does climate affect the way people use our country's land?
- How is climate important to people where you live?

Our country's land

Waterways and ports   Our country depends on shipping for much of its trade. The United States has a long coastline with many bays that make fine harbors for oceangoing ships. Many **ports,** or harbor cities, have been built near these bays. Look at the map on this page. Find some of our country's ocean ports. Why do you think these ports are important to trade with other countries?

Our country also has outstanding inland waterways. Find Chicago and Duluth on the map on this page. Oceangoing ships can sail up the St. Lawrence River and through the Great Lakes to these inland ports. Why do you think this is important to our country's trade?

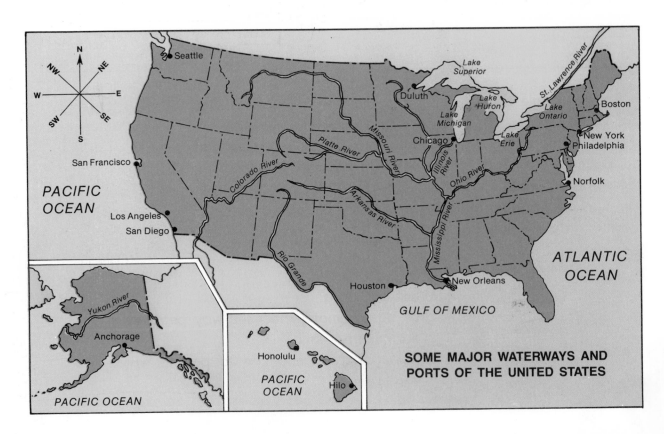

SOME MAJOR WATERWAYS AND PORTS OF THE UNITED STATES

The Mississippi River is an important waterway in our country. Its **source**—the place where a river begins—is in Minnesota. Its **mouth**—the place where a river flows into a larger body of water—is in Louisiana.

A river that flows into a larger river is called a **tributary.** The Ohio River and the Illinois River are tributaries of the Mississippi River. Heavy goods, such as coal and iron ore, can be carried more cheaply on water than on land. Why do you think this is important to trade within our country?

Landforms of the United States Look at the maps of Hawaii and Alaska on this page. The state of Hawaii is made up of several **islands,** or bodies of land that have water on all sides. A large piece of land that has water on *almost* all sides is called a **peninsula** [puh-NIHN(T)-s(uh-)luh]. What parts of Alaska are peninsulas?

Different kinds of land surfaces are called **landforms.** The maps on this page will help you understand the major landforms found in different parts of our country. **Mountains** are raised lands that are much higher than the land around them. Many mountains have high peaks. Find the mountains on the maps of Hawaii and Alaska. How does the mapmaker show that these are raised lands? Some mountains in Hawaii

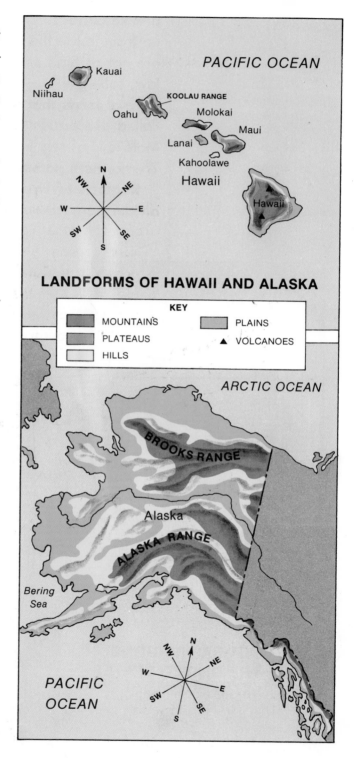

LANDFORMS OF HAWAII AND ALASKA

KEY

■ MOUNTAINS
■ PLATEAUS
□ HILLS
■ PLAINS
▲ VOLCANOES

are **volcanoes.** These are mountains formed of rock thrown up from inside the earth. **Hills** are also raised lands, but they are not as high as mountains. The middle part of Alaska has low, rolling hills.

Level lands that are higher than the land around them are called **plateaus** [pla-TOHZ]. The west side of the island of Molokai has this kind of landform. **Plains** are low flatlands. The northern part of Alaska is a plain.

Regions of the United States There are many ways of dividing our country into parts. Our country is divided into

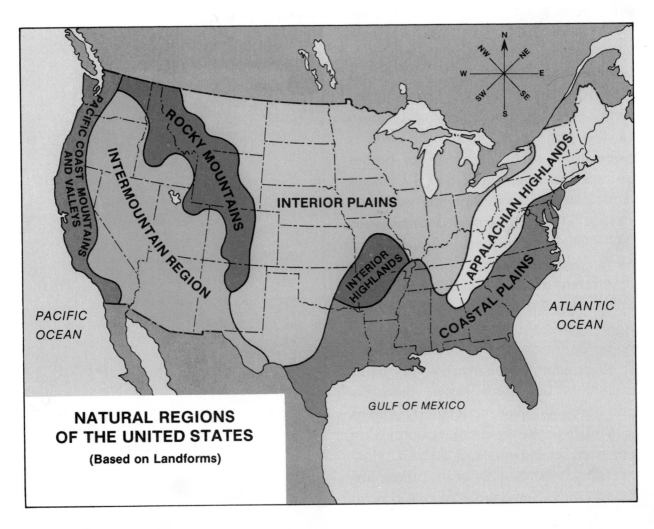

**NATURAL REGIONS
OF THE UNITED STATES**
(Based on Landforms)

states. States are **political regions,** or parts made by people. But our country is also divided into **natural regions,** or parts not made by people.

The map on page 42 shows how our country might be divided based on landforms. Find the Appalachian Highlands on the map. This part of our country is made up of mountains, hills, and plateaus. Where are some other mountains found in our country? What is the part of our country between the Rocky Mountains and the Pacific Coast Mountains called? It is made up of plateaus and **canyons**—deep, narrow valleys with steep sides. What parts of our country are plains?

An understanding of our country's land is useful to the study of our country's history. Such an understanding can help you see why people might have settled in one place rather than in another. It can help you see why some parts of our country are used for farming. And it can help you see how landforms might affect the kinds of jobs that people do.

wrap ·up

- What are some of our country's important waterways?
- What are some landforms found in different parts of our country?
- How might natural regions affect the way people live?

3

Our country's people

Who we are   Our country is sometimes called a nation of **immigrants**. Immigrants are people who come from another continent or country to live in our country. We are all Americans. Yet every American is an immigrant or is an offspring of someone who came from another place.

The first groups of people in what is now the United States came from Asia thousands of years ago. These groups of people are now known as American Indians and Eskimos. At a much later time European people began to come to our country. And many black people were brought here from Africa to work as slaves.

We are one people, but we have many different backgrounds. Look at the circle graph on this page. It will help you understand where our people came from. Where did most United States immigrants come from?

Today our country is made up of people from almost every continent. And immigrants still come to the United States. They follow our way of life, but they also have their own ideas and ways of doing things. How do you think these groups of people have added to the American way of life?

**UNITED STATES IMMIGRANTS
BY PLACE OF ORIGIN, 1820–1974**

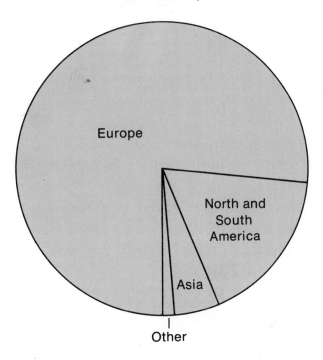

Americans of all ages There are over 200 million people in our country. These people can be divided into groups based on age. People in different age groups have different needs. Our young people need schools. As these people get older they will need jobs. And older people may need more health care than younger people need. Why do you think it is important to know how many of our people are in each age group?

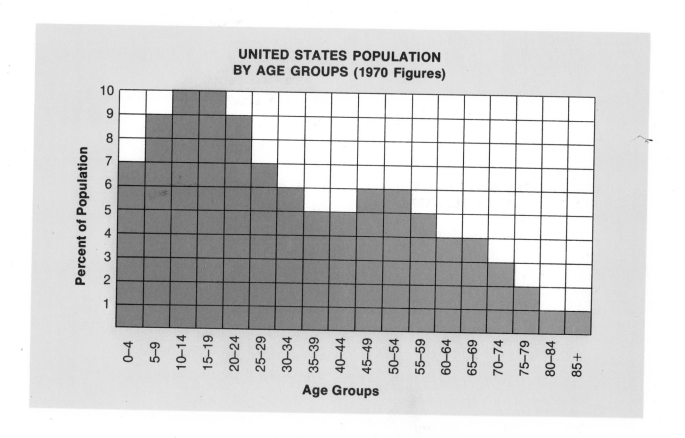

The bar graph on this page shows how our people are divided into age groups. Which age groups have the most people? Which age groups have the fewest people? How might this graph be useful in helping the leaders of our country plan for people's needs?

Where we live Most of our people live in or near cities. New York City has the largest population of any city in our country. But five other cities in our country have more than 1 million people.

The map on this page shows how the population is **distributed,** or spread, throughout the United States. In which part of our country do most people live? Which two states have the fewest people living in them?

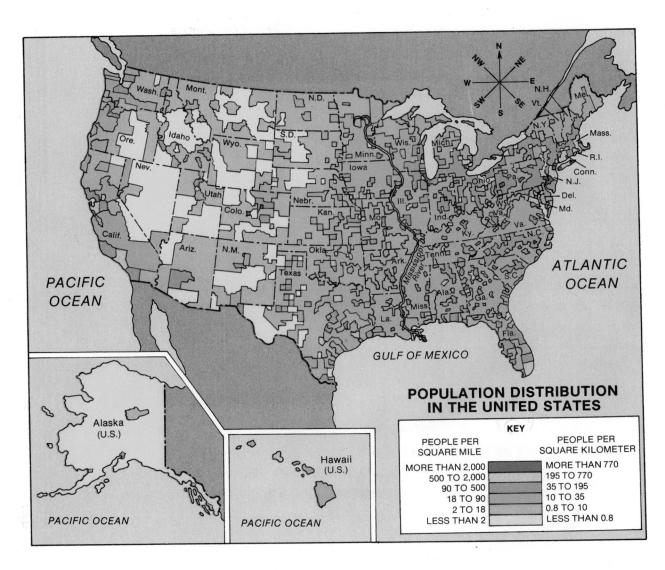

POPULATION DISTRIBUTION IN THE UNITED STATES

KEY		
PEOPLE PER SQUARE MILE		**PEOPLE PER SQUARE KILOMETER**
MORE THAN 2,000		MORE THAN 770
500 TO 2,000		195 TO 770
90 TO 500		35 TO 195
18 TO 90		10 TO 35
2 TO 18		0.8 TO 10
LESS THAN 2		LESS THAN 0.8

What we do The people of working age in our country earn a living in many different ways. The pictograph on this page shows about how many people do certain kinds of jobs. More workers in our country have jobs in **manufacturing,** or making goods, than in any other kind of work. The United States makes more goods than any other country in the world. How does this explain why so many people in our country have jobs in manufacturing?

In 1900 American workers spent about sixty hours a week at their job. Today American workers spend about forty hours a week at work. This means that people have more time to do other things. Many of our people enjoy watching or taking part in sports. Each year many Americans go camping in our country's parks. And many people have hobbies such as music or painting. What other ways can you think of that Americans spend their time away from work?

EMPLOYMENT IN THE UNITED STATES

Job	Number of Workers
Manufacturing	👤👤👤👤👤👤👤👤👤
Trade	👤👤👤👤👤👤👤👤
Government	👤👤👤👤👤👤
Services	👤👤👤👤👤👤
Public Utilities and Transportation	👤👤
Farming	👤👤
Banking, Insurance, and Real Estate	👤👤
Building	👤👤
Mining	ǀ

Each 👤 = 2 Million Workers

wrap·up

- What makes our country a nation of immigrants? because
- Where do most of our people live? in cr nees
- How do people in the United States earn a living? by

47

A Biographical Sketch

Understanding people

Dr. Margaret Mead was one of the best-known **anthropologists** [AN(T)-thruh-PAHL-uh-juhsts], or one who

studies people, in the world. She studied and wrote about people in our country. She also studied and wrote about people in other parts of the world. Dr. Mead was interested in what people believe, how they meet their needs, and how they treat one another. Why do you think these things are important to an understanding of people?

One of the ways Dr. Mead learned about people was through **field study.** This means that she lived among the people she studied. She talked to them and watched what they did. Dr. Mead made field studies of American Indians and of other groups of people in our country. She also studied people in Samoa and in New Guinea. How might these studies have helped Dr. Mead compare different ways of life?

Margaret Mead wrote many books about her work. She believed that all people are important and that no person or group should be favored over any other. She felt that we must understand the past in order to make life better in the future. How do you think Dr. Mead's work has helped people understand one another?

Chapter-End Activities

The chapter-end activities may be done by writing the questions or statements and the answers on a separate sheet of paper or by writing just the answers on a separate sheet of paper, whichever your teacher desires.

Words and Terms

climate   tributary
temperature peninsula
precipitation landforms
source   immigrants
mouth

_____ 1. Water that falls to the earth, generally as rain or snow

_____ 2. A river that flows into a larger river

_____ 3. People who come from another continent or country to live in our country

_____ 4. The place where a river begins

_____ 5. A large piece of land that has water on almost all sides

_____ 6. Different kinds of land surfaces

_____ 7. The place where a river flows into a larger body of water

_____ 8. The kind of weather a place has over a long time

Fact Recall

1. Much of our country's farmland is in the (eastern half, western half) because that part of the United States receives more rainfall.

2. (Manufacturing, Irrigation) makes it possible for farmers to grow crops in dry parts of our country.

3. States and cities are (political, natural) regions because they were made by people.

4. Most immigrants came to the United States from (Asia, Europe).

5. More workers in our country have jobs in (farming, manufacturing) than in any other kind of work.

Concepts and Understandings

1. How do climates and landforms affect the way people in our country live?

2. In what ways are our country's waterways important to trade?

3. How may maps and graphs be used to present facts about our country's people?

Unit End

Main Ideas and Understandings

1. Explain how parallels of latitude and meridians of longitude are used to locate places in our country. What might you learn about our country from a political map? What might you learn about our country from a physical map? How are time lines used to present information about our country's history? Why are charts and graphs useful in the study of our country?

2. How does climate affect the way people use our country's land? How do landforms affect the way people in our country live? Why are graphs and maps useful in the study of our country's people?

Research Ideas

1. Pretend that you are taking a bus trip through part of our country. Your starting point is Denver, Colorado. The chart below shows your schedule. Use a map of the United States to fill in the missing information. Use the distance scale on the map to find the distance between the places listed.

	City and State	Latitude and Longitude	Distance Between Places
1st stop	(a)	41° N 112° W	512 miles 819 kilometers
2nd stop	Albuquerque, New Mexico	(b)	612 miles 979 kilometers
3rd stop	Dallas, Texas	33° N 97° W	(c)
4th stop	St. Louis, Missouri	(d)	651 miles 1 042 kilometers

2. Did you know that Montana is called the Treasure State because of the gold and silver found there? All our states have nicknames. Match each of the following nicknames with its state: Sooner State, Sunshine State, Show Me State, Land of Lincoln, Hoosier State, Aloha State. How did each state get its nickname? What is the nickname of the state in which you live?

Activities and Projects

1. Work in small groups to make maps of the United States. Draw each map on poster board. Make a distance scale and a map key for each map. Each group might make a different kind of map. Here are some suggestions:
   a. A political map showing cities and states
   b. A physical map showing mountains, rivers, and lakes
   c. A climate map
   d. A land-use map
   e. A natural-regions map
   f. A population map

2. Take a census of the people in your classroom. You might ask questions such as the following:

   How many people live in your household?

   What are the age and the sex of each person?

   From what continent or country did the ancestors of people in your household come?

   What do the workers in your household do to earn a living?

You might make charts or graphs to show the results of your census.

The First Americans

Chapter 3   The First Arrivals
Chapter 4   Life Among the American Indians

What group of people do you think has lived in North America longer than any other group? Looking at the picture on page 52 should help you answer the question. This person is a relative of the first people who settled in our country.

In this unit you will learn about the first settlers in North America. You will also learn about the later relatives of these first settlers. And you will find answers to the following questions:

Where did the first people to settle North America come from?

How and why did life for early groups of people in North America change?

How did the different cultural groups of American Indians use their environment to meet their needs?

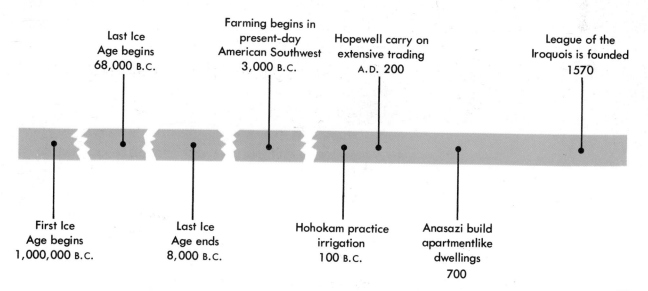

First Ice
Age begins
1,000,000 B.C.

Last Ice
Age begins
68,000 B.C.

Last Ice
Age ends
8,000 B.C.

Farming begins in
present-day
American Southwest
3,000 B.C.

Hohokam practice
irrigation
100 B.C.

Hopewell carry on
extensive trading
A.D. 200

Anasazi build
apartmentlike
dwellings
700

League of the
Iroquois is founded
1570

CHAPTER 3

The First Arrivals

1. Crossing the bridge
2. Early Indian cultures

Learning about the past isn't always easy. A very long time ago there were no written records. But scholars have a number of ideas about the past. They also have certain kinds of evidence for what they believe happened. The tools, weapons, and other things people left behind are part of this evidence.

In this chapter you will learn about where the first people in the Americas probably came from. You will also learn when and why they likely came to the Americas. What else would you like to know about the first people in the Americas? Why would you like to know these things? The early groups of people in the Americas and the later relatives of these people have become known as the American Indians. But they are also sometimes called the first Americans. Do you think this is a good name for these people? Why do you think so?

1

Crossing the bridge

How we learn about the past Much of what we know about the past comes from the work of **archaeologists** [AHR-kee-AHL-uh-juhsts]. These are people who study the remains of those who lived long ago. Sometimes these remains are the bones of early people. And sometimes the remains are **artifacts** [AHRT-uh-FAKTS]. These are things that have been left behind that were made by people. Tools, weapons, and works of art are artifacts. What other kinds of artifacts can you name?

Some remains are very useful for finding out when people may have lived. This is because carbon-14 is found in all living things. By measuring the amount of carbon-14 left in things that were once alive, scientists can tell how old such remains are. This is called **radiocarbon dating**. It tells the age of remains such as bone or hair. Do you think it would tell the age of teeth? Why do you think so?

People come to the Americas The first people to come to the Americas are believed to have come from Asia. We do

Artifacts such as those shown on this page give us clues as to how early people in North America once lived.

not know when they began coming to the Americas. But we know they came long before Europeans reached North America and South America.

Thousands of years ago sheets of ice thousands of feet (meters) thick covered large parts of the earth. Often these ice sheets spread over millions of square miles (square kilometers). There were four major movements of ice, each known as an **Ice Age.** The first movement may have begun about 1,000,000 years ago. The last movement may have started about 70,000 years ago and ended about 10,000 years ago. Some archaeologists believe that groups of people may have started coming to the Americas around the start of the last Ice Age. Others believe people did not come to the Americas until about 25,000 years ago or later.

How they came A narrow body of water connecting two larger bodies of water is called a **strait.** Look at the map on this page. Find the Bering Strait. It is about sixty miles wide. What two oceans does it connect?

Some people believe that thousands of years ago there was a strip of land where the Bering Strait is today. Such a strip of land connecting two larger pieces of land is sometimes called a **land bridge.** Look at the map on this page again. Notice that the ice sheet

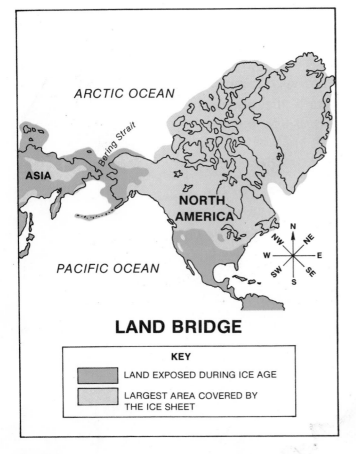

LAND BRIDGE

KEY	
	LAND EXPOSED DURING ICE AGE
	LARGEST AREA COVERED BY THE ICE SHEET

did not cover the land bridge between Asia and North America. How would this situation have helped early people come from Asia to the Americas?

Scientists believe that the ice sheets changed in size and shape as well as moved back and forth. So different parts or amounts of land were covered by ice at various times. For much of the time parts of the land were ice-free. It was in these ice-free places that people and animals could live and move around. How might this help to explain why artifacts are found in some places and not in others?

Why they came   One of the basic **needs** of early people was food. Needs are those things all people must have in order to live. What needs besides food do you think early people had? What needs do you have?

Many archaeologists believe that the groups of early people who came to the Americas were searching for food. These people were likely following animals that they hunted. Look at the map on this page. In what directions did the animals and people travel?

Many kinds of animals that early people hunted are now **extinct** [ihk-STIHNG(K)T]. This means that there aren't any of these kinds of animals anymore. But we know about such animals from **fossils** [FAHS-uhlz] that

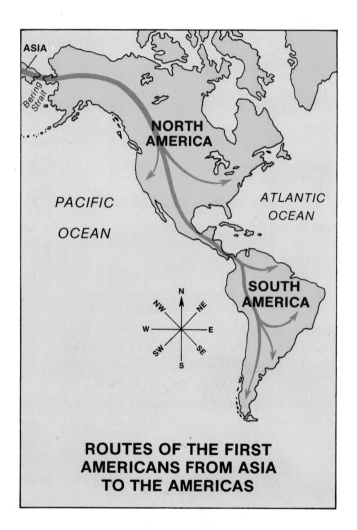

ROUTES OF THE FIRST AMERICANS FROM ASIA TO THE AMERICAS

Mastodons, like the one shown above, were ancient relatives of present-day elephants. Mastodons, which are now extinct, provided early people in North America with food. Do you think mastodons were hard to kill? Why do you think so?

have been found. These are the hardened remains of animals or plants. Animals that once lived in the Americas included large animals such as the **mammoth** [MAM-uhth]. This was an animal something like an elephant, only larger. Early people also hunted a kind of large **bison** [BYS-uhn], or buffalo.

What they brought The early people who came to the Americas brought the clothes they were wearing and the weapons they used for hunting. Because these people hunted large animals, they used spears or arrows with stone points.

These early people also brought their tools for cutting up the animals for food. And they brought their tools for scraping the skins of animals. These skins were used for clothing. What else might animal skins have been used for?

wrap ·up

- Where did the first people to come to the Americas probably come from?
- How did the ice sheets during the last Ice Age probably make it easy for people to move into the Americas?
- How were the first people who came to the Americas trying to meet their need for food?

A Biographical Sketch

A new kind of calendar

Willard Frank Libby was born in Grand Valley, Colorado, on December 17, 1908. At first Libby wanted to be an engineer. But he changed his mind and studied chemistry instead. In 1960 Libby won the Nobel prize for chemistry. A Nobel prize is a reward given

to a person who has done something important in his or her field. It is a great honor to be given such a reward.

When Willard F. Libby finished school, he taught in California for twelve years. He then moved to Chicago, Illinois, and taught at the University of Chicago. It was there that Libby and some of his students developed radiocarbon dating in 1947. This way of dating makes it possible to find out the age of things that were once alive.

When news of Libby's work became known, people were very excited. Remains from all over the world were sent to Libby so that they could be dated. Pieces of wood taken from old buildings, teeth and bones from Ice Age animals, and clothing from Indian graves were just some of the things Libby received. One piece of wood Libby tested came from a king's grave in Egypt. This piece of wood turned out to be nearly 4,000 years old.

Besides the Nobel prize, Libby has received many other honors for his years of work and study. Today radiocarbon dating is thought to be the most important means of finding out the age of something that was once alive.

2

Early Indian cultures

A time of change   You, like other people, live in a certain kind of **environment** [ihn-VY-ruhn-muhnt]. This is the world around you. If the place where you live should change much, you would likely have to **adapt** to, or get used to, a new environment. This is what happened to the early groups of people who came to the Americas.

About 8,000 years ago the climate of North America began changing. It became warmer and drier. What do you think happened to the huge ice sheets that covered parts of North America? What do you think happened to the land bridge that may have connected Asia and North America?

Learning new ways   As the climate became warmer, the large Ice Age animals began dying out. People who depended on these animals for food had to find new ways of getting food. People began to hunt smaller animals such as rabbits and deer. But the amount of food people could get from these animals was less than they used to get from a mammoth. And sometimes these animals were hard to find. So people began to depend more and more on plants for their food. Early groups gathered roots, seeds, berries, and nuts.

As food gathering became important, people did not have to move as often as when they hunted. Why do you think this was so? After a while people learned that some foods could be dried and stored for use later on. Then people could stay in one place longer. Why do you think this was so?

Eventually some early groups in North America learned to grow their own food. Then they began to settle in one place. Why do you think they were able to do this? In time settlements grew larger. These settlements became villages.

Early people in North America depended on animals for much of their food. How have these hunters trapped the bison they are hunting? What are the hunters using to kill the bison?

People in villages learned that some people could do certain things better than others could. So some people planted crops, while others made tools. And some wove baskets, while others shaped **pottery**—things made of baked clay.

Most of the early groups of people who came from Asia to settle in the Americas later became known as American Indians. Each group of early Indians in the Americas adapted to the environment in its own way, depending upon where the group settled. Because of this the **culture**, or way of life, of these early Indians often differed. Houses, clothes, tools, and even languages make up part of a group's culture. What other things can you think of that make up a culture?

People of the desert   One of the early groups of Indians in North America were the **Hohokam** [HOH-hoh-KAHM]. These people lived in the desert where the Gila River and the Salt River meet in what is now southern Arizona. Why do you think they chose to settle where two rivers meet?

The Hohokam used very simple tools to build irrigation canals. It took a large number of people a very long time to build the canals. What are the Hohokam in the picture using to loosen the soil? What are they using to carry the soil away?

The Hohokam were a very peaceful people. They spent most of their time farming. The soil where the Hohokam lived was very rich, but not enough rain fell for growing most crops. So the Hohokam built large **irrigation canals.** These were ditches that brought water from streams and rivers to the fields where crops were planted. In this way the Hohokam were able to grow crops such as corn and cotton.

The Hohokam lived in small villages. They built their houses by digging a hole in the ground and then using wooden poles to form the roof and walls. They covered the poles with branches, twigs, and mud. Do you think houses like this might be cool in the summer? Why do you think so?

To the north of the Hohokam lived a group of Indians known as the **Anasazi** [AH-nuh-SAH-zee]. The Anasazi lived in a part of the present-day United States known as the four corners. This is where the four states of Arizona, New Mexico, Utah, and Colorado meet.

The earliest Anasazi are known as Basket Makers. This is because many baskets have been found in the place where these Indians lived. Like their neighbors to the south, the Anasazi lived in a very dry part of the country. There were few wild plants to gather or animals to hunt. So the Anasazi, like the Hohokam, depended on farming to get most of their food. At first their major crops were corn and pumpkins. Later on these Indians also began to grow beans and cotton.

The early Anasazi lived in pit houses built much like the Hohokam's pit houses. These houses had just one room. Later the Anasazi began building their houses aboveground. These houses were made of mud and straw and had two rooms. One room was used as the family living quarters, and the other room was used for storing food. When a daughter married, another room was added to her parents' house for the new family to live in. This happened again and again, depending upon the number of daughters in a family.

The Anasazi not only joined rooms, they also joined houses. Eventually a town might be made up of one large building. A building might have from 20 rooms to as many as 1,000 rooms. Look at the picture on this page. Why do you think the Anasazi built their homes on the side of a cliff like this?

This picture was taken at Canyon de Chelly National Monument in northeastern Arizona. It shows the ruins built by the Anasazi. The Anasazi used ladders to climb the cliffs so they could reach their homes. In case of an attack they raised the ladders.

Anasazi villages and towns were often built around the old pit houses the early Indians once lived in. Instead of filling the pits, the Indians used them for storing sacred things. Later the Indians made these pits larger and used them as places for praying and dancing to their gods. These underground rooms were known as **kivas** [KEE-vuhz].

The Mound Builders   Many groups of early Indians living in the Ohio River valley and in the Mississippi River valley built huge **mounds**. These were large heaps of dirt and stone. A few of them measured 100 feet (30.48 meters) high and spread over 15 acres (6.07 hectares). Why do you think these people were called Mound Builders?

Hundreds of mounds built by these Indians have been discovered. Some of the mounds were used as graves. Others

The Adenas, earliest of the Mound Builders, built the Great Serpent Mound near present-day Hillsboro, Ohio. The mound measures more than 1,300 feet (396 meters) from head to tail and was used by the Adenas as a place to bury their dead.

were built to serve as the base for temples. These mounds were often built in the shape of circles or squares. And sometimes they were built in the shape of birds, snakes, and other animals. Look at the picture of one of these mounds on page 64. What does the shape of this mound look like to you?

One of the largest and most interesting groups of Mound Builders were the **Hopewell**. The Hopewell built their villages along riverbanks and streams. Here fish, game, fresh water, and rich soil were plentiful. Also there was much clay, sand, gravel, and stone for building their mounds.

The Hopewell traded with other North American Indians in order to get the things they wanted that could not be found in the place where they lived. Copper, seashells, bear teeth, and pearls are just some of the things the Hopewell traded for. Why would living near a river or a stream make it easy for the Hopewell to carry on trade?

Not all the Hopewell Indians worked at the same job. While some members of the group built mounds, others went on trading trips. Still other members built bark-covered houses or took care of the village garden where corn, beans, squash, and tobacco grew. Why do you think the Hopewell divided the work among the members of the group?

wrap ·up

- What does *adapt to the environment* mean?
- What happened to cause early groups of people in North America to change their way of getting food?
- How did the environments of the Hohokam, the Anasazi, and the Hopewell affect their ways of life?

Using Your Skills

Reading a chart

EARLY NORTH AMERICAN INDIAN CULTURES

	Hohokam	Anasazi	Hopewell
Environment	Desert—Very hot and dry with few plants	Semidesert—Warm and fairly dry with some plants	Forest—Warm summers and cool winters with many trees
Food	Corn, beans, squash, cactus fruit, rabbit, and deer	Corn, beans, pumpkins, sunflower seeds, nuts, prickly-pear fruit, rabbit, turkey, and deer	Corn, squash, beans, sunflower seeds, goosefoot seeds, deer, turkey, turtle, and waterfowl
Clothing	Cotton ponchos; sandals made of vegetable fibers	Robes of feathers and of rabbit fur; breechcloths for men; apronlike skirts for women	Robes of cloth, fur, and animal skins; moccasins of animal skins; breechcloths for men; apronlike skirts for women
Housing	Pit houses	Apartmentlike buildings made of adobe	Round and oval wigwams
Arts and Crafts	Red-on-buff pottery; human figures of clay; turquoise jewelry	Black-on-white pottery; basketry; turquoise jewelry	Buff or gray pottery; copper, stone, and bone tools; shell, bone, and pearl ornaments

Use the chart to answer the following questions:

1. What are the names of the three early Indian cultures represented on the chart?

2. Which Indian culture lived where it was hot and dry?

3. What foods shown on the chart were eaten by all three of these Indian cultures?

4. What type of housing did the Hopewell have?

5. What materials did the Hohokam, the Anasazi, and the Hopewell use to make jewelry and other ornaments?

Chapter-End Activities

The chapter-end activities may be done by writing the questions or statements and the answers on a separate sheet of paper or by writing just the answers on a separate sheet of paper, whichever your teacher desires.

Words and Terms

strait
Ice Age
culture
extinct
artifacts

adapt
radiocarbon dating
environment
land bridge

Archaeologists search for __(1)__ to find out about the way of life of early peoples. They use __(2)__ to find out the age of something that was once alive. Some archaeologists believe that the first groups of people came to North America during the last __(3)__. These people probably walked across a __(4)__ as they followed animals, such as the mammoths, that are now __(5)__.

Early groups of people in the Americas had to __(6)__ to the __(7)__, or world around them. The way each group did this determined much about the group's way of life, or __(8)__.

Fact Recall

1. How does radiocarbon dating help archaeologists?
2. How many Ice Ages have there been?
3. What happened about 8,000 years ago as a result of climate changes in North America?
4. What effect did food growing have on the lives of early people?
5. How did Anasazi houses sometimes get to be as large as a town?

Concepts and Understandings

1. Why, according to many archaeologists, did early people come to the Americas?
2. How did the early Indians of North America make use of their natural environment to meet their needs?

CHAPTER 4

Life Among the American Indians

When the first Europeans came to North America, they found many people already living here. Some people believe a little over 1 million Indians were living in the part of North America north of Mexico at that time. Most of these Indians lived in the eastern and the southwestern parts of the present-day United States. Here the Indians carried on much farming. How do you think this made it possible for many Indians to live in these two parts of the country?

The American Indians are divided into different cultural groups. These groups are based on differences in environments. And they are based on differences in ways of life. In this chapter you will learn about five different American Indian cultural groups. You will learn how these Indians met their needs. You will learn about some of their arts and crafts. And you will learn about some of their beliefs.

1

The Pacific Coast Indians

A land of plenty A group of tribes known as the Northwest Coast Indians lived along the Pacific coast of North America. The narrow strip of land on which they lived stretched from southern Alaska to northern California. Ocean breezes brought much rainfall and generally helped to keep the temperatures from being either too hot or too cold.

Thick forests rose from the shoreline of this land. Other plants grew in great numbers. Many streams and rivers flowed throughout the land. Do you think this was a desirable place in which to live? Why do you think so?

The major food of the Northwest Coast Indians was fish. These people caught many salmon, cod, and shellfish. During the fishing season the people caught enough fish to last all winter. The Indians ate some fish right away. And they dried other fish by smoking them. This allowed the fish to be stored for a long time without spoiling. Why would this be important to the Northwest Coast Indians?

The Northwest Coast Indians also met their need for food by hunting and gathering. These Indians hunted seals,

The Northwest Coast Indians depended upon their natural environment to meet their needs. The many waterways and forests where these Indians lived provided them with much food and materials from which to make things. How are the Indians in this picture making use of their natural environment?

This picture shows a Northwest Coast Indian village. Notice the highly decorated doorposts in front of the plank houses.

sea lions, porpoises, and whales for their meat. They also hunted animals of the forests such as deer, bear, and moose. Berries, roots of plants, and seaweed were among the many foods gathered by the Northwest Coast Indians. Why do you think these Indians never grew any of their food?

Clothing and housing   Most of the Northwest Indians wore little clothing during much of the year. What do you know about the weather where these Indians lived that made this possible? The Northwest Coast Indians wore hats and cone-shaped capes woven of bark. These protected the Indians from the rain. In the wintertime the Northwest Coast Indians wrapped themselves in the furs and hides of animals. Where do you think they got these clothing materials?

During the spring and summer the Northwest Coast Indians lived in villages on the coast. But in the winter the Indians moved to large inland villages. Here they were protected from storms that often occurred along the coast.

The Northwest Coast Indians lived in very large houses. These houses were made of wood. Many families lived in one house. The boards used for the roofs and walls of the house could be taken down and moved. This left just the framework of the house standing. Why do you think the Northwest Coast Indians built houses like this?

The wood-carvers The Northwest Coast Indians met their need for food, clothing, and shelter easily. Do you think this allowed the Indians to have extra time to do other things? Why do you think so?

One way the Northwest Coast Indians spent their time was carving beautiful things from wood. Why do you think these Indians chose to make things from wood? The Indians made wooden hammers, spoons, and spears. They carved wooden masks and hand rattles to use during ceremonies. And they carved giant **totem poles** from the trunks of large trees.

Look at the picture of a totem pole on this page. Notice the figures on the pole. The Northwest Coast Indians carved people, birds, and other animals on their totem poles. Sometimes these carvings told a make-believe story. But generally they were used to tell the history of one's own family. How do you think some people today record their family history?

Totem poles were used in many different ways. They were often placed in front of houses for others to see. Sometimes they were used to hold up the roof of a house. And in some cases totem poles were used to mark graves. What is the totem pole in this picture being used for?

Canoes were very important to the Northwest Coast Indians. Most of the time these Indians journeyed by canoe rather than on foot. Why do you think they did this? The Northwest Coast Indians carved their canoes from the trunks of cedar trees or redwood trees.

Wealth and power   Wealth was very important to the Northwest Coast Indians. Wealth meant power. And these Indians believed the best way to show one's wealth was to give a **potlatch.** This was a feast in honor of an important happening such as a wedding, a birth, or a death. At a potlatch the host gave gifts to the guests. How is this different from parties that you have attended? The host might give away such things as canoes, blankets, slaves, fish oil, or even a house. The more the host gave away, the more important the host became in the eyes of the guests.

The Northwest Coast Indians belonged to different classes. The highest class was made up of chiefs. Chiefs were born into their positions and had more wealth than other group members. Next came the younger brothers of the chiefs. Then came the other members of the tribe such as those who fished and carved wood. Slaves were the lowest class. Most of these people were taken by force from other Indian groups.

The California-Intermountain Indians   Another group of Indians also lived along the Pacific coast of North America. Many of these Indians lived in what is now California. And many of these Indians lived in the valleys between the Sierra Nevadas and the Rocky Mountains. Together these Indians were known as the California-Intermountain Indians.

California has a mild climate. Many plants and animals are found there. Do you think this helped the Indians who lived there meet their needs easily? Why do you think so? Some California-Intermountain Indians, however, lived where it was hot and dry. Do you think this made it hard for these Indians to meet their needs? Why or why not?

The Indians of California ground acorn kernels into a fine yellow meal. From this meal, the Indians made bread. Acorn meal could be stored for a long time. Thus the Indians had a constant food supply.

The California-Intermountain Indians met their need for food by hunting, gathering, and fishing. How is this like the Northwest Coast Indians? The California-Intermountain Indians who lived in California depended mostly on acorns for food. Other California-Intermountain Indians depended mostly on seeds, berries, roots, and insects for food. Groups of these Indians also hunted animals such as deer and bear.

A simple way of life During warm weather the California-Intermountain Indians wore little clothing. Men sometimes wrapped a piece of animal skin around their waists. Women sometimes wore skirts made of animal skins. When it was cold, these Indians wore robes made of rabbit fur.

The California-Intermountain Indians built many different kinds of houses. Some houses were large circular houses covered with earth. Others were tiny lean-tos. Indians built lean-tos by pushing sticks into the ground to form a framework. The Indians then covered this framework with grasses. Do you think such houses offered much protection from rain and wind? Why or why not?

The Pomo Indians of California were among the finest basket makers in the world. This basket is an example of their fine art. When the Pomos wove a basket with a horizontal band, they left a break in the design. The Indians believed not to do so would cause the weaver to go blind.

The different tribes of California lived in villages. Anywhere from three to thirty villages were often united under one leader. This leader was chosen because he was thought to be wise. All members of the group were treated equally. How was this different from the Northwest Coast Indians?

The finest baskets The baskets made by the California-Intermountain Indians were among the finest made anywhere in the world. These baskets were cone-shaped and used for storing seeds and nuts. To add color, some tribes wove colored feathers, beads, or shells into their baskets.

Look at the basket shown in the picture on this page. Notice how tightly woven this basket is. Many of the California-Intermountain Indians made baskets like this. These baskets were watertight and thus could be used for cooking.

wrap ·up

- What two different Indian cultural groups lived along the Pacific coast of North America?
- How did the environment of the Pacific Coast help the Indians who lived there meet their needs?
- How did the way of life of the Northwest Coast Indians compare with that of the California-Intermountain Indians?

Using Your Skills

Reading a map

Use the map to answer the following questions:

1. What does this map show?

2. How many Indian cultures are shown on the map? What is the name of each culture?

3. Which Indian culture was located in the northernmost part of North America?

4. Which Indian culture was located in the southernmost part of North America?

5. How many Indian cultures shown on the map were located partly on land that is now part of the United States? What is the name of each of these cultures?

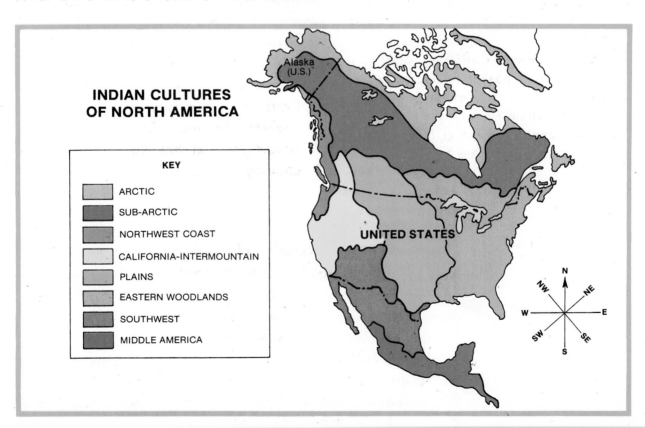

INDIAN CULTURES OF NORTH AMERICA

Alaska (U.S.)

UNITED STATES

KEY

- ARCTIC
- SUB-ARCTIC
- NORTHWEST COAST
- CALIFORNIA-INTERMOUNTAIN
- PLAINS
- EASTERN WOODLANDS
- SOUTHWEST
- MIDDLE AMERICA

2

The Southwest Indians

Food from the desert   Many Indians lived in what is now known as the American Southwest. The present-day states of Arizona and New Mexico and parts of Utah, Colorado, and Texas make up the Southwest. The Indians who lived in the Southwest followed a way of life suited to the world around them.

Some Southwest Indians met their need for food by hunting and gathering. They hunted deer, rabbits, and birds. And they gathered nuts, cactus fruit, and many kinds of berries and seeds. But plants and animals were not plentiful in some parts of the Southwest. Do you think this might have made it difficult to feed a large number of people? Why do you think so? Because food was often hard to find, most Southwest Indians met part of their need for food by farming. They planted corn, beans, squashes, and other crops.

Growing crops, however, was not easy for the Southwest Indians. Why do you think this was so? Some Indians depended upon the flooding of rivers during the rainy season for water for their crops. Other Indians built ditches to bring water from streams to their fields. And some Indians learned dry farming. This way of farming made use of even the smallest amount of water in the soil.

Different kinds of clothing and housing   Some Southwest Indians lived where it was very hot. Do you think they needed much clothing? Why or why not? Other Southwest Indians lived where it was sometimes quite cold. What kind of clothing do you think these Indians needed? Why?

Most of the Southwest Indians wore clothing made of animal skins. These Indians used deerskin to make shirts, skirts, and moccasins. Some Southwest Indians raised cotton. So these Indians also had clothes made of cotton cloth.

This Papago woman collects fruit from a saguaro cactus, just as her ancestors have done for centuries. She is using a pole made from a dead saguaro to knock the fruit to the ground. The Indians made jam, candy, syrup, and wine from the fruit that was collected.

When it was cold, the Southwest Indians wore blankets made of rabbit fur.

The Southwest Indians lived in many kinds of houses. Some Indians built small, one-room houses. These houses had flat roofs and were made of **adobe**. Adobe was made by mixing desert clay with straw. When adobe dried, it was very hard. Houses made of adobe were cool in the summer and warm in the winter. Why would this be important to the Southwest Indians? Other Indians used adobe to hold stones together for building large apartmentlike buildings.

Many Southwest Indians lived in houses called **hogans**. Look at the picture at the bottom of this page. The Indians built such a house by covering a heavy wooden framework with a thick layer of earth. Some Southwest Indians

Some Navajo Indians still live in hogans like the one pictured below. Why do you think hogans are often built in canyons or at the base of cliffs?

Southwest Indian pottery was among the finest made by American Indians in North America. The Indians mixed clay with sand and then built up the sides of the pottery by placing ropelike coils on top of one another. The woman in this picture uses the same method to make pottery today.

lived in **wickiups.** These were houses made of branches and grasses laid over light frameworks of poles. Other Southwest Indians lived in cone-shaped houses made of animal skins. Where do you think these Indians got the animal skins for making their houses?

Arts and crafts The Southwest Indians made beautiful baskets and pottery. The baskets and pottery were used to store food and water. Look at the picture on this page of an Indian woman making pottery. Notice how she is using her hands to shape the clay. Where do you think the materials to make the pottery came from?

The Southwest Indians were also fine weavers. Some Indians wove blankets made of cotton. Where do you think these Indians got the cotton? After sheep were brought to the Southwest, the Indians wove blankets and rugs of wool. What do you think the Indians used the blankets and rugs for?

Beliefs and ideas The Southwest Indians believed that everything in the world around them had its own spirit. Most of their religious beliefs and ceremonies centered around crops, soil, rainfall, and sunshine. Why do you think this was so? The Southwest Indians thought of the earth as the mother of all living things. So the Indians believed that land could not be owned by one person. They believed the land belonged to everyone. Do you think religion was important to these Indians? Why do you think so?

Most of the Southwest Indians were governed by chiefs. The chiefs were often religious leaders. Why do you think this was so? Many chiefs inherited their positions. Others were chosen because they were thought to be wise and strong by the members of the group. For what reasons do you think we choose our leaders today?

Women had a very important role among the Southwest Indians. In many groups women owned the houses, the crops, and the fields. In these groups the mother was the head of the family. The children received their last names from their mother's family. How is this different from the role of women in American families today? How is it the same?

Each August, for nine days, the Hopi Indians of Arizona perform the Snake Dance, just as their ancestors did many years ago. The Indians dance and pray for rain and good crops. Some Indians dance with live rattlesnakes in their mouths.

wrap ·up

- What made it necessary for most Southwest Indians to grow their own food?
- How did the Southwest Indians use their natural environment to meet their need for clothing and shelter?
- How did religion influence the way of life of the Southwest Indians?

3

The Plains Indians

This picture shows the Plains Indians on a winter buffalo hunt. How are the dogs in this picture helping the hunters? Do you think the hunters can move through the snow easier than the buffalo can? What makes you think so?

Land of the buffalo   If you traveled eastward from the Rocky Mountains to the Mississippi River, you would cross the American plains. This part of the country is generally flat, treeless, and covered with grasses. It was here that the Plains Indians lived.

Large herds of buffalo roamed the plains. Some herds were made up of thousands of buffalo. Why do you think so many buffalo lived in this part of the country? The Plains Indians hunted buffalo on foot. Do you think this was dangerous for the Indians? Why do you think so? Often the Indians placed wolfskins over their bodies. This allowed the Indians to get close to the buffalo. Then the Indians used bows and arrows to kill the buffalo. Sometimes the whole tribe participated in a hunt. Then the Indians forced the buffalo into an enclosed area. Or the Indians drove a herd of buffalo over a cliff. Do you think many buffalo were killed at one time this way? Why do you think so?

Food and clothing from the buffalo   The Plains Indians got most of their food from buffalo. Some buffalo meat was eaten right away. Other meat was cut into thin slices and dried in the sun. And some meat was used to make **pemmican**. This was dried meat mixed with berries and melted fat. Meat fixed this way would keep for a fairly long period of time. Why do you think the Indians might have wanted to keep some meat for future use? The Plains Indians also hunted other large animals. They hunted deer, elk, and antelope. They also ate the fruits, seeds, and roots of many plants.

The Plains Indians prepared buffalo skins from which to make clothing. They did this by scraping the skins and then leaving them in the sun to dry. Men wore shirts and moccasins. Women wore long dresses and moccasins. Both men and women wore leggings. When it was cold, the Plains Indians wore robes made of buffalo fur.

Two ways of life   Some of the Plains Indians were **nomads.** This means they did not settle in one place. These Indians lived in small groups called bands. Once a year, in late spring, bands got together to hunt buffalo. Why would hunting in large groups be easier than hunting in small groups?

The Indians that did not settle in one place lived in houses called **tepees.** These houses were cone-shaped and made of buffalo skins sewn together. Tepees could be taken down and moved. Why would this be important to these Indians?

The Plains Indians lived in tepees like the ones pictured below. When the Indians set up camp, it was the women's job to prepare the tepees. This took a great deal of skill. Why do you think an opening is left at the top of the tepees?

Other groups of Indians settled in villages for part of the year. During this time these Indians planted crops such as corn, beans, and squashes. After the crops were **harvested,** or picked, these Indians left the villages to search for buffalo. When it was time to plant crops again, the Indians returned to the villages.

Village houses were large. They were shaped like a dome and were covered with earth. What kind of houses do you think these Indians lived in when they left the villages to hunt? Why do you think so?

When the Plains Indians traveled, they moved their belongings on a **travois** [truh-VOY]. Look at the picture of the travois on this page. What shape is the travois? Why do you think the Indians used dogs to pull the travois?

Hide paintings   The Plains Indians used buffalo skins like we use paper. And they used drawings like we use words. Look at the picture of a hide painting on page 83. Notice each small drawing. These drawings tell the history of a certain time in the lives of the Indians.

The Plains Indians took great pride in painting their tepees. Drawings on tepees might show a great buffalo hunt. Or they might show a time when the owner of the tepee was very

When the Plains Indians traveled, all men, women, and children who were able walked. Men carried only their weapons. Women carried young children and the family's lighter belongings. Where do you think the heavier items were placed?

brave. Why do you think it was important to the Plains Indians to record these things? Why is it important to record things that happen today?

Shamans, dreams, and clubs   All the Plains Indians believed in **shamans** [SHAHM-uhnz]. These were medicine men. The Indians believed shamans brought good to the Indians. The Plains Indians also believed that the sky, waters, and land had special powers. The Indians believed these powers could be passed on to people. One way the Indians believed they could obtain these powers was through a dream.

Each group of Plains Indians had a chief. This leader mainly advised people. Most Plains Indian groups also had clubs. Some clubs were for men. Other clubs were for women. Each club had its own songs and dances. And each club was in charge of certain things. One club that had many members was in charge of keeping order among the other members of the group. Why do you think this was important?

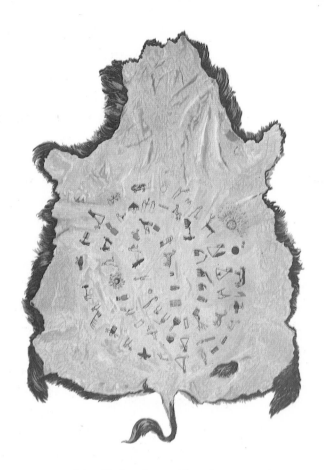

Painted buffalo skins, like the one above, tell us much about the way of life for the Plains Indians. Look at the drawings carefully. What might some of the figures represent?

wrap ·up

- What animal played a very important role in the lives of the Plains Indians?
- How did the Plains Indians use their natural environment to meet their needs?
- How did the way of life of the Plains Indians who were nomads compare with that of the Plains Indians who lived in villages for part of the year?

4

The Eastern Woodlands Indians

A land of forests and streams   A large number of Indians once lived in the part of the present-day United States that is east of the Mississippi River. These Indians were known as the Eastern Woodlands Indians. The land where these Indians lived was covered with thick forests. And many rivers and streams flowed throughout the land.

The Eastern Woodlands Indians hunted deer, bear, elk, and many other kinds of animals. They also hunted wild birds. Why do you think so many animals lived in this part of the country? The Eastern Woodlands Indians also caught many kinds of fish. Look at the picture at the upper left of page 85. What are the Indians using to catch the fish?

The Eastern Woodlands Indians also gathered different kinds of plant foods. They gathered the leaves of some plants and the berries and seeds of others. And they tapped the maple trees that grew in the forests in order to make maple syrup. Do you think the Indians were able to meet their need for food easily? Why do you think so?

Besides hunting, fishing, and gathering, nearly all the Eastern Woodlands Indians farmed. These Indians had to do much work though, before they could plant crops. Why do you think this was so? The Indians cleared fields by cutting down large trees and setting them on fire. They planted crops such as corn, beans, squashes, sunflowers, and tobacco between the tree stumps. Land farmed in this way grew good crops for a limited amount of time. Then the Indians moved to another place. There they did the same things all over again. What do you think happened to the old farm fields the Indians left behind?

The picture on the left shows Algonquian Indians fishing. The Indians used fire to attract the fish. The picture above shows the building of a longhouse. Why is longhouse a good name for this kind of building?

Animals and trees The Eastern Woodlands Indians wore clothing made from animal skins. How do you think the Indians got these skins? Both men and women wore leggings and moccasins made of deerskin. They also used the fur of bears and raccoons to make warm robes and capes. When do you think these were worn?

Some Eastern Woodlands Indians lived in **wigwams.** These were cone-shaped or dome-shaped houses. They were built by driving pointed poles into the ground to form a circle. These poles were then tied together and covered with strips of bark. Where do you think the Indians got the materials for building these houses? Other Eastern Woodlands Indians lived in **longhouses.** These were large houses in which six to ten families lived. Longhouses were also built by covering poles with strips of bark. Look at the picture of a longhouse at the upper right of this page. How is the shape of a longhouse different from that of a wigwam?

The Eastern Woodlands Indians made many things from materials they got from trees. They used tree bark to build canoes. Do you think canoes were important to these Indians? Why do you think so? They also made snowshoes, dishes, and bows and arrows from tree bark and from wood. Why do you think these Indians made so many things from bark and wood?

Tribes and bands   Every tribe of Eastern Woodlands Indians was divided into small groups called bands. The leader of a band was called a **sachem** [SAY-chuhm], or chief. When a chief died, the women of the band were often the ones who decided upon a new chief. What do you think this says about the role of women in some bands?

When chiefs held a meeting, they began by smoking a pipe. This pipe was called a **calumet,** or peace pipe. It stood for peace and friendship. At these meetings, the chiefs often gave long speeches. Because the Indians had no written language, sometimes it was hard for them to remember many things. So the Indians used colored beads woven into designs to help them remember. The same design always had the same meaning. These beads were called **wampum.**

The picture on the left shows a calumet. What did the Indians decorate the calumet with? The picture below shows wampum beads. Indians used wampum to help them remember important events and for money. Instead of trading goods, the Indians often bought goods with wampum beads.

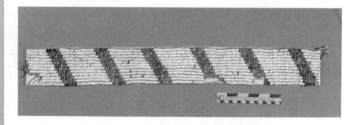

Religious groups The Eastern Woodlands Indians believed that there were both good spirits and bad spirits. The Indians made offerings to both kinds of spirits. They asked the spirits to bring good fortune to the Indians. What kinds of things do you think the Indians might have asked the spirits for?

The Eastern Woodlands Indians held many ceremonies throughout the year. These were times for thanking the spirits for their gifts and blessings. And they were times for large feasts and much dancing. Do we have a certain time of the year when we are thankful for gifts and blessings that we have received? If so, when?

The Eastern Woodlands Indians belonged to medicine societies, which were like clubs. Members of these societies tried to cure people who were sick. Look at the pictures of the wooden masks on this page. The Indians thought such masks had healing powers.

These Iroquois healing masks were worn by members of the False Face Society during certain ceremonies. The Indians carved the masks from living trees to "give life" to the masks.

wrap·up

- In what part of the present-day United States did the Eastern Woodlands Indians live?
- How did the Eastern Woodlands Indians use their environment to meet their needs?
- How did religion influence the way of life of the Eastern Woodlands Indians?

A Biographical Sketch

The League of the Iroquois

A group of Indians known as the Iroquois once lived in the present-day state of New York. The Iroquois were divided into different groups. Five of these groups were the Seneca, the Oneida, the Onondaga, the Cayuga, and the Mohawk. These Indians sometimes fought with one another. And they often fought with neighboring Indian groups. Hiawatha, a Mohawk chief, believed the Iroquois should stop fighting with one another. Hiawatha believed the Iroquois should join together so they would be strong and powerful against their enemies.

Hiawatha went among the villages of the five Iroquois groups telling the leaders about his plan. At first the other chiefs did not like Hiawatha's plan. But after a while all the chiefs agreed. And so the League of the Iroquois was formed.

The League of the Iroquois was governed by fifty chiefs. These chiefs were chosen by the people to act for them. When the chiefs had to decide important matters, they held a meeting. What they decided had to be agreed to by all before it became law.

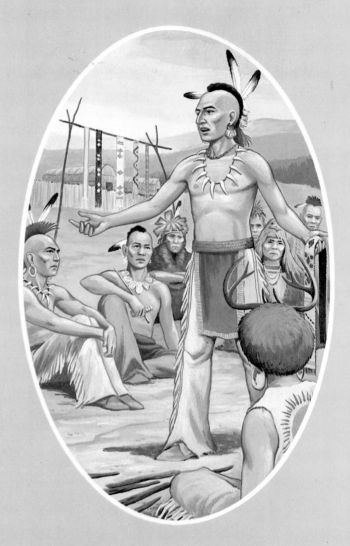

Hiawatha's plan brought peace among the five Iroquois groups. In time the Tuscarora joined the league, making six members. So Hiawatha's dream of the Iroquois becoming strong and powerful became true.

Chapter-End Activities

The chapter-end activities may be done by writing the questions or statements and the answers on a separate sheet of paper or by writing just the answers on a separate sheet of paper, whichever your teacher desires.

Words and Terms

calumet   totem poles   hogans
nomads   longhouses   travois
adobe   potlatch   pemmican

_____ 1. Tall wooden columns that were used to tell a family's history

_____ 2. A large feast where the host gave gifts to the guests

_____ 3. A kind of desert clay that dries very hard when mixed with straw

_____ 4. Dried buffalo meat mixed with berries and melted fat

_____ 5. People who do not settle in one place

_____ 6. A means used by Plains Indians to move their belongings

_____ 7. Large houses in which six to ten families lived

_____ 8. A peace pipe

Fact Recall

1. The major food of the Northwest Coast Indians was (corn, fish, deer).

2. The California-Intermountain Indians made beautiful (pottery, baskets).

3. Growing crops was not easy for the (Southwest, Plains, Eastern Woodlands) Indians.

4. The Plains Indians depended on (hunting, gathering, farming) for most of their food.

5. The Eastern Woodlands Indians used (clay, bark, animal skins) to build their houses.

Concepts and Understandings

1. How did the environments of the five American Indian groups discussed in this chapter influence the way each of these groups met its need for food?

2. How did the environments of the five American Indian groups discussed in this chapter influence the way each of these groups met its need for clothing and shelter?

89

Main Ideas and Understandings

1. Where did the first people to come to the Americas probably come from? When did these people probably first begin coming to the Americas? How did the first people to come to the Americas get here? Why did these people come? What did the first people bring with them to the Americas?

2. How did early people in the Americas adapt to their new environment? How did the growing of crops change early people's way of life? What were the names of three early Indian cultures of North America? Where did these early Indians live? In what way did these Indians meet their needs?

3. How did the Northwest Coast Indians, the California-Intermountain Indians, the Southwest Indians, the Plains Indians, and the Eastern Woodlands Indians use their natural environment to meet their need for food, clothing, and shelter?

Research Ideas

1. Besides radiocarbon dating, archaeologists also use tree-ring dating to find the age of objects that are very old. How does this method work? What part did Andrew E. Douglass play in tree-ring dating? What other methods do scientists use to date objects that are very old?

2. The Mississippians were one of the more advanced of the early Indian cultures of North America. Find out about the Mississippians. Where was the large Mississippian city of Cahokia located? How large was the great mound these Indians built at Cahokia? What eventually became of the Mississippian peoples?

3. Many of our states take their names from Indian words. What is the meaning of each of the following state names: Arizona, Connecticut, Illinois, Michigan, Ohio, and Wisconsin? From what group of Indians did each of these names come? What are other state names and their meanings that come from Indian words?

Activities and Projects

1. Imagine that you have been chosen to take a trip in a time machine. Choose an Indian group that you have just read about to visit. Write a story about your visit. Describe the Indians' way of life. Draw pictures of what you see.

2. Plan an American Indian arts and crafts show. Make objects that represent arts and crafts of each Indian cultural group talked about in the chapter. Label each object as to which group or groups it represents. Tell what each object was used for and what materials the Indians used to make each object.

Unit 3

A Great Interest in America

When people are the first from any country to find a place, they often put a flag in the ground. Why do you suppose they do that?

Hundreds of years ago people from certain countries in Europe marked places that they found in America. Sometimes they used a cross or a stone or some other marker. And sometimes they used a flag. Later, other people from these same countries settled in America. In this unit you will learn about some of the people from Europe who came to America. You will find answers to the following questions:

What were people from Europe seeking when they made journeys to and throughout America?

Why did people from Europe settle in America?

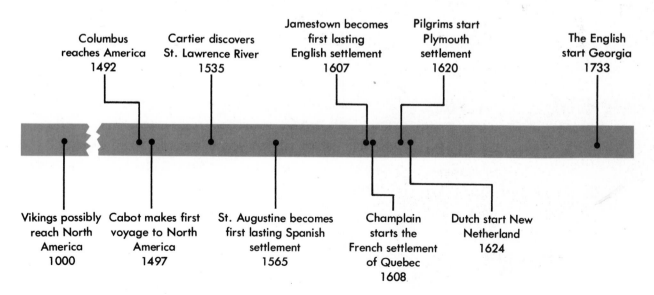

Columbus
reaches America
1492

Cartier discovers
St. Lawrence River
1535

Jamestown becomes
first lasting
English settlement
1607

Pilgrims start
Plymouth
settlement
1620

The English
start Georgia
1733

Vikings possibly
reach North
America
1000

Cabot makes first
voyage to North
America
1497

St. Augustine becomes
first lasting Spanish
settlement
1565

Champlain
starts the
French settlement
of Quebec
1608

Dutch start New
Netherland
1624

CHAPTER 5

The Beginnings of Exploration and Colonization

Have you ever searched for things in a cave? Have you ever searched for things underwater or elsewhere? If so, what did you find?

Today people search for many different things. Long ago people also searched for different things. Some searched for trade routes. Others searched for land. Still others searched for riches. In this chapter you will learn about some people from Europe who searched for these things. You will also learn about some of the first settlements started in the Americas.

1

Interest in the unknown

A great mystery   We know that Christopher Columbus found people living in the Americas. And we know that these people discovered the Americas thousands of years ago during the last Ice Age. But who might have come to the Americas between then and the time of Columbus? The answer to this question is somewhat of a mystery.

Some **historians**—people who study or write history—believe they might have answers to the mystery. So do other people who study the past. Some believe that the Turks might have been the first people after the American Indians to come to the Americas. Others believe that the Japanese, the Egyptians, or the Phoenicians [fih-NIHSH-uhnz] might have been first. Still others believe that the Romans, the Chinese, or the Irish might have been first.

It is possible that any one of these groups of people might have come to the Americas before Columbus did. But there are too few facts to prove that they did. And people have different ideas about who might have come to the Americas and when. Some ideas are based on comparing early coins and pottery found in the Americas with those used elsewhere. Other ideas are based on comparing writing found on stones in the Americas with the writing of early people in other places. Some people have tried to prove their ideas by building boats like those used long ago. And they have tried to sail such boats across the Atlantic Ocean to the Americas. Do you think this is a good way to prove that others could have come to the Americas before Columbus? Why do you think so?

A strong possibility   Some historians and other people believe that people known as **Vikings** came to the Americas before Columbus did. These people lived in Norway, Sweden, or Denmark. Sometimes they are also known as the Norse.

Around 860 a group of Vikings set out on a **voyage** from Norway. A voyage is a journey by sea. After many days the Vikings found the land known as Iceland. Some of them decided to start a settlement there. One of these people was Eric the Red. Later Eric the Red discovered some land he had not known about before. Look at the map on page 97. What land did Eric the Red discover?

More Viking adventures The Vikings began to settle on Greenland. Bjarni Herjolfsson [buh-YAHR-nee-hur-JOHLFS-suhn] was among these people. Once when returning to Greenland from Iceland, Bjarni sailed off course. After a few days, he saw land. People who study stories of Bjarni's journey believe that he saw Baffin [BAF-uhn] Island.

After Bjarni returned to Greenland, he told people about his trip. Bjarni's story made Leif Ericson and other Vikings decide to find out more about this land. Around the year 1000 Leif and the others sailed west from Greenland. They stopped at Baffin Island. Then they sailed farther and found more land. Leif named the land Markland,

The Vikings were seafarers. They built strong, sturdy ships. The Vikings generally sailed these ships along the coasts of Europe and Asia. What do you think it might have been like to sail on a Viking ship?

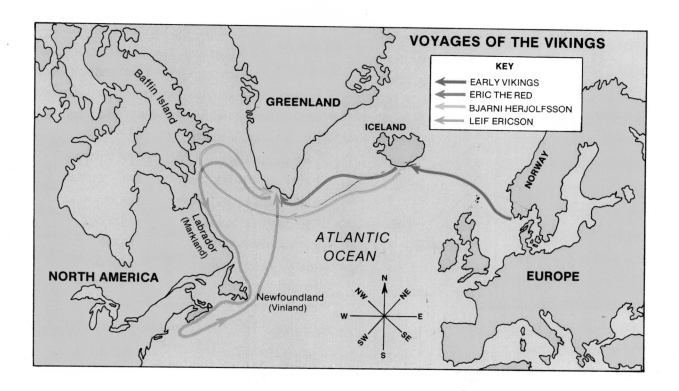

VOYAGES OF THE VIKINGS

KEY
EARLY VIKINGS
ERIC THE RED
BJARNI HERJOLFSSON
LEIF ERICSON

which meant forestland. Find Markland on the map on this page. What is the name of this land today?

After several days Leif sailed on and discovered more land. Leif named this new land Vinland, or Wineland. Find Vinland on the map. What present-day land had Leif Ericson discovered? Near which continent is this land? Not long after Leif discovered Vinland, a group of Vikings settled there. But the settlement did not last long.

Some evidence Much of what is known about the Vikings comes from **sagas** [SAHG-uhz]. These are stories the Vikings told about their journeys. These stories were told over and over again. After hundreds of years the stories were written down. Do you think it was important for the stories to be written down? Why do you think so?

People have been studying about the Vikings for many years. Some historians have read and studied many sagas

These remains were found by Anne and Helge Ingstad at L'Anse aux Meadows in northern Newfoundland, Canada, in 1961. The Ingstads believe that these remains were once Viking houses.

about them. Some people have made a **dig** on land where the Vikings are believed to have lived. This means that archaeologists have dug up the land to look for remains showing that the Vikings once lived there.

Beginning in 1960 some Norwegian archaeologists dug up the remains of two houses in Newfoundland. You can see the remains of these houses in the picture on this page. These remains look much like early Norse houses found in Greenland. Parts of the remains were given a radiocarbon test for dating. The test showed the remains to be between 800 and 1,000 years old. And the sagas say that the Vikings lived in Newfoundland between 800 and 1,000 years ago. So, many people believe that the Vikings did come to the Americas before Columbus did. What do you think? What reasons would you give for your answer?

wrap ·up

- What are some groups of people who might have been the first to come to the Americas after the American Indians?
- What kinds of evidence do historians and archaeologists have to show that the Vikings might have come to the Americas?
- How do you think facts help people who study the past back up their ideas?

Making an outline

Read the story below. Then copy the outline that follows the story. Use the story to complete each line of the outline.

KINDS OF NORSE SHIPS

The Vikings had two kinds of ships. One kind of ship was known as a longship. Longships were made of oak. Each longship had a square sail and about thirty to sixty oars. Longships were used mostly as warships. They were also used for short trips along the coasts of Europe and Asia.

The other kind of Norse ship was known as a knarr [KNAHR], or a knorr [KNUR]. Knarrs were made of pine and oak. Each knarr had a square sail and a few oars. Knarrs were used mostly as trading ships. They were built to carry food and other goods. The Vikings might have used knarrs when they crossed the Atlantic Ocean.

KINDS OF NORSE SHIPS

I. Longships
    A. Type of wood: _____
    B. Type of sail: _____
    C. Number of oars: _____
    D. Uses of: _____
II. Knarrs
    A. Type of wood: _____
    B. Type of sail: _____
    C. Number of oars: _____
    D. Uses of: _____

2

The Spanish take the lead

Estates like the one shown below were found in many places throughout Europe from about A.D. 500 to A.D. 1300. The landowner was a lord, and the workers were peasants. What kinds of work does the picture show these peasants doing?

Life in Europe changes   Hundreds of years ago most of the land in Europe was owned by a few people. Others lived on the land and worked for a landowner. The land of each landowner was able to meet all the needs of those living on the land. Life in most of Europe went on for hundreds of years without much change.

Then slowly things began to change. Some people from Europe took part in the **Crusades.** These were a series of wars between some Europeans and a group of people in southwest Asia. People from Europe saw a different way of life in Asia. They saw new kinds of foods, cloth, and other goods. They took some of these things back to Europe. Before long others in Europe wanted these things. Do you think this led to more trade between Asia and Europe? Why do you think so?

Trade with the East   At first most of the trade between Europe and Asia was carried on by a few people from Italy. This European country had a good location between other European countries and Asia. One of the people from Italy who traded in Asia was Marco Polo. He went to China and

This view is of Venice, Italy, during the 1400s. Venice was one of the cities that controlled much of the early trade between Europe and Asia.

brought back many goods with him. And he told others of the things he had seen in China.

As time passed, some countries in Europe became unhappy over the high cost of goods from Asia. One reason for the high cost was the Italian control of most of the trade. Another reason was that goods carried over land were sometimes stolen by robbers. Also, some people charged money for allowing goods to go through their country.

Some European countries wanted to lower the price of goods by having their own trade routes with Asia. They especially wanted to find a short, all-water route to Asia. Two of these European countries were Portugal and Spain. These countries would gain from an all-water route because they were on the Atlantic Ocean.

Searching for an all-water route Prince Henry the Navigator of Portugal wanted his sailors to find an all-water route to Asia. So he started a school to help them make better ships and to improve their sailing skills.

Some people thought Asia could be reached by sailing south around Africa and then east across the Indian Ocean. Others thought Asia could be reached by sailing west across

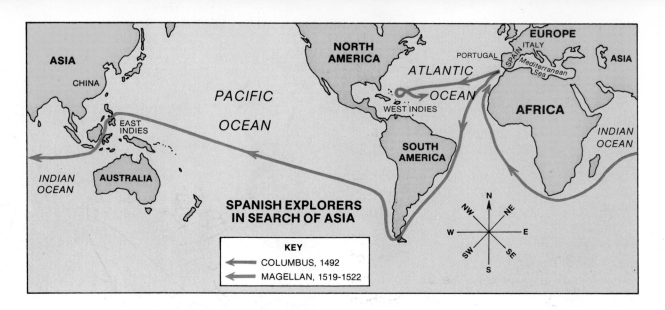

**SPANISH EXPLORERS
IN SEARCH OF ASIA**

KEY
COLUMBUS, 1492
MAGELLAN, 1519-1522

the Atlantic Ocean. One of the latter was Christopher Columbus, an Italian sea captain. Look at the map on this page. What continents were in Columbus's way?

Columbus hoped to get help from Portugal for his trip. But the leaders of Portugal would not help Columbus. So Columbus was forced to look elsewhere for help. He needed ships, a crew, and supplies. Columbus finally interested King Ferdinand and Queen Isabella of Spain in his trip. They were willing to spend the money to try to find a short, all-water route to Asia. Why do you think they were willing to do this? Columbus got three ships for his trip. They were the *Niña* [NEE-nyuh], the *Pinta* [PIHN-tuh], and the *Santa Maria* [SAN-tuh-muh-REE-uh]. In August of 1492 the three ships set sail across the Atlantic Ocean.

Early on the morning of October 12, 1492, Columbus and those with him sighted land. Columbus thought he had found the **Indies,** a group of islands near Asia. So he called the people Indians. But he had really found a group of islands off the coast of the Americas. Because of Columbus's mistake, these islands are now known as the West Indies. Columbus made three more trips but never found an all-water route to Asia. However, Columbus found much more—the Americas.

More Spanish explorations Spain sent **explorers** to different places. Explorers are people who make journeys in search of new things. The leaders of Spain wanted goods from Asia. They also wanted gold and other things. Some explorers searched for a short, all-water route to Asia. Some searched for other things. And some found things they weren't searching for. One of these was Vasco Núñez de Balboa. He discovered the Pacific Ocean. Balboa and those with him are believed to have been the first Europeans to see this ocean.

Ferdinand Magellan [muh-JEHL-uhn] reached Asia by sailing west. He died there, but others of his group returned to Spain by sailing west across the Indian Ocean. This was the first voyage around the world. Why do you think this was an important trip?

Some Spanish explorers were seeking the Fountain of Youth. This fountain was supposed to be able to make old people young again. Juan Ponce de León [PAHN(T)S-duh-LEE-uhn] never found the Fountain of Youth. But he did find a peninsula that he named Florida. Later the first Spanish settlement began there.

An explorer named Álvar Núñez Cabeza de Vaca [kuh-BAY-zuh-duh-VAHK-uh] set out on a journey to

In 1513 Balboa led a group of people across present-day Panama. Balboa was seeking gold that he had been told about by some Indians. After several weeks of travel, Balboa and those with him came to the Pacific Ocean. Balboa claimed the ocean and its shores for Spain. How do you think he felt at that moment?

Florida in 1528. Cabeza de Vaca was going to explore Florida but was shipwrecked near present-day Texas. He went by land across what is now Texas and then back into Mexico.

Another explorer, Hernando Cortes [kawr-TEHZ], went west from Mexico and found a peninsula. Today this land is known as Baja [BAH-hah] California, or Lower California. Several years later Juan Rodríguez Cabrillo [kuh-BREE-(y)oh] sailed along the western coast of Baja California. He went as far as present-day San Diego. So he and those with him became the first Europeans to land on the Pacific coast of the present-day United States.

Looking for gold   Stories about cities of gold interested many of those exploring for Spain. One of these was Hernando de Soto. He went to Florida seeking such cities but never found them. Then he went west and discovered the Mississippi River, which became important to Spain at a later time.

Another person interested in cities of gold was Estéban [ehs-TAY-bahn]—an African brought to America as a slave. He was also known as Estevanico or Estévan. Estéban became the guide for a journey seeking seven cities of gold. These

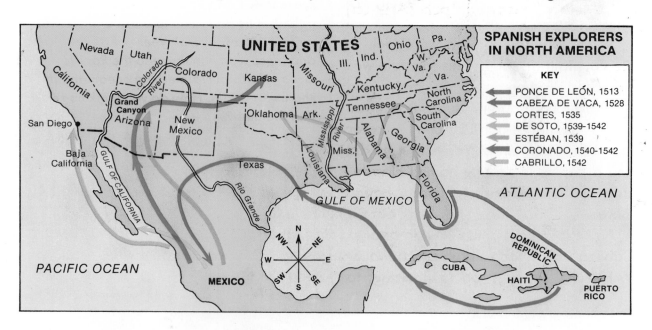

SPANISH EXPLORERS IN NORTH AMERICA

KEY
PONCE DE LEÓN, 1513
CABEZA DE VACA, 1528
CORTES, 1535
DE SOTO, 1539-1542
ESTÉBAN, 1539
CORONADO, 1540-1542
CABRILLO, 1542

were known as the *Seven Cities of Cíbola* [SEE-buh-luh]. Estéban was said to have reached one of these cities but was put to death there.

At a later time Francisco Coronado searched for the Seven Cities of Cíbola. But what he found turned out to be Zuni villages. Coronado continued to look for gold but never found any. However, some of his group discovered the Grand Canyon in present-day Arizona.

Spanish conquerors Not all who went on journeys for Spain were explorers. Some were **conquerors,** or people who use power to overcome others. And some, such as Hernando Cortes, were both. As you read on page 104, Cortes discovered Baja California. He also defeated the Aztec Indians and won all of Mexico for the Spanish.

Francisco Pizarro [puh-ZAHR-oh] was another Spanish leader. Several years after Cortes won Mexico, Pizarro won Peru by defeating the Inca Indians. This gave the Spanish a right to land in South America.

Montezuma, the Aztec emperor, greeted Cortes with gifts, as Cortes marched into the capital city of the Aztec empire. But Cortes was not paying Montezuma a friendly visit. Cortes conquered the Aztecs and carried off their wealth.

wrap·up

- What made people in Europe want to find an all-water route to Asia?
- How did Columbus's voyage of 1492 turn out to be important for Spain?
- Why did Spain keep sending explorers and conquerors to different places?

A Biographical Sketch

A determined leader

Francisco Coronado had not been in Mexico long before he was chosen to lead a journey to the Seven Cities of Cíbola. Coronado set out in the spring of 1540. The pace of the journey was slow. So Coronado, Friar Marcos, and some soldiers set out ahead of the group. Friar Marcos was supposed to know where the Seven Cities of Cíbola were. So he went with Coronado to guide him. After several days, they came to a place that Friar Marcos pointed to as the Seven Cities. But Coronado only saw clay huts! The huts were part of a Zuni village. Coronado was both disappointed and angry.

Coronado had his mind set on finding gold. So he and the soldiers went on. They often stayed at Indian villages. At one village Coronado met the Turk. The Turk told Coronado about a different land of gold.

Coronado was excited about this news. For weeks the Turk guided Coronado and the soldiers. But once again there was no gold! The Turk had used Coronado to get back to his own village. How do you think Coronado felt about this?

Coronado cannot be remembered for finding gold. But he can be remembered for giving Spain a claim to lands in the southwestern part of the present-day United States. And Coronado's group can be remembered for discovering the Grand Canyon.

3

A look at Spanish lands in America

Spanish claims From the time of Columbus to the time of Coronado the Spanish explored and conquered much land in the Americas. This Spanish land was divided into two large parts. One part was called Peru. Look at the map on this page. On which continent was the Spanish land called Peru found?

The other part of the Americas that belonged to the Spanish was called New Spain. New Spain took in much of the West Indies and the Spanish land north of Panama. Look again at the map. On which continent was most of New Spain found?

Concerns in Florida The land in Florida was part of New Spain. This land had been discovered for the Spanish by Ponce de León. But France was also interested in this land. A group of French decided to settle there. When the Spanish king heard about this, he became very upset. Why do you think the Spanish king was upset over the French being in Florida?

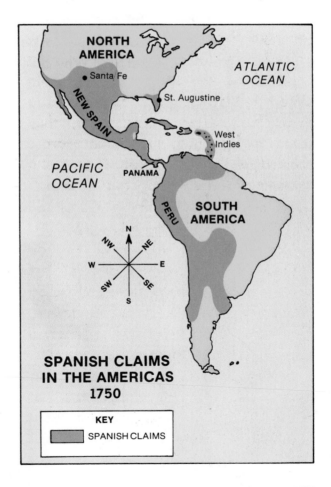

SPANISH CLAIMS IN THE AMERICAS 1750

KEY

SPANISH CLAIMS

A Spanish explorer named Pedro Menéndez de Avilés [muh-NEHN-duhs-day-AHV-uh-LAYS] was planning a trip to Florida. So the Spanish king sent for Menéndez and told him to drive the French out of Florida. Hundreds of people went to Florida with Menéndez. They carried out the king's orders. Then they founded St. Augustine [AW-guh-STEEN] in 1565. So St. Augustine became the first **permanent**, or lasting, European settlement in the United States.

St. Augustine was built as a fort by Spanish soldiers. But it was also used by Spanish **missionaries**—those who wanted to teach their religion to others. The Spanish missionaries did not work just at St. Augustine. They started mission settlements throughout much of present-day Florida, Georgia, and South Carolina. Do you think these settlements helped the Spanish get a better hold on the lands they had discovered earlier? Why do you think so?

This picture shows a street scene in St. Augustine, Florida, hundreds of years ago. What does this picture show about life in this early Spanish settlement?

Land in the Southwest Land in the southwestern part of what is now the United States was also part of New Spain. Much of this land belonged to Spain because of the travels of Coronado.

The Spanish began to settle in present-day New Mexico around 1600. In 1610 Santa Fe was founded as the capital for part of New Spain. Today Santa Fe is the capital of New Mexico. This makes Santa Fe the oldest seat of government in our country. For how many years has Santa Fe been a capital?

Spanish missionaries went throughout the Southwest just as they had in Florida and other parts of the Southeast. They set up churches and settlements in present-day Texas, New Mexico, Arizona, and California. By so doing, they helped the Spanish to settle and to hold this part of our country.

San Xavier del Bac Mission is near Tucson, Arizona. It is the only remaining mission in Arizona. It was started by the Jesuit priest Eusebio Francisco Kino in 1700. How would you describe the building shown in this picture?

wrap·up

- How were Spanish lands in the Americas divided?
- Why have St. Augustine and Santa Fe been remembered as important communities since the days of New Spain?
- Why did the Spanish want to start mission settlements on the land they claimed in North America?

Life in New Spain

Making a living All the Spanish lands in America belonged to the king of Spain. The king divided the land among persons whom he favored. These were people who had wealth or power. Landowners in New Spain kept their land as long as they pleased the king and did what he said.

Farming was an important way of life for many of the landowners in New Spain. Most of the landowners had very large farms called **haciendas** [(H)AHS-ee-EHN-duhz]. Only such large farms were generally able to make money in New Spain. This was because the land was very dry and the soil was generally poor. How do you think having very large farms was helpful under these conditions?

Mining was another way of making a living in New Spain. But as in the case of farming, only a few Spanish made money by mining. This was because the cost of mining gold and silver was very high. So the mines were generally owned by just a few wealthy people.

People who owned haciendas or mines needed lots of workers. Why do you think this was so? Many of the workers were Indians. They were forced by the Spanish to work for them when the Spanish took over the land in New Spain. As the need for more workers grew, blacks from Africa were also used. Both the Indians and the blacks were treated as slaves.

Mission life Missions could be found throughout New Spain. They were set up and supported by the Spanish king. The king hoped the missions would help New Spain to grow in power and wealth. Why do you suppose the Spanish king wanted this to happen?

Look at the picture on the bottom of page 111. Each mission was like a small settlement. It had a church, a school, living quarters, workshops, and store-rooms. And it had a farm. Soldiers generally lived in the settlement to help protect it against persons from other countries.

Indians did much of the work at a mission. They were generally treated better than Indians who worked on large farms or in mines. The missionaries wanted to teach the Indians their faith. And they wanted to make the Indians members of the Roman Catholic Church. So the missionaries helped the Indians in many ways. They taught the Indians to read and write in Spanish. They showed the Indians better ways of raising crops and how to raise cattle and sheep. They also taught the Indians how to spin and to weave.

As a mission did well, a village grew up around it. Then a new settlement would be started in another place. Why do you think this might have pleased the leaders of Spain?

This picture shows a view of a Spanish hacienda. This hacienda is located on land that was once part of New Spain.

Missions played an important role in New Spain from the 1500s to the 1800s. What are some of the activities taking place at this mission?

This portrait is of Antonio de Mendoza, who was appointed the first viceroy of New Spain in 1535. Mendoza was eager to help increase Spanish power in the Americas and to find treasures for the king of Spain. This was why Mendoza sent Coronado on a journey to the Seven Cities of Cíbola.

Governing New Spain The form of government in New Spain was patterned after that in Spain. Why do you suppose this was so? New Spain was ruled by officers chosen by the king of Spain. The king chose a **viceroy,** or chief officer, to be the head of the government of New Spain for him.

Antonio de Mendoza [mehn-DOH-zuh] was chosen to be the first viceroy of New Spain. Mendoza lived in Mexico City—the capital of New Spain. Mendoza's job was to carry out the king's orders. And he was to keep order in New Spain.

New Spain was ruled by a small group of people. Others in New Spain had no voice in the government. How do you think the people who had no voice in the government felt?

The Spanish influence continues Spanish rule in the Americas lasted for several hundred years. Today many things in our country remind us that the Spanish once lived here. The names of the states of Florida, Colorado, Nevada, and California are formed from Spanish words. Many towns, rivers, and mountains in the United States have Spanish names. The remains of Spanish missions can be found in parts of the United States. Many people living in the southwestern part of our country today are Spanish.

Spanish-style houses, like this one in Florida, are a reminder of Spanish influence in North America. Such houses can be seen today in various parts of the United States.

The Spanish are also remembered for other things. They brought horses, cattle, sheep, hogs, and goats to this country. They also brought orange trees, cherry trees, wheat, rice, and peas. The picture of a Spanish-style house on this page shows another Spanish influence. What things about this house catch your attention? What other things remind you that the Spanish lived in our country hundreds of years ago?

wrap·up

- What ways of making a living did those with wealth or power have open to them in New Spain?
- How did the king of Spain influence life in New Spain?
- How did the Spanish contribute to the American way of life?

Chapter-End Activities

The chapter-end activities may be done by writing the questions or statements and the answers on a separate sheet of paper or by writing just the answers on a separate sheet of paper, whichever your teacher desires.

Words and Terms

explorers	viceroy
historians	sagas
missionaries	voyage

_____ 1. A journey by sea

_____ 2. Stories the Vikings told about their journeys

_____ 3. People who make journeys in search of new things

_____ 4. Those who wanted to teach their religion to others

_____ 5. A chief officer chosen by the king to govern New Spain

Fact Recall

1. Many people believe there is enough evidence to show that the (Portuguese, Vikings) might have come to the Americas before Columbus did.

2. Florida was discovered and named for the Spanish by (Ponce de León, Magellan).

3. Much of the southwestern part of the present-day United States was explored for the Spanish by (De Soto, Coronado).

4. The first permanent European settlement in what is the present-day United States was (Santa Fe, St. Augustine).

5. (Missionaries, Soldiers) in New Spain helped the Indians learn new ways of doing things.

Concepts and Understandings

1. Why do some historians and archaeologists believe that groups of people might have come to the Americas between the arrival of the American Indians and the first voyage of Columbus?

2. Why were the leaders of Spain willing to continue to support the activities of explorers and conquerors?

3. How did the king of Spain play an important role in the way of life in New Spain?

CHAPTER 6

The French Arrive in America

1. The French explorers
2. A look at French lands
3. Life in New France

Make believe you are going to spend a summer day at a river. What are some things you might see at the river? What are some things you might do at the river?

Many rivers are important waterways. Two rivers were very important to the French people who explored and settled in America. In this chapter you will learn about these rivers. You will also learn about the lands along these rivers that the French explored and claimed. And you will learn about some of the early French settlements in America.

1

The French explorers

A northern route Spain was the first European country to explore the Americas. But other countries in Europe later followed. France was one of these countries.

At first the leaders of France seemed mostly interested in gaining power in Europe. But during the early 1500s, some people from France went to Newfoundland to fish. They began sending codfish to France. In time the leaders of France became more and more interested in the Americas. Why do you think this was so?

Around the time that the French leaders were becoming interested in the Americas, they heard about Magellan's journey to Asia. This news must have furthered the French interest in finding an all-water trade route to Asia. However, the route that Magellan had taken around South America was both long and hard. So, the French decided to try to find a northern route to Asia. Such a route would be much shorter than going all the way around South America.

The first attempts Giovanni da Verrazano [VEHR-uh-ZAHN-oh] was chosen by the king of France to be the first to try to find a northern route. Verrazano set sail in 1524. He sailed along the Atlantic coast of North America from present-day North Carolina to present-day Nova Scotia. But Verrazano failed to find a northern route and so returned to France.

Ten years later the king of France sent Jacques Cartier [kahr-TYAY] to find a northern route. Cartier sailed around the present-day Gulf of St. Lawrence. He claimed all the land he sailed near for France. The following year Cartier discovered the mouth of the present-day St. Lawrence River. Cartier sailed up the St. Lawrence River but failed to find a northern

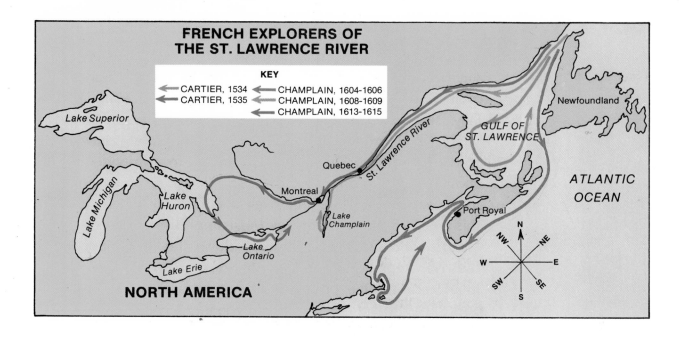

FRENCH EXPLORERS OF THE ST. LAWRENCE RIVER

KEY
← CARTIER, 1534   ← CHAMPLAIN, 1604-1606
← CARTIER, 1535   ← CHAMPLAIN, 1608-1609
                  ← CHAMPLAIN, 1613-1615

Lake Superior
Lake Michigan
Lake Huron
Lake Erie
Lake Ontario
Montreal
Quebec
Lake Champlain
St. Lawrence River
GULF OF ST. LAWRENCE
Newfoundland
ATLANTIC OCEAN
Port Royal
NORTH AMERICA

route. Look at the map on this page. To what present-day city did Cartier sail?

A busy explorer   Samuel de Champlain [sham-PLAYN] was another French explorer. In 1603 Champlain went on his first journey up the St. Lawrence River. The following year Champlain went on another **expedition**. An expedition is a journey that a group of people make with a certain goal in mind. The goal of Champlain's journey was to form a settlement. Champlain sailed along the Atlantic coast of North America. Then he helped start the settlement of Port Royal— now Annapolis Royal, Nova Scotia. This settlement became a trading post.

In 1608 Champlain founded the city of Quebec [kwih-BEHK] on the banks of the St. Lawrence River. Quebec became an important trading settlement. Later Champlain discovered a lake that has since been named Lake Champlain in his honor. A few years later Champlain discovered two of the Great Lakes. Look at the map again. Which two of the Great Lakes did Champlain discover on his trip that began in 1613?

More explorations After Champlain's journeys, the French began to settle the land they claimed in North America. But the French still wanted to find a short water route through North America to the Pacific Ocean. In 1673 they sent a missionary named Father Jacques Marquette [mahr-KEHT] and a fur trader named Louis Joliet [zhawl-YAY] on an expedition. The French had heard from friendly Indians about a river to the west of Lake Michigan. Marquette and Joliet were to explore this river and find out where it went. This river was the present-day Mississippi River.

Marquette and Joliet paddled down the Mississippi River. The river kept flowing south, not west. When Marquette and Joliet reached the present-day Arkansas River, they turned back. They found out from other friendly Indians that the Mississippi River did not lead to the Pacific Ocean.

A large claim Robert de La Salle [luh-SAL] was another French explorer. He led a journey down the Mississippi River in 1682. Look at the map on page 119. What body of water does the mouth of the Mississippi River enter?

Father Jacques Marquette and Louis Joliet were most likely the first French people to explore the Mississippi River. How do you think they might have felt during their travel down this river?

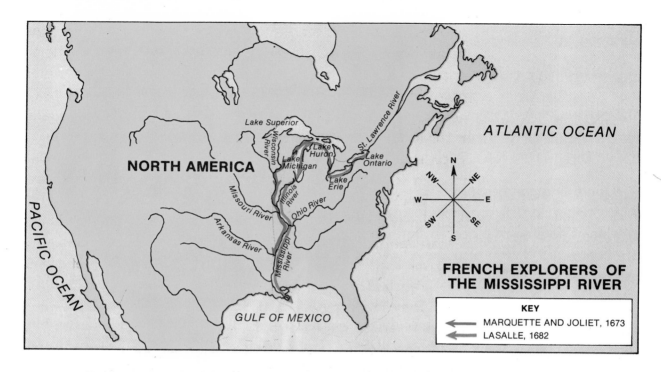

Map labels:
- ATLANTIC OCEAN
- Lake Superior
- Wisconsin River
- Lake Huron
- St. Lawrence River
- Lake Michigan
- Lake Ontario
- NORTH AMERICA
- Lake Erie
- Missouri River
- Illinois River
- Ohio River
- PACIFIC OCEAN
- Arkansas River
- Mississippi River
- GULF OF MEXICO

Compass: N, NE, NW, W, E, SW, SE, S

FRENCH EXPLORERS OF THE MISSISSIPPI RIVER

KEY	
←	MARQUETTE AND JOLIET, 1673
←	LASALLE, 1682

La Salle set up a cross and a tablet at the mouth of the Mississippi River. This meant that he claimed the Mississippi River and all the land watered by it for France. And it meant that he claimed all the land watered by all rivers flowing into the Mississippi River. La Salle named this land Louisiana in honor of King Louis XIV of France.

The French never found a northern route to Asia. But they did find a route through the middle of the present-day United States. This route went from north to south. It went from the St. Lawrence River to the Gulf of Mexico.

wrap·up

- Why did the French want to find a northern route?
- How did Cartier and Champlain help the French claim land in North America?
- How were the French able to find a route through the middle of our country?

Reading a time line

A time line can be helpful in understanding when important things happened. It can help to give one a sense of the order in which things took place. A time line shows how happenings are connected. It can also show how one happening may lead to another.

Use the time line to answer these questions.

1. What does this time line show?
2. What happened in 1524?
3. Did Cartier discover the mouth of the St. Lawrence River or explore the Gulf of St. Lawrence first?
4. What happened in 1608?
5. In what year did Marquette and Joliet explore the Mississippi River to the Arkansas River?
6. How many years passed between the time Marquette and Joliet explored the Mississippi River and the time La Salle explored the Mississippi River?

FRENCH EXPLORATIONS IN NORTH AMERICA

1524	Verrazano explores Atlantic coast of North America
1534	Cartier explores Gulf of St. Lawrence
1535	Cartier discovers mouth of St. Lawrence River
1608	Champlain starts Quebec
1673	Marquette and Joliet explore Mississippi River to Arkansas River
1682	La Salle explores Mississippi River to Gulf of Mexico

2

A look at French lands

French claims   Between the time of Cartier and the time of La Salle, the French claimed much land in the Americas. A small part of this French land was in the West Indies. Find the French land in the West Indies on the map on this page.

The large part of the Americas claimed by the French was called New France. Why do you suppose it was given that name? Look at the map on this page. On which continent was New France found?

Northern New France   Large numbers of animals lived in the forests in the northern part of New France. There were

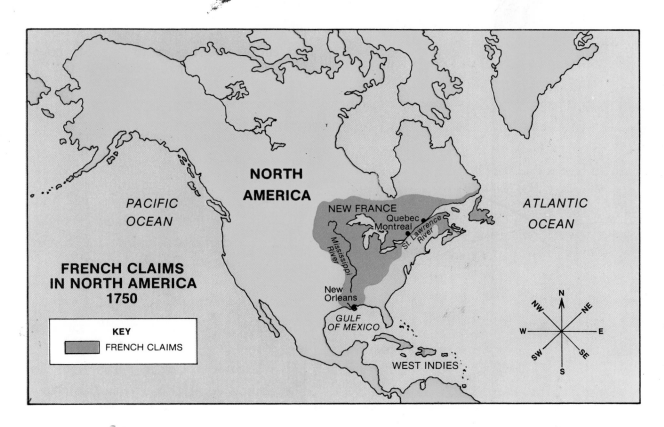

many foxes, otters, muskrats, and beavers. Many people in France and other parts of Europe desired fur coats and fur hats. They especially wanted those made of beaver fur. Do you think this made the furs of northern New France valuable to the French? Why do you think so?

Before long the French became interested in trading animal furs. They began to set up fur-trading posts in different parts of northern New France. Do you think these fur-trading posts helped the French get a stronger hold on the lands they had discovered? Why do you think so?

Quebec was founded as a fur-trading post along the banks of the St. Lawrence River. The French were pleased with the location of Quebec. It meant that they controlled the way by which people entered the northern part of the Americas. Why do you think this was important to the French?

Missionaries helped the French hold their lands in northern New France. Some helped make Quebec the center of New France. Others helped found Montreal, which became an important trade center. Still others helped start settlements in other parts of northern New France.

The Louisiana area The land La Salle named Louisiana was part of New

This picture shows Quebec, Canada, hundreds of years ago. Notice how much of Quebec has been built on a hill. What advantage do you think this might have been to the French?

France. For a while this part of New France did not become settled. Why do you think this was so?

Then in 1718 Jean Baptiste de Bienville [bee-EHN-VIHL] founded New Orleans along the banks of the Mississippi River. The French were as pleased with the location of New Orleans as they were with that of Quebec. New Orleans was not far from the mouth of the river. Large ships could easily sail to and from the settlement. New Orleans quickly became an important trade center for the French.

The French had strong trade centers at both ends of New France. They had Quebec at the northern end. And they had New Orleans at the southern end. The French also had a great system of rivers and lakes between Quebec and New Orleans. And they had many small trading posts and forts along these rivers and lakes. How do you think the French felt about their holdings in the Americas? Why do you think they felt that way?

The French-style building shown above is located in an old section of New Orleans, Louisiana. Such buildings can be seen today in different parts of the United States and Canada.

wrap·up

- Where was New France located?
- How did fur trading play an important part in helping New France to grow?
- Why were Quebec and New Orleans important settlements to the French?

A Biographical Sketch

A hard worker

Samuel de Champlain worked long and hard to help France settle in North America. In 1608 Champlain led an expedition to North America. The goal of this journey was to set up a fur-trading post. Champlain and those with him sailed up the St. Lawrence River. After they landed along the banks of the river, they began clearing land and building shelters. A new French settlement, which Champlain named Quebec, was started!

Champlain helped Quebec become a center for fur trading between the French and the Indians. Then Champlain left Quebec for a while. He helped some friendly Indians fight other Indians with whom they were at war. During this time, Champlain discovered a large lake, now known as Lake Champlain.

Later Champlain returned to Quebec to help the settlement grow. He tried to get people in France to move to New France, especially to Quebec. And he tried to get missionaries to come to work with the Indians. After a while, Champlain left Quebec again. This time he explored other parts of North

America that were unknown to him. During this journey, Champlain claimed more land for New France.

Champlain is often remembered for claiming land in North America for France. And he is often remembered for trying to settle New France. Because of Champlain's hard work, he is sometimes known as the Father of New France. Do you think this is a good title for Champlain? Why or why not?

Life in New France

Land for farming   The French land in North America belonged to the king of France. The king gave rights to this land to trading companies in France. The trading companies then gave the land to a few favored people. These landowners were called **seigneurs** [sayn-YURZ]. The farmers who worked the land were called **habitants** [(H)AB-ih-TAHZ].

The trading companies had hoped that many people from France would come to New France to farm. But, because the landowners controlled the land, there was very little free land. This meant that people who wanted to farm could not own land. Instead, they had to pay rent to and work for a seigneur. In addition, the northern part of New France had very thick forests, poor soil, and a short growing season. So many farmers stayed in France. Much of New France was also very cold during the long winter months. Why might this have kept people from wanting to settle there?

Farms like this one were found in parts of New France. They were generally located near the banks of the St. Lawrence River from Quebec to Montreal.

French fur trappers and many groups of Indians in New France became friends. Some trappers even lived among their Indian friends. How are this Indian and this trapper showing their friendship?

Other ways of making a living

Some people who moved to New France made their living by fishing. However, most people who moved to northern New France made their living by fur trading. Those who trapped furs in northern New France spent much time in the **wilderness.** This is the woods or part of the land that has been changed very little by people. The trappers generally traveled by canoe, like the one in the picture on this page. Besides trapping furs, many of these people also traded with the Indians for furs.

When spring came, the trappers and their Indian friends took their furs to trading centers. At about the same time, ships from France would arrive at the trading centers. Then the Indians would exchange their furs for goods from Europe. The Indians often got goods such as blankets, cloth, beads, spoons, and guns in exchange for their furs. A few weeks later, the Indians and the trappers would load their canoes with the goods they had traded for. Then they would return to the wilderness. And the French ships would return to Europe loaded with the furs.

The desire for furs in Europe made fur trading a very important business in northern New France. It was the best way for people in New France to make a living. And it helped many people in New France. Fur trading helped the Indians and others who trapped the furs to get other goods. And it helped those who traded the furs to earn a living. But fur trading also hurt New France. The people who trapped were often on the move. They lived a carefree life that drew them away from communities and into the woods. How does the way of life of the trappers help explain why there were so few lasting settlements in New France?

The Indians and the missionaries The French and many groups of Indians in North America were on friendly terms. They trusted and respected one another. One reason for this was that the French did not change the land very much. The French spent more time trapping and trading furs than in clearing land for farming and for building settlements.

French missionaries helped to further the good relations between the French and the Indians. The missionaries often lived and worked with the Indians on Indian lands. They treated the Indians well and taught them new ways of doing things. They tried to make the Indians members of the Roman Catholic Church. And they helped the Indians trade at French forts. In what ways do you think that the Indians helped the French?

Governing New France The king of France chose officers to rule and keep order in New France. The king also chose an **intendant** [ihn-TEHN-duhnt], or chief officer, to be the head of the government of New France.

Jean Talon [tah-LOHN] was chosen to be the first intendant of New France. Talon's job was to carry out the wishes of the king. He tried to help the French settle New France. And he worked to help the French gain more power and wealth in North America.

The French influence Today many things in the United States and in Canada help us remember that the French once

Mardi Gras takes place in New Orleans, Louisiana, every year. But other Mardi Gras also take place in some other southern cities.

lived here. Several lakes, rivers, and towns in our country and in Canada have French names. Some people living in the United States and many people living in eastern Canada today are French. These people, especially those living in eastern Canada, generally speak French.

Other things also remind us that the French once lived in North America. French-style houses can be seen in parts of the United States and in Canada. And **Mardi Gras** [MAHRD-ee-GRAH], a large kind of party, was brought to this country by the French. This party takes place in February or March and lasts for about two weeks. During this time there are many parades and dances. The picture on this page shows one part of Mardi Gras. What part does it show? What else can you think of that reminds you that the French lived in North America hundreds of years ago?

wrap •up

- What were some ways of making a living in New France?
- Why did the French have a hard time developing and settling New France?
- How did the French contribute to the way of life in North America?

Chapter-End Activities

The chapter-end activities may be done by writing the questions or statements and the answers on a separate sheet of paper or by writing just the answers on a separate sheet of paper, whichever your teacher desires.

Words and Terms

Mardi Gras	wilderness
expedition	habitants
seigneurs	intendant

Last night I dreamed that I visited New France. First I spent some time along the banks of the St. Lawrence River with some landowners called __(1)__. While there, I helped some __(2)__ farm part of the land. Then I spent some time with a trapper in the __(3)__, or woods. Next, I helped some friendly Indians canoe to a big trading center. I think it was Montreal. There I saw the chief officer, or __(4)__, of New France talking with some other officers. Just before my dream ended, I was in New Orleans. I was taking part in a large kind of party called __(5)__.

Fact Recall

1. Which explorers helped France claim land near the present-day St. Lawrence River?

2. Which French explorers made journeys down the present-day Mississippi River?

3. Which settlement was at the northern end of New France, and which settlement was at the southern end of New France?

4. What were some of the ways by which people in New France made a living?

5. What are some things that help us remember that the French once lived in what are now the United States and Canada?

Concepts and Understandings

1. Why did the leaders of France continue to send explorers to North America?

2. How did the fur-trading business help New France, and how did it hurt New France?

129

CHAPTER 7

The English Get Started in America

1. **English activity begins**
2. **Early successful English settlements**
3. **More English colonies**

Make believe you have just arrived in America in the early 1600s. Your home will be in the settlement you see in the picture on this page. Do you think you might like living in this settlement? Why or why not?

This settlement was started by a group of people from England. People came to America from England for different reasons. Some English people came to America to get rich. Others came seeking religious freedom. Still others came to start a new way of life. In this chapter you will read about some of the English settlements started in North America. And you will read how some of these settlements became permanent places in our country.

1

English activity begins

A shorter route to Asia John Cabot [KAB-uht], an Italian sea captain, was living in England at the time Columbus made his first journey. When Cabot heard about Columbus's journey, he felt that Columbus had sailed too far south. Cabot believed that a northern route across the Atlantic Ocean to Asia would be shorter.

Cabot got the king of England to give him permission to sail for England. Some business people in England helped pay for the trip. Why do you think the king of England and the business people were willing to help Cabot?

In 1497 Cabot set sail for North America. There, he sailed along the coast of present-day Newfoundland and Nova Scotia before returning to England. Cabot never found a short, all-water route to Asia. But he did give England its first claim to land in North America.

A famous sea dog Sometimes English sea captains robbed Spanish treasure ships. These captains were often called **sea dogs.** Sir Francis Drake was a well-known English sea dog.

John Cabot and his crew sailed for North America from Bristol, England, on the Mathew. How do you think Cabot and his crew felt as they prepared to sail on their voyage?

Francis Drake was among the most daring of the English sea dogs. He was knighted Sir Francis Drake after he robbed Spanish treasure ships off the coast of Peru in 1577 and then sailed around the world.

In 1577 Drake left England and sailed around South America. He found some unprotected Spanish treasure ships near Peru. Drake took as much treasure from these ships as his own ships could carry. Then he sailed northwest, not daring to return by the same route he had come. Why do you suppose that was so? Drake finally sailed west across the Pacific Ocean and the Indian Ocean. He sailed around the tip of Africa and back to England. Drake became the first English person to sail around the world.

Attempts to settle The English finally became interested in starting a **colony** in America. A colony is one or more settlements started by people who keep ties with the country from which they came. Sir Humphrey Gilbert was given permission by the queen of England to start a colony in Newfoundland. Gilbert reached Newfoundland in 1583, but the people did not like the cold, bare land that they saw. They tried to return to England but went down at sea.

Sir Walter Raleigh [RAWL-ee] became the next person to try to start an English colony in America. In 1585 he sent a group of people to America. The group started a colony on Roanoke [ROH-(uh-)NOHK] Island off the coast of present-day North Carolina. Find

Roanoke Island on the map on this page. Why do you think the group started a settlement on Roanoke Island? The English soon made enemies of some Indians on Roanoke. The English also began to run out of food. So they left Roanoke and returned to England.

A lost colony Raleigh tried again, in 1587, to start an English colony in America. John White was chosen to be the leader of the new colony. Shortly after the group landed on Roanoke Island, White's daughter gave birth to a baby girl. The baby, named Virginia Dare, became the first English child born in America.

After a while White went to England for more supplies. A war in England kept him from returning to Roanoke for two years. When White finally returned to Roanoke, no one was there. The colony had disappeared. Perhaps unfriendly Indians killed the people, or the people starved. Perhaps they joined a friendly group of Indians. No one knows for sure.

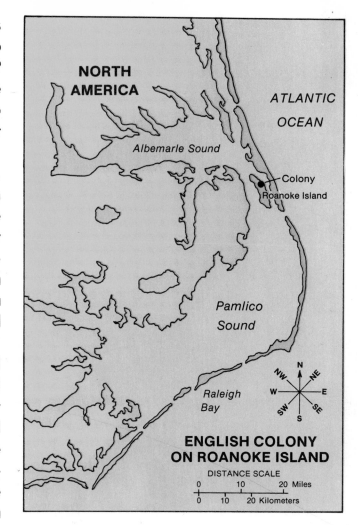

ENGLISH COLONY
ON ROANOKE ISLAND

DISTANCE SCALE

wrap •up

- Why did Cabot want to take a northern route across the Atlantic Ocean?
- How did Gilbert and Raleigh try to help the English hold their land in North America?
- Why did the early attempts by the English to start colonies in America fail?

2

Early successful English settlements

Not giving up   The first tries by England at starting a colony in America failed for a number of reasons. England had troubles at home and was fighting with Spain. And money for starting a colony was not easy to come by. By 1600, however, England was at peace with Spain. And in the early 1600s, some people began to start trading companies. These companies wanted to send people to begin trading settlements in different parts of the world.

One trading company was known as the Virginia Company. It received a **charter,** or a written order, from King James I to start settlements in North America. The king divided much land in North America between two groups of the Virginia Company. One of these groups was the Plymouth Company. The other group was the London Company.

The first permanent settlement   The London Company was the first to send **colonists** to America. Colonists are people who go to live in a new place but keep ties with the country from which they came. In 1607 the people sent by the London Company arrived in North America. They started a settlement along the banks of a river that they named the James River. And they named their settlement Jamestown. In whose honor do you think they named the river and settlement?

Life was rough for the first colonists of Jamestown. The place where they settled was full of fever-carrying insects. Many people became sick and died. Also, the colonists spent too much time hunting for gold instead of farming and building strong houses. The houses they did build were damp.

After a while John Smith took charge as the leader of Jamestown. He did not want to see the colony fail. So Smith

told the people that if they wanted to eat, they would have to work. Smith got the people to build better houses like you see in the picture on this page. And he got the people to dig wells, clear land, and plant crops. Smith also traded with the Indians for food. But then he was badly hurt in a gunpowder accident and had to return to England.

After Smith left Jamestown, things began to get bad again. There was not enough food for everyone. And the people were afraid to look for food outside the **stockade**. This was a line of strong posts that was built around the whole settlement. Why do you think they built a stockade?

Finally, things got better at Jamestown. The people began to raise their own food. Then John Rolfe learned to grow and cure an Indian plant called tobacco. Rolfe sent some of it to England. People there liked it very much. Soon more and more people in Jamestown began growing tobacco. Trade between the colony and England grew. And Jamestown became the first lasting English settlement.

Another permanent settlement In the 1500s King Henry VIII of England had formed the Church of England. Everyone in England had to belong to this new church. But

These buildings are like the ones built by the early colonists at Jamestown, Virginia. How did the colonists use their natural environment to make these buildings?

some people did not like the Church of England. Some of them even wanted to leave the Church of England.

One group of people that wanted to leave the church went to Holland, but they were not happy there either. Several years later they decided to move to America in hopes of finding religious freedom. These people became known as the **Pilgrims.** Because the London Company helped pay for their trip, the Pilgrims returned to England before going to America. Then in 1620 they sailed for America aboard the *Mayflower.* They landed in the harbor of Cape Cod. This was farther north than where they were supposed to land. The Pilgrims became worried because they had no rights to land where they were. So they made an agreement, the *Mayflower Compact,* to govern themselves by majority rule. Do you think this was an important agreement? If so, why?

The Pilgrims looked for a good place to settle. They called the place they chose Plymouth, after the place they had left in England. It had a good harbor, and it had fields that had been cleared by a group of Indians. Why do you think these things were important to the Pilgrims?

Indians helped the Pilgrims get settled at Plymouth. The Indians brought them seeds and taught them how to grow certain crops, such as corn. The summer of 1621 went well for the people from England, and they had a good harvest. So

The Pilgrims were very thankful to be safe on land after being at sea for two months. They were eager to start their settlement. What do you think were some of the first things they had to do?

they invited their Indian friends to a feast that has become known as the first Thanksgiving. Why do you suppose the Pilgrims did that? Why do you think people still hold Thanksgiving feasts once a year?

Still more settlements Another group of people who did not like the Church of England were known as **Puritans.** Some of these people decided to seek religious freedom in America. So they formed their own trading company, called the Massachusetts Bay Company. It got a written order from the king to start settlements in America.

In 1630 the Massachusetts Bay Company sent several hundred Puritans to America. The place where they made their settlements became known as the Massachusetts Bay Colony. Find Salem, Charlestown, and Boston on the map on this page. Why do you think these and other Massachusetts Bay Colony settlements were started where they were?

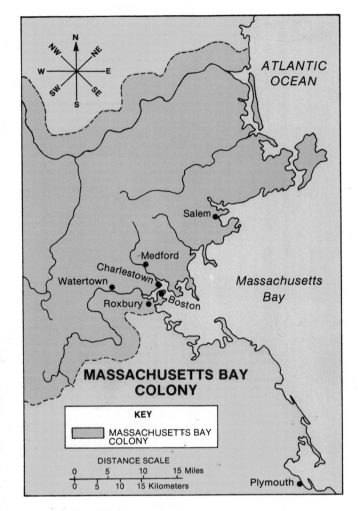

MASSACHUSETTS BAY COLONY

KEY

☐ MASSACHUSETTS BAY COLONY

DISTANCE SCALE

0   5   10   15 Miles

0   5   10   15 Kilometers

wrap·up

- What role did the Virginia Company play in helping the English settle in America?
- Why was Jamestown an important English settlement?
- How did the desire for religious freedom help the English start settlements in America?

Using Your Skills

Reading a map

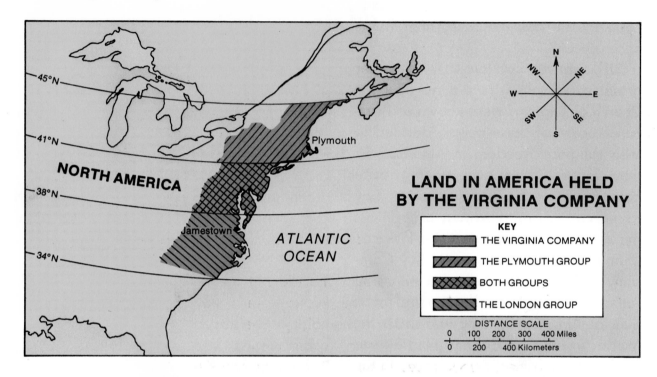

Use the map to answer these questions.

1. What does the map show?

2. Between which lines of latitude was land given to the Plymouth group only?

3. Between which lines of latitude was land given to the London group only?

4. Between which lines of latitude was land given to both groups?

5. Which group had rights to the land where Jamestown was started?

6. Which group had rights to the land where Plymouth was started?

3

More English colonies

A difference of opinion By 1640 thousands of English people were living in the Massachusetts Bay Colony. Some of these people did not always agree with the Puritan leaders of Massachusetts. One of these people was Roger Williams. Williams often spoke up when he did not agree with the leaders. So the leaders decided to send Williams back to England. Why do you think they decided to do that? But before Williams could be sent back, he secretly left one night. Look at the picture on this page. Who helped Williams after he left the colony? Several months after leaving Massachusetts, Williams started the settlement of Providence on land that he bought from the Indians.

Anne Hutchinson was another person who did not always agree with the Puritan leaders of the Massachusetts Bay Colony. She, too, was forced to leave the colony. She settled near Providence. Other people from Massachusetts also began to settle near Providence. In time, Providence and the settlements near it became the colony of Rhode Island. It was

Roger Williams left the Massachusetts Bay Colony so he would not be sent back to England. After traveling alone through the woods for four days, Williams met some friends, who gave him shelter.

a place where people could find religious freedom. Why do you think this was so?

Other dissatisfied people   Thomas Hooker was another person who wasn't always pleased with the way of life in Massachusetts Bay Colony. So he led a group of people out of Massachusetts. Some of these people left to find religious freedom. Others left to find better soil. Why do you think good soil was important to the early colonists? Hooker and those with him started the settlement of Hartford. This was the beginning of the colony of Connecticut.

Other people who were not pleased with Massachusetts left and went north. These people started a number of settlements that finally became the colony of New Hampshire. New Hampshire, Massachusetts, Rhode Island, and Connecticut made up the New England colonies.

The Dutch claim land   In 1609 the Netherlands became interested in finding a northern route through North America. So a Dutch trading company sent Henry Hudson, an English sea captain, to North America. Hudson discovered a river, now known as the Hudson River, in present-day New York. He claimed the land near the river for the Dutch.

The Dutch called the land that Hudson claimed New Netherland. They started the settlement of New Amsterdam, now New York City, at the mouth of the Hudson River. And they set up trading posts along the river. Then in 1655 the Dutch took over New Sweden. This was a colony that had been started by the Swedes in 1638. It was located along the banks of the present-day Delaware River.

New Netherland soon became a successful trading colony. This upset the English. So the English decided to fight the Dutch in 1664. But the Dutch gave up without firing a shot. Most of New Netherland became the English colony of New York. But a small part of New Netherland was given to those who started the English colony of New Jersey.

The picture above shows the Dutch colonist Peter Minuit buying Manhattan Island from some Indians in 1626. The picture on the right shows William Penn with some of his Indian friends.

The Quakers arrive In 1681 the king of England gave William Penn some land in North America. The king named this land Pennsylvania in honor of Penn's father, with whom the king had been friends.

Penn was a **Quaker,** or member of the Religious Society of Friends. Many members of this group went to Pennsylvania with Penn. These people were seeking religious freedom. Penn also allowed thousands of people of many different faiths and from a number of countries to settle in Pennsylvania. Penn treated everyone who settled in Pennsylvania well. By so doing, Penn helped Pennsylvania become one of the largest and most successful colonies.

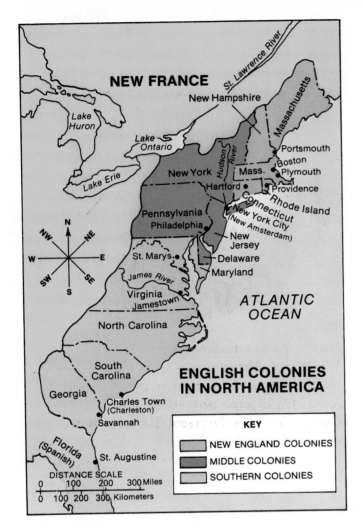

NEW FRANCE

Lake Huron

Lake Ontario

Lake Erie

New Hampshire

Massachusetts

Portsmouth
Boston
Mass. Plymouth
Providence
Rhode Island

New York

Hudson River

Hartford

Connecticut

New York City
(New Amsterdam)

Pennsylvania
Philadelphia

New Jersey

St. Marys

Delaware

Maryland

James River

Virginia
Jamestown

ATLANTIC OCEAN

North Carolina

ENGLISH COLONIES
IN NORTH AMERICA

South Carolina

Georgia

Charles Town
(Charleston)

Savannah

Florida
(Spanish)

St. Augustine

DISTANCE SCALE
0   100   200   300 Miles
0   100 200 300 Kilometers

N NE NW E W SE SW S

KEY

NEW ENGLAND COLONIES
MIDDLE COLONIES
SOUTHERN COLONIES

St. Lawrence River

At first, Pennsylvania had no coastline. So Penn asked for and received some land on the coast. This land later became the colony of Delaware. Delaware, New York, New Jersey, and Pennsylvania made up the Middle colonies.

Settling the South Jamestown was the first lasting English settlement in North America. After a while other settlements were started near Jamestown. These settlements became part of the colony of Virginia.

George Calvert, the first Lord Baltimore, wanted to settle in North America. But he died before receiving land from the king of England. The land was then passed on to Calvert's son, the second Lord Baltimore. He settled at St. Marys, where he hoped to make a settlement for Roman Catholics. Look at the map on this page. What became the name of the colony in which St. Marys was started?

Several years after Lord Baltimore was given land, the king gave some land to eight other people whom he favored. This land became known as Carolina. From its early days, Carolina began to grow in two different ways. The northern part was settled mostly by people from Virginia and other colonies to the north. These people started small farms. The southern part of Carolina was settled mostly by people from England and other countries of Europe. These people started large farms. In time, Carolina was divided into the colonies of North Carolina and South Carolina.

James Oglethorpe was interested in helping people in England who could not pay what they owed others. These people were often put in prison and left there. Oglethorpe wanted to take these people to North America so they could make a new start in life. The king gave Oglethorpe the land between South Carolina and Florida. Look at the map on page 142. Which country did Florida belong to? Why might the king of England have been somewhat eager to have people settle the land north of Florida? The land that Oglethorpe and those with him settled became the colony of Georgia. Georgia, Virginia, Maryland, North Carolina, and South Carolina made up the Southern colonies. The English then had thirteen colonies settled along the Atlantic coast of the present-day United States.

The friendship developed between the English colonists and the Indians helped the English establish permanent colonies. After James Oglethorpe arrived in the colony of Georgia in 1733, he became friends with the Indians living there.

wrap·up

- Why were the colonies of Rhode Island, Connecticut, and New Hampshire started?
- How were the Middle colonies started?
- How were the Southern colonies started?

A Biographical Sketch

Some *thoughts of her own*

Anne Hutchinson was a very religious person. She moved to the Massachusetts Bay Colony from England because she felt that God had told her to do so. The Hutchinsons had not been in Massachusetts long before Anne began to hold meetings for women in her home. Later some men also began to attend these meetings. At these meetings Hutchinson would repeat the Sunday sermon from notes she made. The church leaders liked the meetings because many women were not able to attend church. But then Hutchinson began to give her own ideas about the sermons. Sometimes these ideas were not the same as those of the church leaders. This caused problems in the colony. Why do you think this was so?

The leaders of the church took Anne Hutchinson to court. They charged her with saying things against the church. She might just have received a warning if she had not said what was on her mind. But instead, she made a long speech about her thoughts. After she finished her speech, the leaders decided to **banish** her from Massachusetts. That meant she had to leave the colony.

When spring came, the Hutchinsons left Massachusetts. They settled in what later became Rhode Island.

Anne Hutchinson believed that no church held the power to tell people what to believe. She also believed that people had the right to think for themselves. By standing up for what she believed, Anne Hutchinson helped to further the idea of religious freedom in America. Today this is one of the important rights that people in our country have.

Chapter-End Activities

The chapter-end activities may be done by writing the questions or statements and the answers on a separate sheet of paper or by writing just the answers on a separate sheet of paper, whichever your teacher desires.

Words and Terms

charter   stockade
Puritans   colony
colonists   sea dogs

1. English captains who robbed Spanish treasure ships were often called ____.

2. A ____ is one or more settlements started by people who keep ties with the country from which they came.

3. Trading companies needed to get a ____, or a written order, before they could start settlements in North America.

4. People who go to live in a new place but keep ties with the country from which they came are called ____.

5. A ____ was a line of strong posts that was built around a whole settlement.

Fact Recall

1. Twice Sir Walter Raleigh tried to start an English colony at this place in America.
   a. Long Island
   b. Roanoke Island

2. This place was the first permanent English settlement.
   a. Jamestown
   b. Boston

3. Plymouth was settled by this group of people.
   a. Roman Catholics
   b. Pilgrims

4. This colony was started by people who left Massachusetts.
   a. Georgia
   b. Rhode Island

5. The colony of New York was first settled by these people.
   a. the Dutch
   b. the Quakers

Concepts and Understandings

1. Why did some early English settlements in America fail while others succeeded?

2. How were the thirteen English colonies in America started?

Unit End

Main Ideas and Understandings

1. Why do many people believe that the Vikings came to the Americas before Columbus did? Why did the leaders of Spain continue to send explorers and conquerors to different places? Why was St. Augustine an important Spanish settlement? What are some of the contributions made to the Americas by the Spanish?

2. For what reason did the French want to find a northern route to Asia? How were the French able to find a route through the middle of our country? In what ways did fur trading play an important role in New France? What are some of the contributions made to North America by the French?

3. For what reason did Cabot want to take a northern route to Asia? For what reasons did the early attempts by the English to start colonies in America fail? Why was Jamestown an important English settlement? How were the thirteen English colonies in North America started?

Research Ideas

1. Some of the Spanish missions in present-day Florida, Texas, New Mexico, Arizona, and California still exist. Find out the names of some of these missions. Where and when was each of these missions started? What person or persons started each of these missions?

2. Quebec, Quebec; Montreal, Quebec; and New Orleans, Louisiana, were important trading centers in New France. Find out about these three cities today. What is the population of each city today? What are some major industries in each city? What are some special attractions in each city?

3. Some people played important roles in the settling of the thirteen English colonies in North America. Find out what each of the following people did: Sir George Carteret, Pocahontas, Squanto, Peter Stuyvesant, and John Winthrop. From which country did each of these people come? With which English colony was each of these people involved?

Activities and Projects

1. Make a chart comparing the exploring and settling activities of Spain, France, and England in the Americas. You might compare the following categories on your chart: reason for exploring, lands claimed, and reasons for settling. You might want to add other categories to your chart.

2. Work in teams to prepare questions for a quiz program about the explorers and colonists presented in this unit. Have each team ask their questions aloud. Have the members of another team take turns answering. You might have one member of each team keep score by counting one point for each correct answer.

Unit 4

The Thirteen American Colonies

You have seen pictures of the first English settlements in our country. And most likely you have seen pictures of George Washington and others who helped the thirteen English colonies gain their freedom from England. But more than 150 years passed between the first settlements and the time the colonies gained their freedom. How much do you know about these years? This unit will help you learn how people lived during colonial times. You will find answers to the following questions:

What groups of people lived in the English colonies?

How did these people fill their needs and wants?

How was the way of life the same in all the English colonies in America? How was it different?

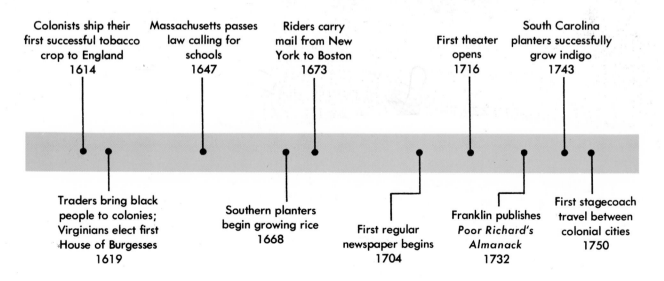

Colonists ship their first successful tobacco crop to England
1614

Massachusetts passes law calling for schools
1647

Riders carry mail from New York to Boston
1673

First theater opens
1716

South Carolina planters successfully grow indigo
1743

Traders bring black people to colonies; Virginians elect first House of Burgesses
1619

Southern planters begin growing rice
1668

First regular newspaper begins
1704

Franklin publishes *Poor Richard's Almanack*
1732

First stagecoach travel between colonial cities
1750

CHAPTER 8

Life in the New England Colonies

1. Making a living
2. The people and their activities

Do you think you could help to build your own house? Could you help to grow your own food? Could you help to make your own shoes and clothing? Or could you help to make a living by fishing or whaling? You might have done all these things if you had been a New England colonist!

The people who settled in Connecticut, Massachusetts, New Hampshire, and Rhode Island were alike in several ways. Many of the people made their living in the same ways. Many of the people belonged to the same church. And all the people shared the problems of filling their needs and wants in the area we still call New England. In this chapter you will learn about the early New England colonists and their way of life.

1

Making a living

Farming the rocky soil   People in all the English colonies were farmers. But farming was hardest in New England. The growing season there was short. Deep forests covered much of the land. And the soil was thin and full of rocks. Why do you think most New England farm fields were small?

At first the New England colonists prepared fields around each town. A family had one or more fields in which to grow corn, oats, vegetables, and fruits. Some people also grew **flax**—a plant from which linen cloth is made. Animals grazed on **commons,** or land everyone could use.

After many years New Englanders divided the fields around towns into farms. Families built houses on their own land, away from the towns. People fenced in their land with stone walls. Where do you think they found stones for the walls?

New England farms were small. Even so, it took every family member except young children to do the work. No matter how hard the people worked, they could not raise all the food they needed. Some food eaten in New England was **imported,** or brought in from other places.

Part of each day's chores in a New England household included working in the fields or in a garden such as this one.

Shipbuilders did most of their work on land. To launch a finished ship, the workers knocked down part of the wooden structure around the ship. Then the ship slid gently into the water.

Taking to the sea   Most colonial settlements in New England were near the ocean. Do you think New England people often went fishing to help feed their families? Why do you think so? Many people who could not make a living by farming began fishing for a living. Colonial and European people wanted fish. So the New England colonies **exported,** or sent to other places, both salted and dried fish.

During the 1700s many New England people began hunting whales. People in colonial times used whale oil in lamps. They used wax from one kind of whale to make candles. And they used whalebone to make buttons.

People who went fishing or whaling needed ships. Many New Englanders made a living by building ships. These ships were as good as English ships but cost less. New England shipbuilders used lumber from the forests. English shipbuilders had to import lumber. Why do you think people all over the world bought New England ships?

The beginnings of industry   New England people needed many things. But it cost a lot to bring English goods across the ocean. So colonists made many things themselves.

They carved furniture, tools, plates, and spoons from wood. They spun flax and wool into thread, which they then wove into cloth. They made their own shoes, candles, and soap. What is the person in the picture at the top of this page doing?

Some people found that they could do certain things better than others could. So some people began to **specialize,** or to do just one kind of work. One person might do all the blacksmith work in a town. Another might grind all the corn. Some people such as candlemakers and tailors traveled from one town to another. Why do you think they did this?

Some places had many people who did the same kind of work. The people worked in their own homes making goods such as cloth or shoes to sell. The work of many people was needed to make some kinds of goods. So people worked together to make such goods as ships, iron, and bricks. Cities such as Boston, Massachusetts, had many craftspeople. Printers, cabinetmakers, and many other skilled people worked in cities. Why do you think most craftspeople wanted to work in cities?

Trading with the world New England had plenty of some things but not enough of other things. So many colonists became **merchants.** These

The person shown above is demonstrating how colonists dipped candlewicks into hot wax or tallow. Colonists generally made candles in their own homes. Other items were made by craftspeople in shops such as the metal shop shown below.

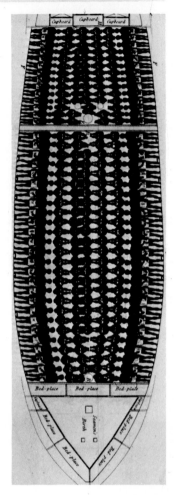

were people who traded with others. Some merchants traded with the Indians. Others owned ships that carried fish, lumber, and whale oil to other colonies and to Europe. Then the ships returned to New England. They brought flour, meat, clothing, tools, and other goods. Why do you think merchants were important in New England?

Some New England ships carried people coming to live in the colonies. Some of the people were **indentured** [ihn-DEHN-churd] **servants.** These were people who agreed to work for others in return for their fare. A servant generally worked four to seven years. Then the person became free.

A few Europeans were kidnapped and brought to the colonies. But most Europeans came by choice. However, black people from Africa had no choice. Beginning in the 1600s merchant ships carried black Africans. Some black people became indentured servants, but most became slaves.

Slaves were crowded into ships like the one in the picture on this page. Many slaves died during the trip across the ocean. Those who lived were sold or traded to people who became their masters. Few slaves were owned by New Englanders. These people did not need slaves, since their families generally did most of the work themselves. But many slaves were owned by people in the other English colonies.

These diagrams show how a slave trader planned to pack as many slaves as possible into one ship. Where on this ship were slaves forced to sit up? Where were slaves forced to lie down?

wrap·up

- What were some of the major goods made in the New England colonies?
- Why did fishing, whaling, and shipbuilding become important in colonial New England?
- Why was trading with other places important to the New England colonies?

Using Your Skills

Reading a chart

SHIPS SAILING FROM BOSTON

TO	1715	1755	1769
England	48	35	66
Other countries in Europe	19	31	21
Africa	unknown	unknown	4
West Indies	200	137	150
Other places in the thirteen English colonies in America	177	122	457
Total	444	325	698

1. What does this chart show?

2. Where did most of the ships sailing from Boston go in 1715? In 1755? In 1769?

3. In what years did more ships sail from Boston to England than to other countries in Europe?

4. To what places did the number of ships sailing from Boston increase the most between 1715 and 1769?

5. By how much did the total number of ships sailing from Boston increase between 1715 and 1769?

2

The people and their activities

Many colonial houses were covered with boards that overlapped slightly to keep out wind and rain. Glass for the windows of a house like this one would probably have been imported from England. Poorer colonists sometimes used oiled paper instead of glass for windows.

Visiting a New England town What would you do if you could move backward through time? Right now make believe that such a trip is possible. Imagine that you are visiting a small colonial town in New England. Towns were the center of most activities in early New England.

One of the first things you would notice is public land in the center of town. In some towns this land was known as a common and in others as a **village green**. The land was used by all the people for recreation and other things. Do you think this was a good idea? Why or why not? Around the public land you would see many buildings.

Most New England buildings were wood. Why do you think colonists used wood for building? Stone chimneys were built into the walls or up through the middle of buildings. How do you think such chimneys helped keep buildings warm?

Some of the buildings were houses, barns, sheds, or shops. Other buildings you would likely see were a school and a **meetinghouse,** or church. And you would see an **inn.** An inn was a public place where people could sleep, eat, and drink. What do we call such buildings today?

Meeting the people   Almost all the people you would meet in an early New England town would be English Puritans. Some of these people had been born in England. Others had parents or grandparents who were English.

The Puritans believed in wearing simple clothing. Most girls and women wore dark dresses with white collars and cuffs. Most boys and men wore short jackets with white collars and cuffs. They also wore long stockings and loose-fitting pants that came just below the knees. Most people wore plain leather shoes that were made to fit on either foot. Why do you think shoes were made this way?

This is how a New England town might have looked in the 1600s. How does this town compare with the community in which you live?

Colonial families, like the one shown above, spent their evenings working or relaxing around the kitchen fireplace. Building a new house involved the help of many neighbors. All the people who helped with a house-raising were rewarded with a feast afterward.

By the 1700s a number of people who were not Puritans were living in New England. Some of these people were Presbyterians or Baptists. A few others were Jewish, Quaker, or Roman Catholic. As more people came to New England, the Puritans became less strict. Why do you think this happened? During the 1700s New Englanders dressed much like their neighbors in the other English colonies.

New Englanders at home The Puritans also believed that houses should be simple. So their houses were very plain inside. Early colonists had little furniture. Some people had only a table, a chair, some benches, a bed, and a chest.

The kitchen was the warmest and brightest room in most houses. Sometimes it was the *only* room! The colonists always kept a fire burning in the large kitchen fireplace. Throughout the house you could smell food cooking. New Englanders often ate stews of deer, squirrel, or rabbit meat. Where do you think they got these animals? They roasted fish, beef, and pork. Sometimes they ate vegetables and fruits from their gardens or from the woods. And every day they ate corn prepared in some way. Why do you think the people depended on a good corn crop every year?

Working and having fun   The New England Puritans were serious people who believed in hard work. But they also had fun. This was partly because they joined together to do hard or tiresome work, such as building houses or harvesting crops. What work are the people in the picture at the bottom of page 158 doing? When the work was finished, the people shared a meal, told stories, or sang songs. In what ways do people today mix work with fun?

Over many years the people in New England towns became rather successful. They had more food, more goods, and more money than in the early years of the colonies. Do you think life was easier for the people? Do you think people had more free time? Why do you think so?

New England men spent some of their free time at inns. Women were often not allowed to do this. At inns the people visited with neighbors and talked with travelers. For many years this was the only way to get news from other places. There were very few newspapers in New England during the 1600s.

New Englanders used some of their free time to read. Everyone read the Bible. The people also read books and poems about subjects such as history and religion. Some people enjoyed reading about journeys to other colonies. During the 1700s travelers and businesspeople often carried newspapers with them. Why do you think people in small towns were eager to read these newspapers?

Attending church and school   Religion was very important to the early New England Puritans. Every Sunday Puritans attended services at the meetinghouse. In some towns people had to pay a fine if they did not come to the services! A few people found it hard to stay awake through services that often lasted several hours. So people with long sticks walked through each meetinghouse. A rap on the head from one of these sticks kept a sleepy Puritan wide awake!

Pupils in colonial schools read from hornbooks. A hornbook consisted of a flat wooden paddle and a piece of paper protected by a thin layer of cow's horn.

Education was also important to the Puritans. They wanted everyone to be able to read the Bible. Some women taught reading and writing in their homes to neighborhood children. And some parents taught their children themselves. But many parents did not have time to teach their children. Why do you think this was true? So New England colonies passed laws calling for towns of a certain size to have schools.

Pupils in early New England schools studied mostly reading, writing, and arithmetic. Pupils had to memorize everything. And teachers often used switches on pupils who did not learn their lessons! The picture on this page shows how a New England school might have looked.

Many New England children went to school for a few years. After that they were too busy at home to attend school. Many girls did not go to school, because some Puritans thought schooling was only for boys. How does your school compare with an early New England school?

Governing the New England colonies People who lived in the New England colonies had many problems. The people did not always agree about things like work, land, and taxes. They needed leaders to make decisions for all the people. Do people today need leaders? Why do you think so?

One such leader was the king of England. The king, and people the king named to help him, made many important decisions for all the colonies. However, each colony also had a **legislature.** This was the group of people that passed laws. Why do you think laws were needed?

New England towns also had local leaders. Voters in each town chose **selectmen.** These people ran the town government. Selectmen called town meetings at which people talked about such things as how to use public land. What other things do you think they might have talked about?

Anyone could attend and speak at a town meeting. But not everyone could vote. White men who were Puritans and who owned land could vote. After many years white men from other churches could also vote. But women, black people, Indians, and indentured servants could not vote at all. During the years that only Puritans could vote, all the leaders of New England were Puritans. So all laws were based on Puritan beliefs. Why do you think this was so?

wrap ·up

- How would you describe the people who were the early New England colonists?
- How did the beliefs of the Puritans affect their way of life?
- How is your community different from a New England colonial community? How is it the same?

A Biographical Sketch

The first English colonial poet

Sailing across the ocean took many weeks in the year 1630. So the shores of Massachusetts looked inviting to English Puritans coming to make new homes in North America. Among these people was a sickly young woman named Anne Bradstreet. Within twenty years she would become the first poet in the English colonies.

Anne and Simon Bradstreet had more money than some colonists. Even so, their life in early Massachusetts was hard. Making a living and keeping house for eight children kept the Bradstreets very busy. Anne Bradstreet sometimes had to wait until everyone else fell asleep. Then she had time to read and write poems.

Some people in the 1600s thought women should leave all reading and writing to men! But Anne Bradstreet's family did not believe that. Some members of her family sent her writings to England. There her first book of poems was printed in 1650. It was the first book of poems written by an English colonist. And it was the first major book of poems written by an English woman.

Anne Bradstreet wrote about nature, religion, her family, sickness, and other things. Some people still read her poems today. These poems help to show what the life and thoughts of an early New England Puritan were like.

Chapter-End Activities

The chapter-end activities may be done by writing the questions or statements and the answers on a separate sheet of paper or by writing just the answers on a separate sheet of paper, whichever your teacher desires.

Words and Terms

legislature   commons
specialize   flax
merchants   inn

_____ 1. Land that everyone could use
_____ 2. To do just one kind of work
_____ 3. People who traded with others
_____ 4. A public place where people could sleep, eat, and drink
_____ 5. The group of people that passed laws

Fact Recall

1. Soil in New England was generally thin and (rich, rocky).
2. Many New England colonists (fished, grew rice) for a living.
3. Many skilled colonial craftspeople worked in (small towns, cities).
4. New England merchants exported (food, lumber).
5. A great number of (Swedes, Puritans) lived in the New England colonies.
6. One food that everyone in New England ate was (corn, tomatoes).
7. New Englanders made hard or tiresome work fun by (joining together, hiring help).
8. Many New Englanders enjoyed reading books and poems about history and (art, religion).
9. The (president, king) made many important decisions for all the colonies.
10. New England town meetings were an important part of (religion, government).

Concepts and Understandings

1. Why did the New England colonists depend on trade to provide many of the goods the people needed?
2. How did the Puritans and their beliefs affect the early way of life in the New England colonies?

163

CHAPTER 9

Life in the Middle Colonies

1. **Economic activities of the people**
2. **How the people lived**

The people who settled in the Middle colonies brought many things to America. Have you heard stories about a jolly fat man who brings presents to children? Have you ever seen pictures of small houses built of logs? When was the last time you ate a cookie? The idea of Santa Claus, log cabins, and the word *cookie* came from people who lived in the Middle colonies.

The Middle colonies were Delaware, New Jersey, New York, and Pennsylvania. The people who lived in these places came from several countries. They spoke different languages and belonged to different churches. But they all worked to help make life more pleasant and rewarding. In this chapter you will learn about how the people in the Middle colonies lived.

Economic activities of the people

The breadbasket of the colonies   The people who came to the Middle colonies found a land of wide river valleys and thick forests. They found rich soil and a fairly long growing season. Many of these people were very good farmers. They knew that planting a different crop in a field each year helps the soil. And they knew how to **fertilize,** or how to add things to the soil that plants need to grow. Why do you think this was important?

Farmers in the Middle colonies grew more food than their families needed. So the farmers raised **cash crops**. These are crops that are raised to be sold. The cash crops of the Middle colonies were wheat and other grains, vegetables, fruits, and farm animals. The most important cash crop was wheat. People raised so much wheat and made so much flour that the Middle colonies were sometimes called the breadbasket of the colonies. Do you think this was a good name for this area? Why or why not?

This was a familiar sight in the Middle colonies at harvest time. Neighbors, hired helpers, indentured servants, and relatives all worked to help harvest the grain quickly.

Trappers were some of the first colonists to move beyond the edge of colonial settlements. Many of them learned from the American Indians how to stay alive in the wilderness.

Farms in the Middle colonies were much larger than those in New England. What reasons can you think of that might explain this? Many people were needed to help with the farm work. Every member of a farm family helped. Many farmers had to use hired helpers or indentured servants. And on a few huge farms slaves were used to do much of the work.

Making a living from the waters and the forests Many people in the Middle colonies lived near rivers or lakes. These people sometimes fished to help feed their families. Some people who lived near the ocean fished for a living. But most people found that they could make more money by farming or doing other things than by fishing. How was this different from New England?

People in the Middle colonies depended on ships for fishing and for trading. So some people made a living by building ships. Where do you think these people got lumber for shipbuilding?

Some people made a living by hunting and trapping. These people searched for such animals as beavers and deer in the forests where no other colonists lived. Merchants traded with hunters and trappers and with Indians for the animal skins. The skins were quite valuable. They were used to make fur hats and fine leather goods.

Manufacturing in the Middle colonies People in the Middle colonies, like people in New England, made many things for themselves. Why do you think the people did this? Many of the people in the Middle colonies specialized. A large number of these people worked with farm goods. Some people, like the person in the picture at the top of this page, worked as millers. Millers ground corn and wheat into flour. Some people worked in bakeries making bread or in dairies making butter and cheese. Why do you think so many people in the Middle colonies worked with farm goods?

The miller shown above directs grain into a hopper, or container. The blacksmith shown below may have other apprentices besides the one shown. What protective clothing is the blacksmith wearing?

The two largest cities in all the English colonies were in the Middle colonies. These cities were New York City, New York, and Philadelphia, Pennsylvania. Many parents sent their children to these cities to become **apprentices.** Apprentices worked with master craftspeople for several years. Then apprentices could go into business for themselves. Do you think this was a good way to learn how to do a job? Why or why not?

The craftspeople in the Middle colonies were well-known in other places. They made some of the best guns people could buy. They also made iron, bricks, glass, tools, wagons, furniture, and fur hats. Where do you think they got the skins used to make hats?

Conestoga wagons like the one shown in the background of this picture were developed in Pennsylvania. How did the Conestoga wagon protect its cargo from the weather?

Getting goods to market   Farmers needed to get their farm goods to places where people could buy those goods. Some farmers used boats to carry farm goods. Others used large covered wagons. The picture on this page shows how these wagons looked. Why do you think farmers used different ways to carry goods?

Some farmers sold their goods. Others traded them for things they needed. Many farmers sent their goods to New York City or to Philadelphia. By 1750 Philadelphia was the largest and busiest city in the English colonies. There merchants exported wheat and other grains, flour, biscuits, meat, and live animals. They made money from the sale of these goods. People used this money to buy other things merchants imported. These were things the people needed or wanted but could not make enough of themselves.

wrap ·up

- Why was farming important in the Middle colonies?
- How would you describe the major goods made in the Middle colonies?
- Why was trade important to the people of the Middle colonies?

Reading bar graphs

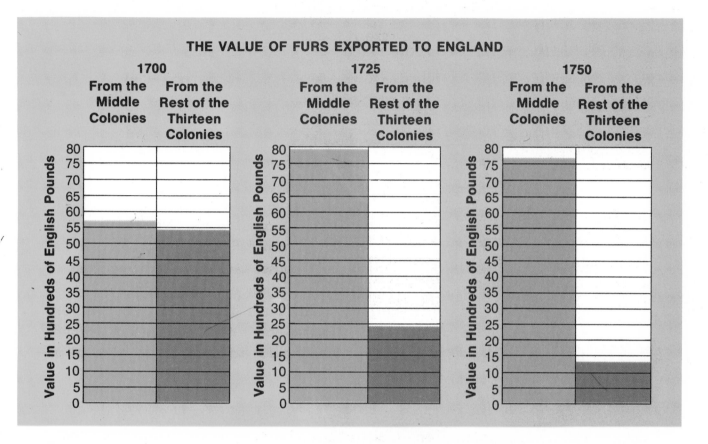

THE VALUE OF FURS EXPORTED TO ENGLAND

Use the graphs to answer the following questions:

1. What do the graphs show?

2. What was the value in British pounds of furs exported to England from the Middle colonies in 1700? In 1725? In 1750?

3. What year shows the smallest difference between the value of furs exported from the Middle colonies and of those exported from the rest of the thirteen colonies? What year shows the greatest difference?

4. By how much did the value of furs exported from the Middle colonies increase between 1700 and 1725? By how much did it decrease between 1725 and 1750?

2

How the people lived

"Seeing" the Middle colonies   Make believe once again that you can take a trip through time. This time you are visiting the Middle colonies. To find the centers of activities here, you would have to visit several kinds of communities.

Cities such as New York and Philadelphia were the busiest centers of activities. Why do you think this was so? The picture on this page shows how New York might have looked in colonial days. Streets and waterfronts in such cities were often full of busy people.

Some people in the Middle colonies lived in towns. But more people lived on farms than in towns. Why do you think this was so? You would see farm buildings made of stone and wood. Some people built houses and barns into the sides of hills. Why do you think people made buildings this way?

Some people lived in the **backcountry.** This was the very edge of land that colonists had settled. In the backcountry people were often many miles from towns or from other

People who gathered along the waterfront in old New York included sailors, ship captains, merchants, shoppers, and anyone else who enjoyed the excitement of waterfront activity. How would you describe the style of dress worn by the people shown here?

farms. The people there cleared small fields and used logs to make cabins and other buildings. Why do you think people in the backcountry made buildings this way?

A variety of people The people who settled in the Middle colonies came from many different backgrounds. During the 1600s the people were generally from the groups that had started each colony. But by the 1700s many different groups of people lived in each of the Middle colonies.

Many English, Welsh, Swedish, and Finnish people lived in New Jersey and Delaware. Some people known as the Scotch-Irish also lived there. These were Scotch people whose families had lived in Ireland for many years.

Many English and Dutch people lived in New York. And a number of black slaves worked on large farms along the Hudson River. In New York City there were many different groups of people. Some of these people were the English, the Dutch, black slaves and free blacks, the Germans, the Jewish, and the French. Why do you think so many different kinds of people settled in a large city like New York?

The colony with the greatest variety of people was Pennsylvania. The people who first settled there were Quakers. The Quakers themselves were English, Welsh, Irish, Dutch, and German. Then the Quakers invited people from throughout Europe to settle in Pennsylvania too. Many Scotch-Irish people lived in the backcountry, and many Germans lived on farms. Even more people from different backgrounds lived in Philadelphia than in New York City. How does this make colonial Philadelphia like large American cities today?

Some ways of life in the Middle colonies People in the Middle colonies followed different ways of life. Many people followed the way of life they had known in their homeland. Why do you think they did this? The Dutch came from a country of clean, neat houses and dairy farms. There they had enjoyed good food and drink, had worn brightly colored clothing, and had formed schools for their children. The Germans also came from a farming country. They, too, had enjoyed good food. In Germany the people had decorated their houses with bright colors. They had taught their children how to farm. How do you think people from these countries lived in the Middle colonies?

Some people, such as the Quakers, followed a way of life taught by their church. The Quakers believed in hard work. They wore plain clothing and lived in simple houses. They attended weekly services at their meetinghouse. But they thought people of other churches should be able to worship as they pleased. The Quakers taught their children to read and write. They taught them other skills, too, such as how to keep business records. How were the Quakers like the Puritans of New England? How were they different?

The Quakers, or the Society of Friends, encouraged men and women to share the duties of leadership in their meetings.

Some people lived in a way that depended on the place where they settled. People in the backcountry built rough cabins. They had to make many things themselves. These people depended on foods they could grow or could get by hunting. They had done few of these things in Europe. Why do you think they learned to do these things in the backcountry?

Using free time People in the Middle colonies had plenty of work to do. And they had several ways of mixing work with pleasure. Many of the people joined together to make hard work fun, just like the New Englanders did. People who lived in the backcountry or on farms often did this. What kinds of work do you think they did in this way?

People from cities, towns, and farms met at **markets** and **fairs**. These were places where people could buy, sell, or trade goods. Markets and fairs were also places to have fun. There people played games, ran races, and ate. What things might people today do at markets or fairs?

During the 1700s many people enjoyed reading. They read books and newspapers. They also read **almanacs**. These were small, yearly magazines with information about many subjects. Some of these magazines also had

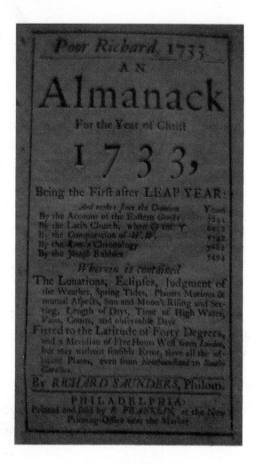

This is the title page of the first edition of Poor Richard's Almanack. *Although Benjamin Franklin wrote his almanacks himself, he pretended that someone else had written them. What name did he use?*

jokes, stories, and wise sayings. Some people in the Middle colonies belonged to singing or dancing groups. People in cities enjoyed gathering at inns or coffeehouses to talk with one another. Those who were rich sometimes attended plays and concerts.

Communicating with one another   People who wanted to travel or to send goods to other colonies often used ships. But many ships were slow and crowded. And a number of people lived far from cities and other communities built along waterways. So people needed other ways to travel and to send goods, news, and mail.

Early stagecoaches had hard wooden seats and no springs. Riders ate and slept at inns like the one shown here.

Many colonies built roads. Some roads, such as the Great Pennsylvania Wagon Road, were built to help farmers carry goods. Roads were made longer as people moved farther from cities and towns. Why do you think such roads became important to travelers as well as to farmers?

Roads known as **post roads** were built for riders carrying mail. Such roads connected cities in New England with New York City and Philadelphia. Some mail routes also became stagecoach routes. Stagecoaches, like the one in the picture on page 174, were used for more than a hundred years.

Government in the Middle colonies Government in the Middle colonies was much like that of New England. The king of England made many important decisions. And legislatures in each colony passed laws. The people voted for their local leaders, but not everyone could vote. Only free white men who owned a certain amount of land or had property of a certain value could vote. How was this like the right to vote in New England?

Some places in the Middle colonies held town meetings. People in these places chose selectmen and other leaders. In some places people lived a long way from towns and from one another. Where do you think this was true? Local government in many of these places was set up by counties. A county was made up of all the towns, farms, or other settlements within a certain area. People chose county leaders who had many of the same powers that selectmen and town leaders had.

wrap ·up

- What were some of the groups of people who settled in the Middle colonies?
- How would you describe the different ways of life in the Middle colonies?
- How is your community like a community in the Middle colonies? How is it different?

A Biographical Sketch

A *pioneer of freedom of the press*

People who read newspapers today know that the papers do not always agree with the government. Papers sometimes say that the government is wrong or that people in the government are not honest. Newspapers were not always allowed to do this, as John Peter Zenger found out in 1735.

Zenger printed a newspaper in New York City. The newspaper said many things about the governor, William Cosby. The paper said that Governor Cosby was greedy and that he did many dishonest things. Governor Cosby thought that the newspaper had harmed his **reputation**, or good name. So he ordered soldiers to burn copies of Zenger's newspaper in the street. Then he had John Peter Zenger thrown into jail.

Zenger remained in jail for about nine months. He was not allowed to meet with his family and his friends. He could only talk with them through a hole in the cell door. But Anna Catharine Zenger kept the printing office open. So the newspaper was printed even while Zenger was in jail.

When Zenger went to court, his lawyer talked to the **jury,** or group of people chosen to hear the case. He asked them to decide if what Zenger had printed was the *truth*. The jury thought about the things Governor Cosby had done. They ageed that the paper had printed the truth, and they set Zenger free. Thanks to the Zenger case, newspapers today can print things both for and against the government. But they should be careful to tell the truth.

Chapter-End Activities

The chapter-end activities may be done by writing the questions or statements and the answers on a separate sheet of paper or by writing just the answers on a separate sheet of paper, whichever your teacher desires.

Words and Terms

almanacs   cash crops   post roads
fertilize   millers   apprentices

1. Farmers who ____ add things to the soil that plants need to grow.

2. Many farmers in the Middle colonies grew ____, or crops raised to be sold.

3. Young people who were ____ worked with master craftspeople for several years to learn a job.

4. Many colonists enjoyed reading ____, or yearly magazines with information about many subjects.

5. Some colonial roads were ____, or roads built for riders carrying mail.

Fact Recall

1. Some of the important cash crops of the Middle colonies were wheat and other grains and ____.
   a. cotton
   b. farm animals

2. Some of the goods made by craftspeople in the Middle colonies were guns, glass, wagons, furniture, and ____.
   a. fur hats
   b. silk cloth

3. Some of the people who settled in the Middle colonies were English, Dutch, Scotch-Irish, or ____.
   a. German
   b. Italian

4. The Quakers believed that people who belonged to other churches should ____.
   a. move to another colony
   b. be able to worship as they pleased

5. Local government in some parts of the Middle colonies was set up by ____.
   a. states
   b. counties

Concepts and Understandings

1. Why did both farming and manufacturing become important in the Middle colonies?

2. Why did different groups of people in the Middle colonies follow different ways of life?

CHAPTER 10

Life in the Southern Colonies

1. **Large-scale and small-scale farming**
2. **The southern way of life**

Where would you expect to find both the oldest and the newest of the thirteen English colonies? Where would you be likely to meet both the richest and the poorest people? Where do you think you would see both the grandest and the plainest of houses? You would have found all these things in the Southern colonies.

The South was a place full of great differences. People in Maryland, Virginia, North Carolina, South Carolina, and Georgia were from many different backgrounds. They made their living in a number of different ways. But they all wanted to make life better for themselves and their families. In this chapter you will learn about how people in the Southern colonies lived.

1

Large-scale and small-scale farming

The largest farms in the colonies
Farming was important in all the English colonies. But nowhere were farms so large and farm crops so valuable as in the Southern colonies. There people owned **plantations.** These were huge farms on which people grew one or two major cash crops.

Most plantations were found near the ocean or along rivers that flowed into the ocean. People in Maryland, Virginia, and North Carolina found good soil there for growing tobacco. But swamps covered much of the lowland near the ocean in South Carolina and Georgia. So landowners in these places grew rice on the lowland. Then on higher land they grew **indigo** [IHN-dih-GOH], a plant used for dying cloth blue. Do you think it was a good idea to grow two cash crops? Why or why not?

People in England paid high prices for tobacco, rice, and indigo. So southern landowners tried to grow as much of these crops as they could. But such crops needed much care from the time they were planted until they were sold. Why do you think it took many people to do all the work on plantations?

The slaves in this picture are processing indigo plants. This work involved several steps and needed many workers. The final product was a blue-dye powder that was very popular in England and in the English colonies.

Finding workers for plantations At first, people who owned plantations used hired helpers and indentured servants. But it cost a lot of money to hire workers. And indentured servants left as soon as their term of work was over. Large landowners could make more money if they had cheap workers who would not leave after a few years. So they began using slaves.

Black people first arrived in Virginia in 1619. Some of these people were indentured servants who became free land-owners. But as plantations grew, more and more slaves were brought in. By 1760 there were more than 300,000 black people in the English colonies. Why do you think more than three fourths of these people lived in the Southern colonies?

Slaves did most of the work needed to grow cash crops and to prepare them for sale. Slaves also worked to grow the food eaten by all the people on a plantation. Some slaves worked in plantation houses. Others became good crafts-people. What kind of work is the person in the picture on page 181 doing? Slaves with certain skills were sometimes hired to do work for other people. This was one of the few ways slaves could earn money for themselves.

Other ways of farming in the Southern colonies Most southern farmers never made enough money to buy plantations. But a number of people owned small farms. These farmers mainly grew food for their own family. Some, how-ever, also grew small amounts of cash crops. Each farm family, with one or two hired helpers or indentured servants, did all the work. Why do you think such farms had few or no slaves?

Many small farmers moved to the backcountry. Land there was cheaper than land near the coast. People in the southern backcountry got their food by farming the river valleys and by hunting animals. Family members had to work together to clear fields from the forestlands. How were the ways of get-

This person is demonstrating one of the steps used in making cloth during colonial times. In the background are some other items that were important for doing work in colonial times. What are some of these items?

ting food in the backcountry of both the Southern and the Middle colonies alike?

Some people in the southern backcountry raised cattle and hogs. They allowed the animals to run wild most of the time. Once a year they rounded up the animals. They used some of the animals for food. They took the others to markets to be sold.

Manufacturing and trade Thick forests of pine trees grew in the South. People used pine trees in making **naval stores.** These were things, such as tar and pitch, that were used in making and repairing wooden ships. Why do you think naval stores were some of the most important goods made in colonial times?

Many of the goods needed on plantations were made by slaves. These people made such things as bricks,

How does this picture of Charleston, then known as Charles Town, help to stress the city's importance as a trading center?

barrels, and iron goods. They also made clothing for other slaves. But rich people wanted fancy things for themselves. Ships from England brought furniture, clothing, china, and artwork directly to plantation docks. Why did the location of southern plantations make this easy to do? The ships then took cash crops back to England to be sold.

People in cities bought many goods from the merchants and craftspeople who worked there. The most important city in the Southern colonies was Charleston, South Carolina. The picture on this page shows how Charleston looked in the 1700s. What kind of work are the people in the picture doing?

wrap·up

- What were the major products of the Southern colonies?
- Why did plantation owners use many slaves?
- Why was trade important to people in the Southern colonies?

Reading a map

1. What does this map show?

2. What colony had the largest amount of land settled before 1700?

3. What colony had no land settled before 1700?

4. In which colony did the amount of land settled between 1700 and 1763 increase the most?

5. Which colony had almost all its land settled by 1763?

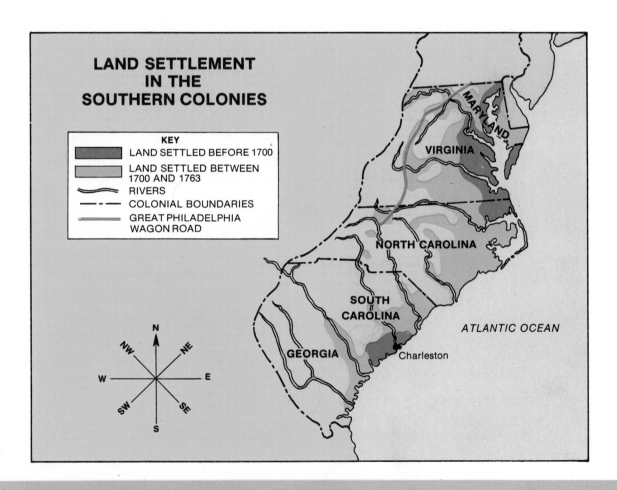

LAND SETTLEMENT
IN THE
SOUTHERN COLONIES

KEY
◼ LAND SETTLED BEFORE 1700
◼ LAND SETTLED BETWEEN 1700 AND 1763
∼ RIVERS
–·– COLONIAL BOUNDARIES
— GREAT PHILADELPHIA WAGON ROAD

MARYLAND

VIRGINIA

NORTH CAROLINA

SOUTH CAROLINA

ATLANTIC OCEAN

GEORGIA

Charleston

N
NW   NE
W   E
SW   SE
S

2

The southern way of life

Tobacco

Orchard

Blacksmith

Barn and Stable

Slave Quarters

Kitchen

Carriage House

Kitchen Garden

Main House

Storage Barn

Wharf

Southern plantations were not all alike, but they had many of the buildings that are shown here. What are some of the important buildings on this plantation?

Viewing the Southern colonies If you could visit the Southern colonies, you would see many familiar sights. The busy docks and streets of southern cities would look much like those of Boston or New York. The farms and backcountry cabins might remind you of places in Pennsylvania.

You would also notice several differences. The weather in the South was generally warmer than in the other parts of the English colonies. So many southern houses were built to keep them from becoming too hot. One way people did this was by building chimneys on the outside of walls. How was this different from the way New Englanders built chimneys?

The greatest difference between the English colonies in the South and elsewhere was the many plantations in the South. A large plantation might have looked like the one shown in the picture on this page. Notice that the kitchen is separate from the main house. This kept cooking smells and the heat of the kitchen fireplace away from the house. Sometimes kitchens and houses were connected by covered walkways. Why do you think this was done?

Visiting a colonial plantation
Most of the people who owned plantations were English. These people tried to live their lives in much the same way that rich people in England did.

Plantation families arose early. The men spent much of each day doing business, keeping records, and riding around the plantation. In many families women took over these duties when men were away or when they died. In other families women took charge of the house and the kitchen. They often cared for anyone on the plantation who became ill.

Children spent many hours a day studying. But since plantations were so large, many people in the South lived far from one another. How do you think this made it hard for the children to attend a school? Many families hired a **tutor,** or a private teacher, who lived on the plantation. Children studied reading, writing, arithmetic, music, and dancing. Older children were often sent to England to attend schools there.

Since people lived so far from their neighbors, they were glad to have company. People often had large dinner parties and dances. Look at the clothing worn by the people in the picture on this page. How is this clothing different from that worn in New England or in the Middle colonies?

Wealthy southern colonists dressed in the latest styles from Europe. They usually bought imported clothing from merchants rather than make their own. They also followed the European fashion of wearing wigs.

Beyond the main house   There were many other people who also lived on a plantation. Most of these people were slaves. These people had to depend on their masters for most of the things they needed. Why do you think this was so?

Masters gave their slaves plain linen clothing to wear. They also gave them food, such as bacon, corn, and buttermilk. Some slaves were allowed to raise vegetables for their families. Slaves also were given the parts of animals that their masters would not eat. These were such parts as the feet and ears of pigs. Slaves learned to use spices to make such food taste better. Some foods that people today enjoy were once made by slaves, either for themselves or for their masters.

Slave families tried hard to make a better life for their children. They told the children stories, sang songs, and made toys for them to play with. But many slave families were separated when masters sold family members to other owners. How does this help explain why many slaves tried to escape from their masters during colonial times?

The head cook often had one of the most responsible plantation jobs. How does this kitchen compare with a kitchen today?

A look at southern colonial cities   Many people who owned plantations spent some time each year in the nearest city. A number of these people came to carry on business. Many people came to Charleston, South Carolina, and to Savannah, Georgia, to spend the whole summer. The sea breezes in these cities were more pleasant than the hot, damp air of the lowland rice plantations.

These buildings are in Charleston, South Carolina. The idea of building porches on homes was popular in Charleston long after the colonial years were over.

Houses in southern cities were generally built of wood or of brick. Some of the houses had separate kitchens just as plantation houses did. Other city houses were built just one room wide but three or four stories high. Such houses had many windows and large porches. Why do you think some houses were made this way?

People in southern colonial cities enjoyed art shows and concerts. Many people came to southern cities to have **portraits,** or pictures of themselves, painted. How do people today have pictures of themselves made? The first theaters built in the English colonies were built in the South. So, many people there also enjoyed seeing plays. People arrived at theaters wearing the latest fashions from England. This meant fancy clothing and wigs for both men and women. Do you think such people generally had lots of money? Why do you think so?

Living in the backcountry The people who lived in the southern backcountry had different backgrounds. Many of the people were English. These people were the small farmers who found that they could not make a living near large plantations. They followed rivers into the backcountry until they found land they could buy. Why do you think people looked for land along rivers?

Many settlers were Quaker, German, and Scotch-Irish. These people came from the Middle colonies. They followed the Great Philadelphia Wagon Road to settle in Maryland, Virginia, and North Carolina. A number of Scotch, Welsh, Irish, Swiss, and free black people also settled in the southern backcountry.

The backcountry people of the South either grew or hunted their own food and made their own clothing. They helped one another do hard work. They also held dances, shooting matches,

Virginia's House of Burgesses was the first representative assembly, or lawmaking body made up of members elected by the voters, in the English colonies. The House of Burgesses was patterned after the lawmaking body of England.

and fairs for fun. How did this way of life compare to the life of plantation owners? How was the backcountry life the same in all the English colonies?

Governing the people   One kind of governing body that all the English colonies used began in the South. This was the part of the legislature that was made up of members chosen by the citizens to act for them. The first such lawmaking body in the English colonies was the **House of Burgesses** in Virginia. The first members of this body were chosen in 1619. What lawmaking bodies can you think of that are chosen by our country's citizens today?

People in the South lived far apart. So local government throughout the South was set up by counties. Where else in the English colonies was government partly set up this way?

In the Southern colonies, only free white men who owned a certain amount of land or property could vote. The amount of land was more than most small farmers and backcountry people owned. So the people who could vote and the people who held public office were generally rich people. Do you think this was a good idea? Why or why not?

wrap·up

- How would you describe the groups of people who settled in the Southern colonies?
- How was the way of life of slaves different from the way of life of their masters?
- How is your community like a southern colonial plantation, city, or backcountry settlement? How is it different?

A Biographical Sketch

A *man of many interests*

Colonial planters could have had many hours of free time every day. But people like William Byrd II did not take it easy during the day. There were too many things to be done.

William Byrd II owned Westover, a large tobacco plantation in Virginia. Much of his land was planted with crops. Byrd himself took charge of the planting of tobacco. But he was never too busy to watch over the planting of flower gardens and orchards, also.

Part of Byrd's land lay near a waterfall on the James River. There he built a sawmill and a flour mill. Byrd also planned a settlement there because he was sure the place was a good location for a city. Today that settlement has grown to be Richmond, the capital city of Virginia.

William Byrd kept close watch on Westover. But he was also busy with government matters. He became a member of the House of Burgesses when he was just eighteen. He held several other public offices in the colony of Virginia during his lifetime.

On many mornings Byrd got up as early as three or four o'clock. This was to make sure he had time to read and study before breakfast. Byrd took time to write during evenings when he was not giving a party or attending one. Among his many writings was a **diary** [DY-(uh-)ree]. A diary is a record kept each day of happenings and thoughts. Today William Byrd's diary helps people understand what life was like in the Southern colonies.

Chapter-End Activities

The chapter-end activities may be done by writing the questions or statements and the answers on a separate sheet of paper or by writing just the answers on a separate sheet of paper, whichever your teacher desires.

Words and Terms

tutor	House of Burgesses
naval stores	indigo
portraits	plantations

1. Many people in the Southern colonies owned large ____, on which they grew one or two major cash crops.
2. People used ____ for dying cloth blue.
3. Shipbuilders used ____ in making and repairing wooden ships.
4. A southern family might have hired a ____ to teach the children.
5. The lawmaking body in Virginia was the ____.

Fact Recall

1. The three major cash crops of the Southern colonies were ____.
   a. corn, beans, and rice
   b. tobacco, wheat, and rice
   c. tobacco, rice, and indigo

2. As plantations grew, most plantation owners used ____ to do most of the work.
   a. slaves
   b. indentured servants
   c. hired helpers

3. Many small farmers moved to ____ where land was cheap.
   a. the backcountry
   b. the coast
   c. the Middle colonies

4. Plantation families invited guests for ____.
   a. markets
   b. house-raisings
   c. dinner and dancing parties

5. The people who settled in the southern backcountry were from ____.
   a. the same European country
   b. many different backgrounds
   c. New England

Concepts and Understandings

1. Why did plantation owners in the Southern colonies depend on trade with England?

2. Why did different groups of people in the Southern colonies follow different ways of life?

Unit End

Main Ideas and Understandings

1. What were some of the ways by which people in the thirteen English colonies in America made a living? Why were some ways of making a living done in all the English colonies? Why were some ways of making a living done in only certain colonies?

2. What kinds of work did colonial merchants do? What goods did these merchants export from the colonies? What goods did they import to the colonies? Why did people in the thirteen English colonies depend on trade for many of the things they needed and wanted?

3. What were some of the major groups of people that settled in the English colonies in America? How did some of these groups of people affect the way of life in the places where they settled?

Research Ideas

1. Large numbers of German people came to Pennsylvania in the 1600s and 1700s. Many of these people settled in what is now Lancaster County. Later relatives of the German people still live there. These people are known as the Pennsylvania Dutch. Why are these people called Dutch if their relatives were Germans? What are the Pennsylvania Dutch known for? How do these people live today?

2. Every year many people visit Williamsburg, Virginia. Part of Williamsburg has been **restored**, or made

to look very much as it did long ago. Find out about Williamsburg. Why was this city important in colonial times? Why did many people move away from Williamsburg after the colonial period? How did people go about restoring the city? What do visitors see today in Williamsburg?

3. At the end of the colonial period the four largest cities in the thirteen English colonies were Philadelphia (40,000 people), New York City (25,000 people), Boston (15,000 people), and Charleston (12,000 people). How large are these cities today? By how many people have these cities grown? How does the size of a colonial city compare to the size of your community or to the size of a city near your community? How do the sizes of the four largest colonial cities compare to the sizes of the four largest cities in our country today?

Activities and Projects

1. Pretend that you live in one of the thirteen English colonies. Keep a diary for two or three days. Write in your diary what things you think you might do and what thoughts you might have if you really lived in that colony.

2. Find out what games colonial children played. Then hold a Colonial Games Day. Dress as you might have if you were a colonist. Invite other classes in your school to your Games Day. Explain to them the games you are playing.

Unit 5

The Road to Independence

The United States flag stands for the land, the people, and the government of our country. The stripes stand for the first thirteen states of our country. The stars stand for the number of states in our country today. What are some ways that people honor our country's flag?

Our country's flag reminds us that the United States was not always like it is today. Americans had to fight for the freedom they wanted. In this unit you will learn about our country's fight for freedom. You will also learn about the problems our country faced after winning its freedom. And you will find answers to the following questions:

Why did the colonists want their freedom from Britain?

How did the colonists win their freedom from Britain?

How was our country's government formed?

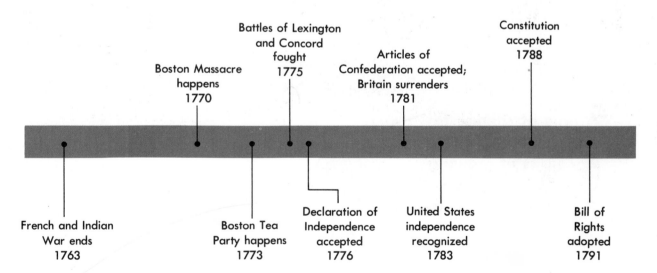

Battles of Lexington and Concord fought 1775

Boston Massacre happens 1770

Articles of Confederation accepted; Britain surrenders 1781

Constitution accepted 1788

French and Indian War ends 1763

Boston Tea Party happens 1773

Declaration of Independence accepted 1776

United States independence recognized 1783

Bill of Rights adopted 1791

CHAPTER 11

Changing Relations with Britain

1. **A time of change for the colonists**
2. **Signs of growing trouble**
3. **A desire for freedom**

What does freedom mean to you? It might mean staying up very late. Or it might mean watching as much television as you like. Freedom meant different things to the colonists. It meant being able to govern themselves. And it meant having rights that they thought all people should have. Why do you think freedom was important to the colonists?

For many years the colonists had enjoyed much freedom under the rule of Britain. But then Britain began to tighten its governing of the colonies. This caused problems between Britain and the colonists. In this chapter you will learn why Britain wanted more control over the colonists. You will learn how the colonists felt about this. And you will learn why the colonists broke away from Britain.

1

A time of change
for the colonists

Fighting for the land For many years the French had carried on fur trade along the upper Ohio River. The British wanted to build up their own fur trade on that land. And the British wanted to build settlements in the Ohio Valley. So the French built forts to protect their fur trade and their land claims from the British. How do you think the British felt about these forts?

In 1753 the governor of Virginia gave a message to a young army officer named George Washington. Washington was sent to tell the French to leave the Ohio Valley. The French refused. So on May 28, 1754, fighting broke out between French soldiers and Virginia colonists. This was the start of a war to decide who would control North America.

The British outnumbered the French in North America, but many Indians fought on the side of the French. Why do you think this was an advantage for the French? Why do you think this war was called the French and Indian War? At first the war went badly for the British. One reason for this was that the colonies were not united. They often

In 1749 a group of French soldiers and American Indians buried lead plates along the Ohio River. On each plate was printed the following: "This land belongs to the king of France." However, this same land was also claimed by the king of England.

197

disagreed with one another. How might this have hurt the British? How might this have helped the French?

A plan for working together In June of 1754 a meeting was held at Albany, New York. At this meeting, Benjamin Franklin explained his plan for getting the colonies to work together. He called his plan the Albany Plan of Union.

Franklin's plan, however, failed. The British government was afraid the plan would cause it to lose some of its power over the colonists. And the colonists were afraid they might lose some of their freedom. Even though the plan was not accepted, it caused many colonists to think about working together. Why do you think this was important?

Fighting the war The British government decided the French had to be forced out of the Ohio Valley. So a British army led by General Edward Braddock was sent to America. In July of 1755 Braddock and his soldiers fought a large battle near Fort Duquesne [doo-KAYN]. The British soldiers were badly beaten, and General Braddock was killed.

During the next two years the French captured many British forts. But in 1757 Britain decided to send new army leaders to

This picture shows the battle between British forces and French forces near Fort Duquesne. The British were badly beaten. By looking at the picture, what reason can you give why the British might have suffered heavy losses?

America. Under these new leaders the British began defeating the French. Then in 1762 Spain entered the war on the side of France. But it was too late for the Spanish to be of any real help to the French. Peace finally came in 1763, with the signing of the Treaty of Paris. Look at the maps on this page. What lands did Britain gain from France? What lands did Britain gain from Spain?

Peace brings trouble The colonists were proud of the part they had played in the French and Indian War. Their soldiers had fought long and hard to help the British win the war. And since the French no longer were a threat in the Ohio Valley, the colonists were eager to build new settlements there.

The British, however, looked at the end of the war differently. They had gained new lands that had to be governed.

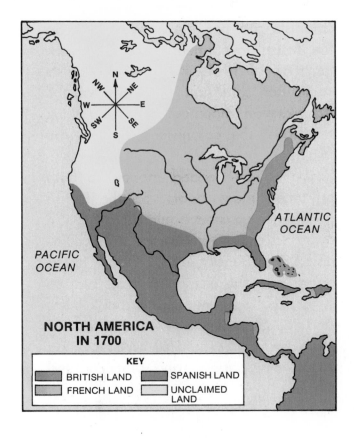

NORTH AMERICA IN 1700

KEY
- BRITISH LAND
- FRENCH LAND
- SPANISH LAND
- UNCLAIMED LAND

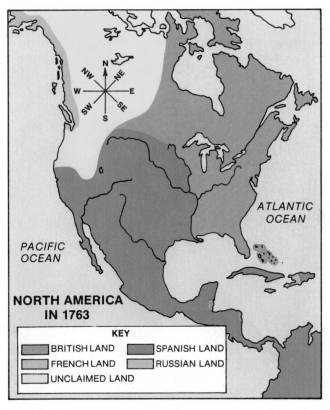

NORTH AMERICA IN 1763

KEY
- BRITISH LAND
- FRENCH LAND
- UNCLAIMED LAND
- SPANISH LAND
- RUSSIAN LAND

The Stamp Act required that a stamp be placed on printed goods to show that the tax had been paid. How are the colonists in the picture above showing their anger over this tax? What does the handbill in the picture below urge the colonists to do?

And they had debts that must be paid. The British decided that the colonists should help them with these problems.

The Indians who lived in the Ohio Valley did not want the colonists to settle there. Why do you think this was so? Pontiac, the chief of the Ottawa, led a group of Indians against British forts and settlements. Pontiac's War, as it was called, lasted for several months.

The British tighten their control Pontiac's War proved to the British government that the new lands in America needed to be under tight control. The British also thought the colonies would be easier to govern if the colonists did not move westward. So the British government passed the Proclamation of 1763. It said the colonists could not settle on land west of the Appalachian Mountains. Do you think this upset the colonists? Why do you think so?

The British needed money to help pay their many debts. So the British government passed a number of acts in order to collect money from the colonists. The Sugar Act of 1764 taxed goods brought into the colonies such as sugar, coffee, wine, silk, and linen. And the Stamp Act of 1765 said that taxes had to be paid on wills, playing cards, newspapers, and other printed matter.

The colonists protest   People who lived in Britain had to pay taxes. But they could vote for others to **represent,** or speak for, them in the government. The colonists did not have anyone to speak for them in the British government. So the colonists were angry. They were being taxed without being represented.

Throughout the colonies, people formed groups called the Sons of Liberty. Members of the Sons of Liberty gave speeches about the rights that the colonists thought they should have. The Sons of Liberty helped form a **boycott** against British goods. This meant that people refused to buy goods brought to America from Britain. Do you think this hurt British trade? Why do you think so?

The merchants in Britain were very upset over the boycott. To help these people, the British government ended the Stamp Act. The colonists were so happy that they paid no attention to a new act. This new act was called the Declaratory Act. It said that the British government had the right to pass whatever laws were needed to govern the colonies.

Then in 1767 the British government passed new laws to raise money. These were the Townshend Acts. They placed a tax on tea, paper, glass, paint, and lead. And they allowed British officials to enter a colonist's home at any time. How do you think the colonists felt about this?

wrap ·up

- What was the cause of the French and Indian War?
- How did the French and Indian War cause a change in the way Britain governed the colonies?
- How did the colonists react to the changes in Britain's way of governing them?

Reading a map

During the late 1700s the British colonists in America were trying to work out their problems with Britain. At the same time a Roman Catholic priest from Spain was working with Indians along the coast of California. His name was Father Junípero Serra [hoo-NEE-puh-ROH-SEHR-uh]. Study the map, and then answer the questions.

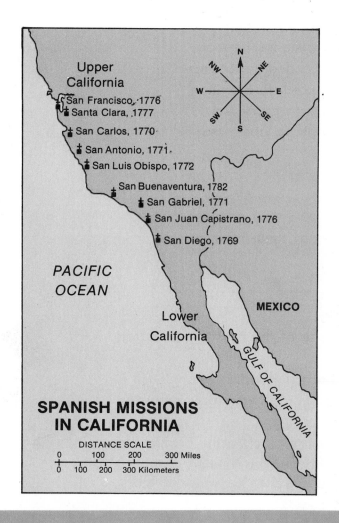

SPANISH MISSIONS IN CALIFORNIA

1. What does the map show?
2. What was the name of the first mission started by Father Serra in California?
3. What was the name of the mission Father Serra started that was located the farthest north?
4. How many missions did Father Serra start between 1770 and 1772? What were their names?
5. About how many miles (kilometers) separated San Francisco from San Diego?
6. What was the total number of missions started by Father Serra in California?

2

Signs of growing trouble

Trouble in Boston   The colonists were very upset over the Townshend Acts. A boycott had helped put an end to the Stamp Act. So the colonists decided to use the same means again. This second boycott started in Boston and then spread quickly throughout the colonies. Colonial merchants refused to buy or use any British goods. Do you think this caused Britain to lose money? Why or why not?

The British government was angry that its laws were not being obeyed. So Britain sent more soldiers to the colonies to see that the laws were carried out. But the people of Boston did not like having British soldiers in their city. Many times the citizens of Boston threw stones and snowballs at the soldiers and called them names. Then on March 5, 1770, a large fight broke out between a group of colonists and a group of British soldiers. The soldiers fired their guns into the crowd. Crispus Attucks, Samuel Maverick, James Caldwell, Samuel Gray, and Patrick Carr were killed. This happening became known as the Boston Massacre.

The citizens of Boston were very angry over the Boston Massacre. They demanded that British troops withdraw from the city. And they demanded that the British soldiers who were involved in the Boston Massacre be tried for murder. Today there is a monument in Boston honoring the five colonists who were killed in the Boston Massacre.

After the Boston Massacre feelings between Britain and the colonies improved. British soldiers were moved out of Boston. And the Townshend Acts were removed, except for the tax on tea. This was kept by the British government to show that it had the right to tax the colonies. Why do you think this was important to the British government? Some colonists, however, still felt that they should not have to pay taxes to Britain.

Committees of Correspondence Samuel Adams was a citizen of Boston. He felt very strongly about the rights of people. He thought the laws Britain passed were very unfair. Adams believed the colonies needed to work together.

In 1772 a group of colonists, led by Samuel Adams, formed a **Committee of Correspondence**. This was a small group of people who told the citizens what the British were doing. Soon other groups formed throughout the colonies. Members spread news about what was happening in different towns. This way people could be ready to act if need be. How do you think these groups helped the colonies work together?

This picture shows Samuel Adams meeting with other members of the Committee of Correspondence to discuss ideas and to write letters. Such meetings were often held in secret.

Trouble over tea In 1773 the British East India Company had more tea than it could sell. So Britain passed the Tea Act. This act stated that only the British East India Company could sell tea in America. How would this help the tea company? The Tea Act made the colonists very angry. They could buy tea at a cheaper price because the tax on tea was lowered. But they did not think it fair that only this one company was allowed to sell tea in America.

Again the colonists showed their anger against Britain. They agreed not to allow British ships carrying tea to enter American harbors. The colonists even set fire to some British ships. In Boston, colonists boarded British ships and threw thousands of dollars worth of tea overboard. This happening has come to be called the Boston Tea Party. Look at the picture on this page. How are the colonists dressed? Why do you think they are dressed this way?

Britain acted quickly to punish the colonists, especially those in Boston. The British government passed a number of laws. One of these laws closed Boston Harbor until the tea that had been destroyed was paid for. Still another law took

In 1773 members of the Sons of Liberty boarded three British ships and destroyed the tea on board. Do you think the people on shore approved? Why do you think so?

self-government away from the people of Massachusetts. It said that the people could no longer hold town meetings. And it said that the people of Massachusetts had to provide housing for more British soldiers.

People throughout the colonies were shocked at these laws. They wanted to help the people of Boston. So nearby towns sent meat, fish, and oil to the people of Boston. Connecticut sent sheep. Pennsylvania sent flour. The Carolinas sent rice. And all the colonies sent money. What do you think might have happened if the colonies had not come to the aid of Boston? Do you think the colonies were beginning to work together? Why do you think this was important?

The First Continental Congress The colonists decided they must do something to protect the rights they thought they should have. So they planned a meeting at which people from each colony would get together and decide what to do. The meeting was called the First Continental Congress. It began in Philadelphia, Pennsylvania, on September 5, 1774. Fifty-six members were present. Georgia was the only colony that did not send anyone to the meeting. John Adams, Patrick Henry, and George Washington were among the leaders

In 1774 the First Continental Congress met at Carpenter's Hall in Philadelphia, Pennsylvania. This famous building can still be seen in Philadelphia today.

who attended. Do you think this meeting of people from twelve colonies was important? Why do you think so?

The people at the First Continental Congress did four important things. First, they said that they would be loyal to the king of England. But they also said that Britain did not have the right to pass laws governing the colonists without their consent. Second, they agreed to stop importing and exporting goods from Britain. Third, they sent a message to King George III of England. They asked the king to stop the laws that took away the rights the colonists thought they should have. Finally, the members arranged for a second meeting to take place in the spring of 1775. This meeting would be held if matters between Britain and the colonies had not improved. Do you think the members of the meeting were hoping things could be settled between Britain and the colonies? What makes you think so?

King George III was only twenty-two years old when he became king of England. He ruled Britain from 1760 to 1820. He faced many problems during that time.

wrap·up

- Why did the colonists place a second boycott on British goods?
- Why did the Boston Massacre and the Boston Tea Party take place, and what happened because of each of these events?
- Why was the First Continental Congress an important meeting?

3

A desire for freedom

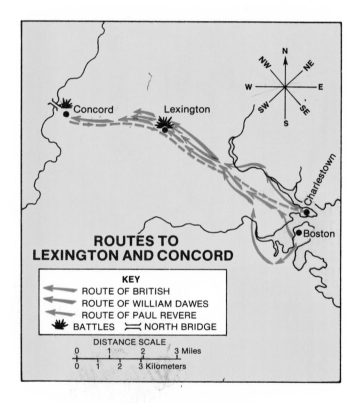

**ROUTES TO
LEXINGTON AND CONCORD**

KEY
ROUTE OF BRITISH
ROUTE OF WILLIAM DAWES
ROUTE OF PAUL REVERE
BATTLES   NORTH BRIDGE

DISTANCE SCALE
0   1   2   3 Miles
0   1   2   3 Kilometers

Ready to fight   People throughout the colonies talked about a possible war with Britain. Groups of men met daily to train and march. Such groups of citizen-soldiers were to be ready to fight at a minute's notice. So they were given the name **minutemen.** Why do you think it was important to these men to be prepared in case of war?

In April of 1775 Thomas Gage, the British general in Boston, decided to act. He planned to send soldiers to Concord to destroy the weapons and gunpowder stored there by the minutemen. On their way to Concord, the soldiers were to capture the colonial leaders who were in Lexington. These leaders were Samuel Adams and John Hancock.

The colonists learned of General Gage's plan. So on the night of April 18, Paul Revere and William Dawes rode through the countryside. They spread the word that the British soldiers were coming. The minutemen prepared to fight. Meanwhile Adams and Hancock managed to get away from Lexington. Look at the map on this page. Why do you think Paul Revere and William Dawes followed different routes?

Shots are fired   On April 19, 1775, the British marched into Lexington. Some seventy minutemen were waiting for them on the village green. No one knows for sure which side fired first, but eight minutemen were killed and ten were wounded.

The British soldiers continued on to Concord. There they destroyed the weapons that the minutemen had not had a chance to hide. Fighting broke out, and the British were forced to turn back.

But news of the fighting had spread quickly. Minutemen hid behind trees, stone walls, barns, and houses along the route. Throughout the day they shot at the British soldiers who were marching back to Boston.

The Second Continental Congress   On May 10, 1775, the Second Continental Congress began in Philadelphia. By the middle of September all the colonies were represented, including Georgia. Many people from the first meeting returned. Other leaders such as John Hancock, Benjamin Franklin, and Thomas Jefferson were also present.

This picture shows the British soldiers returning to Boston from Concord. Why was this a difficult march for the British?

Many people at this meeting were still hoping that it was not too late to settle their differences with Britain. But they thought it important to be ready in case matters were not settled. So they called for the raising of an army. George Washington was made head of this army.

Closer to independence   On June 17, 1775, the first real battle between the colonists and the British took place in Boston. It was called the Battle of Bunker Hill, even though most of the fighting took place on nearby Breed's Hill. The minutemen wanted to drive the British soldiers out of Boston. Even though the minutemen did not win the battle, British losses were very high. This caused the colonists to believe that they might have a chance of winning a war with Britain.

After hearing about Bunker Hill, the members of the Second Continental Congress sent a letter to King George III. They told the king that they were still loyal to him. And they said that they hoped feelings between Britain and the colonies would improve. But the king refused to read this letter. He said the colonists had failed to obey the British government. How do you think the Congress felt when King George refused to read the letter?

At this time many colonists were still unwilling to break away from Britain. Early in 1776, though, something happened that helped some of these people change their minds. Thomas Paine wrote a small book called *Common Sense*. Paine's book told the colonists that they should break away from Britain. After reading *Common Sense*, many people decided to fight for **independence,** or freedom, from Britain.

Independence is declared   On June 7, 1776, Richard Henry Lee of Virginia spoke before the Second Continental Congress. He stated that the colonies should be free and independent states. The members at the meeting voted to accept Lee's idea. Look at the picture at the right on page 211. No-

The picture at the left shows Thomas Paine holding his pamphlet Common Sense. At the right is a picture of a well-known painting showing the presentation of the Declaration of Independence.

tice the five men standing together. These men were chosen to prepare a written message stating that the colonies were free.

Thomas Jefferson wrote the Declaration of Independence. This paper made freedom from Britain the goal of the colonists. It stated that the colonists were no longer ruled by Britain. And it gave reasons why they wanted their freedom. What do you think some of these reasons were? The members of the meeting accepted the Declaration of Independence on July 4, 1776. How do people in our country today honor this important date?

wrap·up

- Why did fighting occur at Lexington and Concord?
- How did Thomas Paine influence the colonists' thinking about declaring their independence?
- Why is July 4, 1776, an important date in the history of our country?

A Biographical Sketch

A brave soldier

Many blacks fought in the War for Independence. One of these blacks was Peter Salem. Salem lived in Framingham, Massachusetts. He believed that the colonies should be free. So when fighting broke out between the colonists and the British, Salem joined the minutemen.

Salem had been with the minutemen only a few days when he took part in the Battle of Concord. But it was in Boston that Peter Salem became a hero. During the Battle of Bunker Hill, Salem fought well. He even shot Major John Pitcairn, a British officer. After the battle, Salem was honored by George Washington for this heroic deed.

Salem continued to serve his country well. He took part in other important battles between 1775 and 1780. When the War for Independence ended, he returned to his home in Massachusetts. He was proud of the part he had played in the war.

Peter Salem was a brave person and a fine soldier. He was willing to fight for what he believed. He fought to make America a land of freedom.

On August 16, 1816, Peter Salem died. But he was not forgotten. In 1882 the people of Framingham built a monument to honor him. The words on the monument read

Peter Salem
A soldier of the Revolution
Concord
Bunker Hill
Saratoga
Died, August 16, 1816

Chapter-End Activities

The chapter-end activities may be done by writing the questions or statements and the answers on a separate sheet of paper or by writing just the answers on a separate sheet of paper, whichever your teacher desires.

Words and Terms

minutemen   represent
boycott   Stamp Act
Sugar Act   Boston Tea Party
    Committee of Correspondence
    Declaration of Independence

1. The ____ taxed goods brought into the colonies such as sugar, coffee, wine, silk, and linen.

2. The colonists did not have anyone to ____, or speak for, them in the British government.

3. A ____ was formed to let colonists know what the British were doing in different towns of the colonies.

4. During a ____ the colonists refused to buy or use British goods.

5. During the ____ colonists destroyed thousands of dollars worth of tea.

6. Citizen-soldiers who were ready to fight at a minute's notice were called ____.

7. The ____ stated that the colonies were free and independent states.

Fact Recall

1. What was the cause of the French and Indian War?

2. What was the cause of Pontiac's War?

3. What was the cause of the Boston Massacre?

4. For what actions are Paul Revere and William Dawes remembered?

5. When did the Second Continental Congress accept the Declaration of Independence?

Concepts and Understandings

1. How did the French and Indian War affect relations between Britain and its colonies in America?

2. Why did the thirteen British colonies in America declare their independence from Britain?

CHAPTER 12

Fighting for Freedom

1. The two sides
2. The early fighting
3. Winning the war

The colonies had declared their independence from Britain in 1776. But it was quite another matter for Americans to obtain that independence. To do so, they had to fight a war with the most powerful country in the world. Why do you think Americans had different feelings about such a war?

The war between the United States and Britain is often called the **War for Independence.** Its outcome was very important to the history of our country. Why do you think this was so? In this chapter you will learn how Americans felt about fighting a war with Britain. You will learn of some advantages and some disadvantages for both the British and the Americans. You will learn about some important events of the war. And you will learn what the outcome of the war meant to the United States.

1

The two sides

A time to choose On July 8, 1776, the first public reading of the Declaration of Independence was made in Philadelphia, Pennsylvania. Riders carried the news throughout the newly formed states. Bells rang, and people cheered. For some people it was a day of rejoicing. For others it was not. But for everyone it was a time to make a choice. The choice was between being true to the king of England or joining the fight for independence. Do you think this was an easy choice to make? Why or why not?

Some people favored the British cause. They did not want to break ties with Britain. These people were called **loyalists**. Other people favored the American cause. These people were called **patriots**. Still others did not take sides. Do you think the different views that people held might have caused problems among Americans? Why do you think so?

A divided people It is thought that during the War for Independence about one third of all Americans were loyalists. These people lived in every state and were from all walks of life. Most loyalists were well-to-do. They

The Declaration of Independence was read to the people of New York City on July 9, 1776. The people responded by tearing down a statue of King George III. The lead from the statue was used to make musket balls for the American Army. How do you think the people in the picture felt about America's declaring its independence?

were the large landowners and people such as doctors and lawyers. Leaders of the Church of England and former officers of the British government were also loyalists. Why do you think these people were on Britain's side during the war?

After the Declaration of Independence, many Americans looked upon loyalists as enemies of the United States. Many loyalists were put in jail, and large numbers of them had their land and homes taken away. Many also lost their jobs, could not vote, and were forced to pay higher taxes than other people paid. Because of the way they were treated, nearly 80,000 loyalists left the country during and after the war. Many of those who remained did not talk about how they felt, but they secretly hoped for a British victory. Why do you think these people were silent about their feelings?

In New England and in the middle states, most patriots were members of the lower and middle classes. These people had to work hard to earn a living. They were not happy with the way things were. They wanted a change. In the southern

American Minuteman

American Soldiers

American Officers

states quite a few large tobacco planters were patriots. Some of these people were important leaders of the American cause. These southern landowners were very much against the British government for taking away rights they thought they should have. It is generally believed that about one third of the total American people were patriots. How does this number compare to the number of people who favored the British cause?

Many Americans decided not to take part in the war for different reasons. Some of these people were against war of any kind. Others weren't interested in the matters that had brought about the war. These people were more interested in their own daily lives than in fighting for independence.

The strength of each side When the War for Independence began, many people believed that Britain would win. The British Navy was the finest in the world. And the British Army was made up of well-trained soldiers who had fought in many battles. Britain had much money to spend on supplying

The picture on these pages shows uniforms worn during the War for Independence. How were the American uniforms like those of the British? How were they different? Notice the uniform of the German soldier. Such soldiers fought for the British.

British Officers

German Soldier

British Soldiers

217

its army with weapons, gunpowder, food, and clothing. And many loyalists and Indians were willing to fight on the side of the British.

The American fighting forces, on the other hand, left a lot to be desired. The American Navy was less than a year old. And the American Army was made up of soldiers who were generally not well trained. Each state also raised a **militia** [muh-LIHSH-uh], or group of citizens trained as soldiers. Members of the militia generally served for only three to six months. Do you think these short terms of duty helped or hurt the American cause? Why do you think so?

Life in the American Army was very rough. American soldiers often had too little food, clothing, and medical supplies. This was because the Second Continental Congress, which served as the government during the war, had no power to tax. This meant that it could only *ask* the states for money and supplies. And even though the states gave some money, it was never enough to pay for the war. Many soldiers left the army before they were supposed to and returned to their homes. How do you think their leaving affected the size of the American fighting forces?

American soldiers, however, did have some things in their favor. They were better suited to fighting in America than the British, who were trained in European ways of fighting. And American Army leaders generally had more ability than the British Army leaders. How do you think both of these things helped the Americans?

Both sides get help Even though it appeared that Britain was stronger than the United States, Britain soon faced many problems. Britain had to fight a war far from home. This meant that the British government had to ship soldiers, food, arms, and clothes across the Atlantic Ocean. This trip took from four to ten weeks. Often the soldiers were weak and sick when they arrived. And sometimes supply ships were lost at sea. How do you think such losses hurt the British cause?

Another problem that Britain faced was that many people in Britain were against the war. They were not willing to go to a faraway land to fight for something they weren't interested in. So the British government hired German soldiers to fight on its side.

The Americans, on the other hand, were fighting on their own land. And they were fighting for a cause they believed in. The major problem for the Americans was a lack of money for supplies. Look at the pictures on this page. They show the kinds of money printed by the Continental Congress during the war. The value of this money dropped until it was worth very little. So the United States asked for help from Britain's greatest enemy—France. The French were eager to get back at the British for the French and Indian War. So France secretly sent supplies to the United States. Later France helped the United States in other ways.

On June 22, 1775, the Continental Congress called for $2 million worth of paper money to be printed. Paul Revere designed and printed this money for the Congress. Such money came to be called Continental Currency.

wrap·up

- Who were the loyalists and the patriots?
- What were some of the advantages and disadvantages that each side had at the beginning of the War for Independence?
- Why did Britain and the United States have to get help from other countries?

2

The early fighting

The British capture New York City   Many battles of the War for Independence took place near the Atlantic coast of the United States. Why do you think this was so? One such battle took place in New York City. The British were very interested in New York City. It had a good location and a fine harbor. What part do you think these things played in the British desire to set up their headquarters there?

One of the first things the British had to do was take control of New York City. So on July 2, 1776, General William Howe and an army of British soldiers landed on Staten Island in New York Harbor. Ten days later Howe's brother arrived in New York with more soldiers and many British ships. By the middle of August there was a very large army of well-equipped British soldiers in New York City.

The Americans, however, knew how important New York City was to the British. General Washington and an army of American soldiers were already stationed on Long Island across the bay from the British. Washington's army was much smaller than that of the British. And only about one third of Washington's soldiers were well trained.

On August 27 the British Army attacked. The Americans suffered many losses and were defeated badly. This British victory was followed by even more British victories around New York City. The British plan had worked. They had taken control of New York City.

New hope for the American soldiers   After being defeated in and around New York City, the American soldiers were very discouraged. Whole companies of soldiers deserted the army. Washington guided what was left of his army across the Delaware River into Pennsylvania in search of safety.

The picture on the left shows General Washington and the American Army after their defeat on Long Island. The picture below is of a famous painting showing Washington leading the American soldiers across the ice-filled Delaware River on Christmas night, 1776.

Washington, however, did not give up hope. On Christmas night he moved his soldiers back across the Delaware River into New Jersey. Look at the picture at the right on this page. What hardships do you think the soldiers faced that night? Early the next day they attacked the German soldiers who were fighting for the British at Trenton. The victory was an easy one for the Americans, who took the soldiers by surprise.

About a week later Washington led another surprise attack. He left his campfires burning to outsmart the British. Then he moved his army to Princeton, New Jersey. The Americans

The picture below shows General Burgoyne surrendering to General Gates after the British defeat at Saratoga. What is Burgoyne offering Gates as a symbol that the British soldiers had laid down their weapons? Colonel Daniel Morgan, dressed in white, helped the Americans win the victory.

defeated the British and drove them out of the town. Why do you think the victories at Trenton and at Princeton gave the American soldiers new hope?

The turning point of the war
The British were not pleased with the way the war was going. So they drew up a plan to separate the New England states from the other states. They would do this by taking over important American bases in New York State.

However, in October of 1777 the British plan was upset. American soldiers surrounded the British near Saratoga, New York. There was no way for the British to escape, so they gave up and laid down their weapons.

The Battle of Saratoga has often been called the turning point of the war. The Americans had defeated a major part of the British Army. By doing so, they showed the world that they could stand up to the British. After the victory at Saratoga, France openly entered the war on the side of the Americans. How do you think this helped the American cause?

wrap·up

- Why did the British want to take control of New York City?
- Why were the battles of Trenton and Princeton important to the American Army?
- Why is the Battle of Saratoga called the turning point of the war?

A Biographical Sketch

A brave woman

Lydia Darragh [DAR-ah] was living in Philadelphia, Pennsylvania, when the British took over that city in September of 1777. The British set up their headquarters across the street from Lydia's house. One day about two months later, a British officer came to Lydia's house. The officer told Lydia that some British officers would hold a meeting in her house that evening.

Lydia sent her family to bed early, as she had been ordered to do. She then let the British officers into the house and went to her room. But she did not go to sleep. Instead, she listened through the keyhole to hear what the officers were saying. She learned that the British planned to attack General Washington's army, which was thirteen miles outside of Philadelphia. The attack was to take place on the night of December 4. Lydia knew that she had to try to warn the Americans. But she also knew that the British would hang her if they found out. How do you think Lydia felt?

The next day Lydia asked the British for a pass to go outside Philadelphia to buy flour. But instead of getting flour, Lydia set off to find General Washington.

As Lydia walked along the road, she met some of Washington's soldiers. She told the officer in charge what she had learned about the British plan. The officer quickly went to tell General Washington the news.

On the night of December 4, the British marched out of Philadelphia as planned. But they later returned defeated. Why do you think the British plan had failed? Lydia Darragh had saved many American lives by her brave act. And she had helped the United States in its fight for freedom.

223

3

Winning the war

Valley Forge   The British Army spent the winter of 1777–1778 in Philadelphia, Pennsylvania. The British had much money to buy supplies. So British soldiers were well housed, well clothed, and well fed. But matters were quite different for General Washington and the American Army at nearby Valley Forge. The American Army had very little money. Supplies had to be carried to Valley Forge by wagon over dirt roads. Often the wagons broke down. Sometimes the supplies were stolen. The soldiers lived in simple huts that did not protect them from the bitter cold. They did not have enough food, clothing, blankets, or shoes. During that terrible winter at Valley Forge nearly 3,000 American soldiers died.

Even though General Washington was faced with many hardships at Valley Forge, he worked hard to build a better army. He placed Baron von Steuben [vahn-ST(Y)OO-buhn] in charge of training the soldiers. Baron von Steuben was a very good soldier who came from Prussia to help the American

The winter at Valley Forge was one of hardship and suffering for the American Army. How are some of the soldiers in this picture trying to keep warm?

cause. He taught the American soldiers how to handle guns, how to march, and how to fight battles. He turned the American Army into a well-trained group of soldiers. Why would this be important to the Americans?

Foreign aid In February of 1778 the United States entered into an agreement with France. The king of France agreed to send ships, weapons, gunpowder, and gold to the United States. The United States and France each promised not to make peace with Britain unless the other country agreed. Why do you think this was an important agreement?

By the end of 1780 Spain and Holland had entered the war against Britain. Britain's enemies were no longer just in the United States. How do you think this made the British cause in the United States more difficult?

The United States received goods and money from Europe. Soldiers from Europe also came to the United States. They came because they believed in the American cause. Casimir Pulaski [KAZ-ih-mihr-puh-LAS-kee] from Poland and the Marquis de Lafayette [MAHR-KEE-de-LAHF-ee-EHT] from France were among those Europeans who came to the United States. These people and others served the United States well. The outcome of the War for Independence

Many soldiers from Europe came to the United States to help the Americans in their fight for freedom. Casimir Pulaski, shown in the top picture, and the Marquis de Lafayette, shown in the bottom picture, were two of these soldiers.

225

might have been very different if Americans had not received help from other countries. Why do you think this is so?

Two American heroes There were many outstanding American heroes in the War for Independence. One of these heroes was George Rogers Clark. He decided to try to stop the Indian attacks on Americans living in the Ohio Valley. The British had directed these attacks since the very beginning of the war. They gave weapons and gunpowder to the Indians. Why do you think the British did this? Clark and a small group of soldiers took control of three important British forts in the Ohio Valley. Having these forts gave Americans a claim to a major part of the Ohio Valley. Do you think this was important? Why do you think so?

Another outstanding American hero was John Paul Jones, an officer in the American Navy. Jones led a brave attack against a large British warship off the coast of Britain. The British gave up after several hours of fighting. Jones had proved that the Americans could fight at sea. Look at the picture at the upper left of page 227. How can you tell the American ships from the British ships?

The war in the South Late in 1779 the war moved to the South. The American Army tried to drive the British out of Savannah, Georgia. However, even with the help of French soldiers, the American plan failed. Soon afterward the British took over Charleston, South Carolina. Two important southern states were then in the hands of the British.

In August of 1780 the Americans were badly defeated at Camden, South Carolina. General Gates was in charge of the American Army in the South. He lost two thirds of his soldiers in that battle. After Gates's defeat, Nathanael Greene was put in charge of the American Army in the South. He caused the British to suffer heavy losses.

The end of the war In 1781 General Cornwallis moved the British Army to Yorktown, Virginia. General Washington and the American Army followed, with a large number of

The picture above shows the Bonhomme Richard, *commanded by* John Paul Jones, *in battle with the* British ship, Serapis. *John Paul Jones is known as the Father of the* American Navy. *The picture on the right shows the British surrendering at Yorktown. Though the fighting stopped here, it took two more years for a peace treaty to be signed.*

French soldiers. A group of French warships sailed into Chesapeake Bay. The British were trapped. Cornwallis knew there was no way to escape. So he surrendered on October 19, 1781.

After six years of fighting, the war was finally over for the Americans. But Britain's war with France, Spain, and Holland went on for two more years. Look at the picture at the lower right of this page. It shows the British soldiers being led between a line of French soldiers and a line of American soldiers. How do you think the British felt at that moment?

The Treaty of Paris   In 1782 a new British government was formed. This new government was friendly to the United States. The Americans were ready for peace. So Benjamin Franklin, John Adams, and John Jay went to Paris to begin peace talks with the British. The two countries signed the Treaty of Paris on September 3, 1783.

The Treaty of Paris contained a number of points. Britain recognized the independence of the United States. All land from the Atlantic Ocean to the Mississippi River and from Canada to Florida was to be part of the United States. Spain was given Florida. Americans were given fishing rights off the coast of Newfoundland. Loyalists who had lost land or homes during the war were to be paid for their losses. And British soldiers and ships were to withdraw from the United States.

The Americans were very pleased with what they had gained from the Treaty of Paris. They got nearly everything that they had asked for. What do you think was the most important thing that Americans gained? Why do you think so?

wrap·up

- How did other countries help the United States in its fight for independence?
- Why did the British surrender at Yorktown, Virginia, in 1781?
- How did the Americans gain from the Treaty of Paris?

Using Your Skills

Reading a map

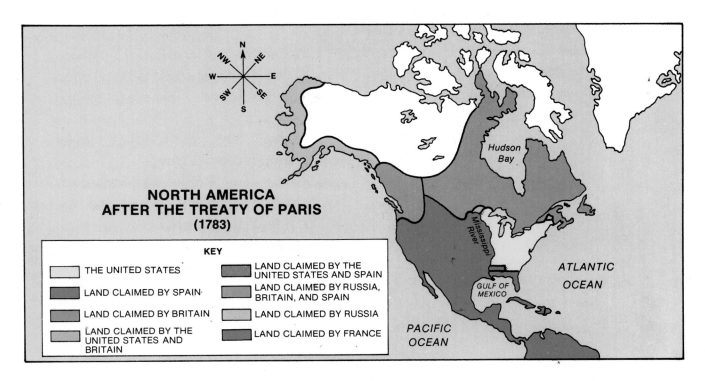

NORTH AMERICA
AFTER THE TREATY OF PARIS
(1783)

KEY

THE UNITED STATES

LAND CLAIMED BY SPAIN

LAND CLAIMED BY BRITAIN

LAND CLAIMED BY THE
UNITED STATES AND
BRITAIN

LAND CLAIMED BY THE
UNITED STATES AND SPAIN

LAND CLAIMED BY RUSSIA,
BRITAIN, AND SPAIN

LAND CLAIMED BY RUSSIA

LAND CLAIMED BY FRANCE

Hudson
Bay

Mississippi River

GULF OF
MEXICO

ATLANTIC
OCEAN

PACIFIC
OCEAN

Use the map to answer the following questions:

1. What does the map show?

2. How many countries claimed land in North America after the Treaty of Paris? What were the names of these countries?

3. Which country claimed the most land in North America after the Treaty of Paris? Which country claimed the least land?

4. Which countries claimed the same lands in North America in 1783?

5. How far west did the United States extend after the Treaty of Paris?

Chapter-End Activities

The chapter-end activities may be done by writing the questions or statements and the answers on a separate sheet of paper or by writing just the answers on a separate sheet of paper, whichever your teacher desires.

Words and Terms

Valley Forge   Saratoga
Treaty of Paris   patriots
loyalists   militia
Yorktown   New York

_____ 1. People who favored the British cause

_____ 2. People who favored the American cause

_____ 3. A group of citizens trained as soldiers

_____ 4. The city where the British wanted to set up their headquarters

_____ 5. The battle referred to as the turning point of the war

_____ 6. The place where Washington's army spent the winter of 1777–1778

_____ 7. An agreement by which the British recognized American independence

Fact Recall

1. After the Declaration of Independence, many Americans looked upon loyalists as (friends, enemies) of the United States.

2. Britain had (much, little) money to buy supplies for its army.

3. After the Battle of Saratoga, (France, Spain) openly entered the war on the side of the Americans.

4. (George Rogers Clark, John Paul Jones) was an outstanding hero in the American Navy.

5. The British surrender at (Yorktown, Camden) ended the War for Independence in America.

Concepts and Understandings

1. Why was it necessary for the Americans to seek help from foreign countries during the War for Independence?

2. Why was the Treaty of Paris important to the United States?

CHAPTER 13

Forming Our Government

1. **From colonies to states**
2. **The need for a strong government**
3. **Our American Republic**

In 1782 the Great Seal of the United States became an official symbol of our country. It stands for many ideas that were important to those who fought for and believed in our country's freedom. Look at the picture of the Great Seal on this page. What are some of the things shown on the seal that stand for the first thirteen states of our country?

During the War for Independence, the states agreed on a set of laws for governing our country. But our country's government under these laws proved to be very weak. So in 1787 a meeting was called to work out the problems of the government. At this meeting a new plan of government for the United States was written. In this chapter you will learn why the first government of the United States did not work. You will also learn how a new plan of government that is still in use today was written.

From colonies to states

Americans had had some experience in self-government before the Declaration of Independence. This helped them in drawing up state constitutions. Some states used their colonial charter as the basis for their constitution, but most states drew up a completely new constitution.

New governments for the states One of the first tasks facing the newly formed states in 1776 was the need to set up state governments. The states believed it was important that the laws for these governments be put into writing. Why do you think this was so? By 1780 each of the thirteen states had written a **constitution,** or plan of government. Most of these state constitutions were written by the lawmaking body of each state. The citizens of the states were not given the chance to vote on the plan for their state. But in Massachusetts the citizens voted on whether or not to accept the plan for their state.

Almost every state constitution had a **bill of rights.** This is a listing of freedoms and rights that cannot be taken away from the people by the government. The bill of rights in many states listed freedom of speech and the right to a fair trial. What other freedoms or rights do you think might have been listed in a bill of rights?

In nearly every state the **governor,** or head of the state government, was not given much power. Most of the power was given to the lawmaking body of each state. The people of each state voted for the members of the lawmaking body. But only those people who owned property could vote. Thus many people did not have a say in their state government.

The Articles of Confederation In 1776 the United States needed a government that could handle the important matters facing a new country. And our country needed a government that could lead it during its war with Britain. So in 1777 the **Articles of Confederation** were presented to the states. These were a set of laws setting forth the powers of both the United States government and the state governments. Before these laws could go into effect, all thirteen states had to accept them.

It took the states four years to accept the Articles of Confederation. The major reason it took so long was a problem over land claims. Look at the map on this page. Which states had claims to lands west of the Appalachian Mountains? States without western land claims wanted lands west of the Appalachian Mountains to belong to all the states. But Maryland would not accept the Articles of Confederation until all the states gave up their western lands.

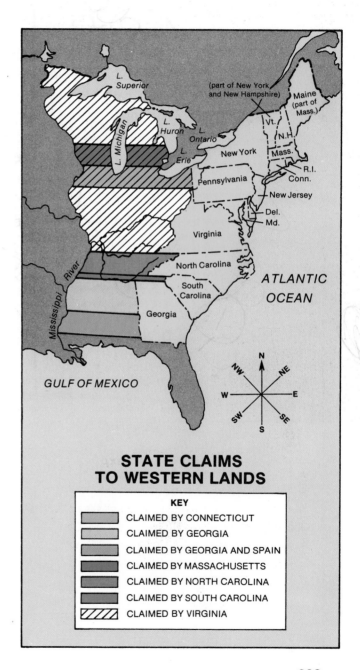

STATE CLAIMS TO WESTERN LANDS

KEY
CLAIMED BY CONNECTICUT
CLAIMED BY GEORGIA
CLAIMED BY GEORGIA AND SPAIN
CLAIMED BY MASSACHUSETTS
CLAIMED BY NORTH CAROLINA
CLAIMED BY SOUTH CAROLINA
CLAIMED BY VIRGINIA

On February 1, 1780, New York gave up its western lands. Connecticut soon followed. Then on January 2, 1781, Virginia also gave up its western land claims. Maryland then agreed to accept the Articles of Confederation. On March 2, 1781, the Articles of Confederation were put into use. They served as our country's plan of government until 1789.

Plans for the new land When all the states had given up their western lands, the land then belonged to the United States government. This land became a **territory,** or land that is part of our country but not yet a state. Much of this land was called the Northwest Territory. Our country's government decided to divide the Northwest Territory into parts. Then the government could sell the divided lands to people who wished to settle there. Why do you think the government wanted to do this? In order to divide the Northwest Territory, the government passed a law called the Land Ordinance of 1785. This law divided the land into square parts called **townships.** Each township was divided into smaller parts called **sections.**

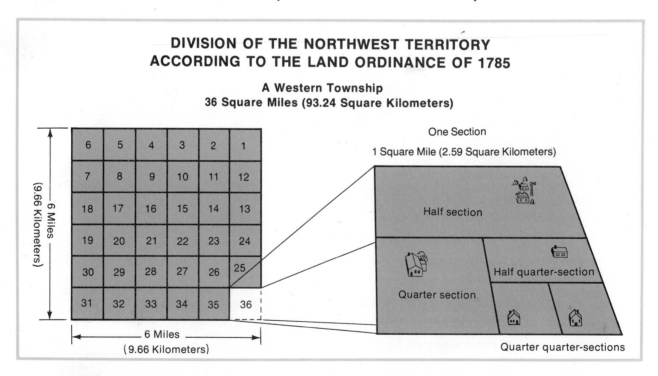

DIVISION OF THE NORTHWEST TERRITORY ACCORDING TO THE LAND ORDINANCE OF 1785

A Western Township
36 Square Miles (93.24 Square Kilometers)

6 Miles (9.66 Kilometers)

6	5	4	3	2	1
7	8	9	10	11	12
18	17	16	15	14	13
19	20	21	22	23	24
30	29	28	27	26	25
31	32	33	34	35	36

6 Miles
(9.66 Kilometers)

One Section
1 Square Mile (2.59 Square Kilometers)

Half section

Quarter section

Half quarter-section

Quarter quarter-sections

Look at the drawing on page 234. How many sections were in each township?

Besides dividing the land in the Northwest Territory, the government had to decide how to govern the land. So in 1787 the government passed a law called the Northwest Ordinance. This law stated that the Northwest Territory should be divided into no fewer than three nor more than five territories. And this law set up rules for a territory to become a state.

The law stated that when a territory had 60,000 people, it could draw up its own plan of government. Then the territory could ask to become a state. Each new state would have the same rights and powers as the first thirteen states. Why do you think this was important? The Northwest Ordinance also stated that people who lived in the Northwest Territory should have schools. And it stated that these people could not own slaves. As our country gained more land, this law was used again and again for adding new states to our country.

After the War for Independence many Americans began to move west of the Appalachian Mountains. The United States government helped in the settlement of these western lands by passing the Land Ordinance of 1785 and the Northwest Ordinance of 1787. What are these settlers taking with them to their new home?

wrap·up

- What is a bill of rights?
- What were the Articles of Confederation?
- Why were the Land Ordinance of 1785 and the Northwest Ordinance of 1787 important?

A Biographical Sketch

Man of the people

Thomas Jefferson was a very important person in the history of our country. He was known throughout the world as someone who believed in freedom for all people. As a child, Jefferson loved the outdoors. And he loved to learn about new things. When Jefferson was seventeen, he attended the College of William and Mary in Williamsburg, Virginia. After college he studied law and became a lawyer. Jefferson became interested in government, and in 1769 he was elected to the House of Burgesses.

This was only the beginning of many years of government service for Jefferson. He is best remembered as the author of the Declaration of Independence. But he also helped to write many laws that guided our country in important matters. As a member of Congress, Jefferson introduced a plan for the use of coins that is still used today. In 1781, under Jefferson's leadership, Virginia gave up its claims to western lands. These lands became part of the Northwest Territory. Jefferson's ideas for governing the Northwest Territory were used in writing the Northwest Ordinance of 1787.

Jefferson served our country as secretary of state and as Vice-President. And Jefferson was President of the United States from 1801 to 1809. Then he returned to Monticello, the home that he had designed in Virginia. Jefferson later started the University of Virginia. Thomas Jefferson died on July 4, 1826. What other happening do you know of in Thomas Jefferson's life that also took place on a fourth of July?

2

The need for a strong government

Problems of a weak government
The years following the War for Independence were hard ones for the United States. Our country's government under the Articles of Confederation was able to take care of some important problems. But it was not strong enough to take care of others.

The United States government under the Articles of Confederation had certain powers. Look at the chart on this page. What powers did the United States government have under the Articles of Confederation? Why do you think it was important for the United States government to have these powers and rights?

The thirteen states were afraid to set up a government that was too strong. They wanted most of the power to remain with the states. So the Articles of Confederation had many weaknesses. One weakness was that the United States government did not have the power to tax. Another weakness was that there was no government leader to see that the laws were carried out. And still another weakness was that all the states had to agree before any part of the Articles of Confederation could be

**POWERS GIVEN
TO THE UNITED STATES GOVERNMENT
BY THE ARTICLES OF CONFEDERATION**

Make peace or war

Set up post offices and charge postage

Set standards for weights and measures

Coin money

Control trade and manage affairs with the Indians

Borrow money

Send representatives to other countries

Receive representatives from other countries

Admit new states into the Union

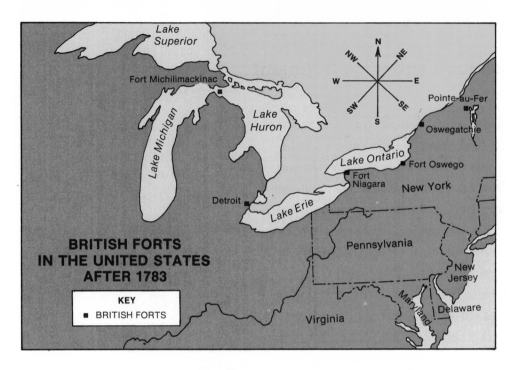

BRITISH FORTS
IN THE UNITED STATES
AFTER 1783

KEY
■ BRITISH FORTS

changed. How would this make it hard to bring about needed changes?

Problems between states During the years following the War for Independence, our country was really not united. People thought of themselves as Virginians or as New Yorkers, not as Americans. The United States was like thirteen small countries rather than one large country. Do you think this might have caused problems? Why or why not?

Under the Articles of Confederation the United States government did not have the power to control trade between the states. Some states placed a high **tariff,** or tax, on goods brought into their state. Other states had low tariffs. Some states taxed goods from one state but did not tax goods from other states. Such acts caused bad feelings between the states. And our country's government was powerless to do anything about it.

Problems with other governments The United States also had problems with foreign governments. By the terms of the Treaty of Paris, Britain had agreed to give up all forts in the United States. But Britain still held some forts in the United States. Look at the map on page 238. How many forts did Britain still hold after the war? What problems do you think this might have caused?

Another problem between the United States and Britain had to do with trade. Before the war many Americans had made their living from trade with Britain and with the British West Indies. But after the war Britain allowed few American ships to enter British ports. And Britain stopped all American trade with the British West Indies. Why do you think this caused great hardships for many Americans? John Adams was sent to London to try to settle these problems with Britain. Adams wanted the British to sign a treaty with the United States. But Britain was unwilling to do so. British leaders said that thirteen treaties would be needed to settle such matters with the United States. Why do you think the British said this?

The United States also had problems with Spain. The port of New Orleans was in the hands of the Spanish. So Spain

In 1785 John Adams was sent to Britain as a representative of the United States. This picture shows Adams meeting with King George III. Adams remained in Britain for three years but was unsuccessful in getting the British to sign a treaty with our country.

could refuse to allow the United States to use the port. This would mean that western farmers would have no way of getting their goods to markets in the East. The United States wanted Spain to promise that New Orleans would remain open to use by our country's people. But the United States government was not strong enough to deal with Spain on this important matter.

Problems over money   After the War for Independence, the United States faced serious money problems. Under the Articles of Confederation the United States government did not have the power to deal with our country's money matters. Each state was allowed to print its own money. People in one state often did not accept money printed in another state. What problems might this have caused?

Many soldiers who had fought during the War for Independence had not been paid for their services. When the war was over, these people had no money. Times were also bad for farmers. The prices of farm goods dropped sharply after the war. How do you think this hurt the farmers? **Debtors,** or people who owed money, wanted the states to print a large amount of paper money. Then the debtors could use the paper money to pay their bills. But when a lot of paper money is printed, the value of the money goes down. Do you think **creditors,** or people to whom money is owed, want this kind of money? Why or why not?

The state of Massachusetts refused to print paper money. This meant that many farmers would lose their farms because they could not pay their bills. Some farmers decided to act to save their farms. They chose Daniel Shays as their leader. Look at the picture on page 241. It shows a group of nearly 2,000 farmers that Shays led in an attack on the courthouse in Springfield, Massachusetts. The farmers demanded that the courts let them keep their farms. Soldiers were sent to stop this uprising.

The attack that Daniel Shays led on the Springfield courthouse was called Shays' Rebellion. What are the soldiers in the picture doing to try to stop this attack?

People throughout the United States became worried. Happenings like the one in Springfield showed that something had to be done. Many people felt a stronger government was needed to deal with problems both within our country and with other countries.

wrap •up

- What were some weaknesses of the United States government under the Articles of Confederation?
- What problems did the United States have with Britain and with Spain after the War for Independence?
- Why were there serious money problems in the United States after the War for Independence?

3

Our American Republic

Benjamin Franklin, pictured above, was the oldest member at the Constitutional Convention. James Madison, pictured below, is called the Father of the Constitution. Both these men played a major role in forming our country's government.

Three important meetings   In the spring of 1785 George Washington held a meeting at his home. The reason for this meeting was to settle differences between Virginia and Maryland over the use of the Potomac River. This meeting was such a success that those present decided to hold another meeting in September of 1786. That meeting would take place in Annapolis, Maryland. Each of the thirteen states was invited to send someone to Annapolis. Five states did so. At the Annapolis meeting Alexander Hamilton wrote down some of the weaknesses of the Articles of Confederation. Then those present decided to hold another meeting to see if something could be done about these weaknesses. That meeting would be held in Philadelphia, Pennsylvania.

On May 25, 1787, people from twelve states met in Philadelphia. Rhode Island did not send anyone because it did not want the government under the Articles of Confederation changed. George Washington was chosen to be in charge of the meeting. Benjamin Franklin, Alexander Hamilton, and James Madison were some other important leaders who attended. The people who attended this meeting came with the idea of making the Articles of Confederation stronger. But instead, they soon decided to write a new plan of government for the United States. So this meeting has become known as the Constitutional Convention.

Disagreements arise The leaders who wrote the Constitution had to decide what plan of government was best for our country. They did this by using what they knew from history. They also used what they had learned while the United States was under the rule of Britain. At first the leaders could not agree as to what plan was best. One of the problems they faced was how to set up the Congress. People agreed that each state should choose members to send to Congress. But they did not agree as to how many members each state should have. Some thought the number of members from each state should depend upon how many people lived in that state. Why do you think the large states favored this plan? Other people thought that all the states should have the same number of members in Congress. Why do you think the small states favored this plan?

Finally the leaders found a plan that was accepted by the large states and by the smaller states. They decided

The United States Capitol is the building in Washington, D.C., where the members of Congress meet. Parts of the Capitol are open to the public. Each year as many as 10 million people from many different countries visit the Capitol. How does this picture show that Americans are proud of their Capitol?

The House of Representatives and the Senate usually meet separately. But sometimes they meet together in a joint session.

that Congress would have two houses. One house would be called the **House of Representatives.** The number of members from each state would depend upon the number of people living in that state. The other house of Congress would be called the **Senate.** Each state would have two members no matter how many people lived in the state.

Even though most people accepted this plan, it brought up another important matter. The southern states wanted to count slaves when deciding how many members a state should have in the House of Representatives. The northern states did not agree. Why do you think this was so? Finally the leaders at the meeting decided that five slaves would be counted as three free people. Both the northern states and the southern states agreed to this.

The new plan Under the Articles of Confederation, the government had only one branch—the Congress. But the members of the Constitutional Convention decided upon a government with three branches. The **legislative branch** was set up to make the laws. This branch is made up of the two houses of Congress. The **executive branch** was set up to carry out the laws. The President of the United States heads this branch. And the **judicial branch** was set up to explain our country's laws. It makes sure that the laws agree with the Constitution. This branch also tries certain kinds of court cases. A number of different courts make up this branch. Each of the three branches of our government can check the power of the other two branches. In this way no branch can become too powerful. Do you think this is a good idea? Why or why not?

The members of the Constitutional Convention wanted to set up a strong United States government. At the same time, they did not want to destroy the power of the states and of the people. So they worked out a plan whereby the United States government has certain powers and the state governments have certain powers. The people choose those who govern them. Our United States government is called a **republic.** This means that the power to govern comes from the people who vote for those who hold public office.

The Constitution gives the United States government a number of important powers. Among these powers are the following: It can control trade between the states and with other countries. It can coin money. It can sign treaties and make peace or war. It can keep an army and a navy. And it can set up post offices. State governments cannot do these things. Why do you think these important powers were given to the United States government rather than to the states? How do these powers compare to the powers given to the United States government and to the state governments under the Articles of Confederation?

The members of the Constitutional Convention remembered how hard it was to make changes in the Articles of Confederation. They wanted to make it easier to change the Constitution. But they did not want to make it too easy. So they drew up a careful plan whereby **amendments,** or changes, can be added to the Constitution. This plan has been used a number of times, but only to make very important changes in our government. Do you think the members were wise to make it possible, but hard, to change our country's government? Why or why not?

Accepting the Constitution Look at the picture on this page. It shows the signing of the Constitution, which took place on September 17, 1787. Thirty-nine members at the meeting in Philadelphia signed the Constitution. Then the people had to decide whether or not this plan of government would ever be put into use.

The citizens of each state chose a group of people to meet and decide whether or not to accept the Constitution. Nine states had to accept the new plan of government before it became the law of the land. How was this different from the number of states that were needed to accept the Articles of Confederation?

This picture is of a famous painting showing the signing of the Constitution. The original painting hangs in our country's Capitol. Who are some of the people you recognize in the picture?

Some people did not think that the Constitution was the best plan of government for our country. They tried to keep the states from accepting it. But on December 7, 1787, Delaware became the first state to accept the Constitution. And by June 21, 1788, eight other states had also accepted it. So the Constitution was put into use. It is still the plan of government for our country today.

Demands for a bill of rights   A number of states, however, were not completely pleased with the Constitution. These states demanded that a bill of rights be added. So, soon after the Constitution was put into use, ten amendments were added. They are known as the Bill of Rights. The Bill of Rights lists those freedoms and rights that all United States citizens have. And it states that the government cannot take these freedoms and rights from the people.

Among the rights given to all United States citizens by the Bill of Rights is freedom of speech. The Bill of Rights also says that all United States citizens are free to go to the church of their choice. And it says that people have the right to meet and to ask the government to correct what is wrong. The Bill of Rights also states the rights of a person tried in court. These and other rights listed in the Bill of Rights protect every United States citizen. Why do you think it was important to the people to have the Bill of Rights added to the Constitution?

wrap ·up

- What kind of government is a republic?
- How do the powers of the United States government under the Constitution compare with the powers of the United States government under the Articles of Confederation?
- Why is the Bill of Rights so important?

Using Your Skills

Reading a diagram

Use the diagram to answer the following questions:
1. What does the diagram show?
2. In what ways can an amendment be offered?
3. In what ways can an amendment be accepted?
4. In how many ways can amendments become part of the Constitution?

HOW AN AMENDMENT BECOMES PART OF THE CONSTITUTION

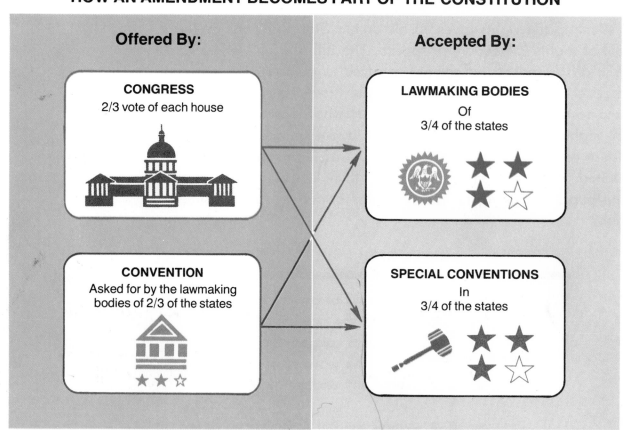

Offered By:

CONGRESS
2/3 vote of each house

CONVENTION
Asked for by the lawmaking bodies of 2/3 of the states

Accepted By:

LAWMAKING BODIES
Of
3/4 of the states

SPECIAL CONVENTIONS
In
3/4 of the states

Chapter-End Activities

The chapter-end activities may be done by writing the questions or statements and the answers on a separate sheet of paper or by writing just the answers on a separate sheet of paper, whichever your teacher desires.

Words and Terms

republic
territory
amendments

Senate
bill of rights
tariff

constitution
House of Representatives

1. By 1780 each state had a ____, or plan of government.

2. A ____ is a listing of freedoms and rights that cannot be taken away from the people by the government.

3. A ____ is land that is part of our country but not yet a state.

4. After the War for Independence, some states placed a high ____, or tax, on goods from other states.

5. The Congress of the United States is made up of two houses—the ____ and the ____.

6. A kind of government in which the power to govern comes from the people is called a ____.

Fact Recall

1. What were the Articles of Confederation?

2. What law provided for the governing of the Northwest Territory?

3. What problems did the United States have with Britain after the War for Independence?

4. What are the three branches of the United States government?

5. What are the first ten amendments to the Constitution known as?

Concepts and Understandings

1. Why was a stronger United States government needed than that provided for by the Articles of Confederation?

2. How are the powers of the United States government separated among the three branches of government?

3. Why is the United States government set up by the Constitution called a republic?

Unit End

Main Ideas and Understandings

1. How did Britain change its way of governing the colonies after the French and Indian War? How did the colonists react to this change? What was the purpose of the First Continental Congress? Why is July 4, 1776, an important date in the history of our country?

2. What were some advantages and disadvantages the British had and the Americans had at the beginning of the War for Independence? Why is the Battle of Saratoga called the turning point of the war? How did other countries help the United States during the War for Independence? Why was the Treaty of Paris important?

3. What were the Articles of Confederation? What did the Land Ordinance of 1785 and the Northwest Ordinance of 1787 provide for? What were some of the weaknesses of the United States government under the Articles of Confederation? What kind of government is set up by the United States Constitution?

Research Ideas

1. Americans have honored our country's past leaders in many ways. Find out how George Washington and Thomas Jefferson are honored. What buildings, monuments, and other structures have been built or named in honor of these two men? What are other ways in which they have been honored?

2. Many people were important in our country's fight for freedom. Find out what Mary McCauley, Prince Estabrook, Ethan Allen, Haym Salomon, Salem Poor, Thaddeus Kosciusko, and Johann Kalb did to help our country win its independence. Why was Benjamin Franklin sent to France during the War for Independence? For what reasons do we remember Phillis Wheatley and Deborah Sampson?

3. Throughout the history of our country the Constitution has been changed a number of times. How many amendments have been added to the Constitution? What does each amendment provide for? When did each one go into effect?

Activities and Projects

1. Work in groups to make murals showing important events that led to or occurred during the War for Independence. Place the murals around the classroom in the order in which each event occurred. Write a report or perform a play to go along with your mural.

2. Draw and cut out symbols that represent American freedom. You may want to draw such things as the American Flag, the Liberty Bell, the Statue of Liberty, and the Great Seal of the United States. On the back of each symbol explain its meaning. Use these symbols to make mobiles.

Unit 6

Our Country Moves Forward

In 1789 our country stretched from the Atlantic Ocean to the Mississippi River. Suppose our country had not gained any more land. How might our country be different today? By 1850, however, the United States had gained a great deal more land. Many other changes had also taken place. Americans had changed their ways of traveling, of working, and of thinking. This unit will help you learn about the changes in our country from 1789 to the 1850s. You will find answers to the following questions:

How did our country's government become strong?

How did the feelings that many Americans had for our country affect life in the United States during this time?

How did our country grow in land size?

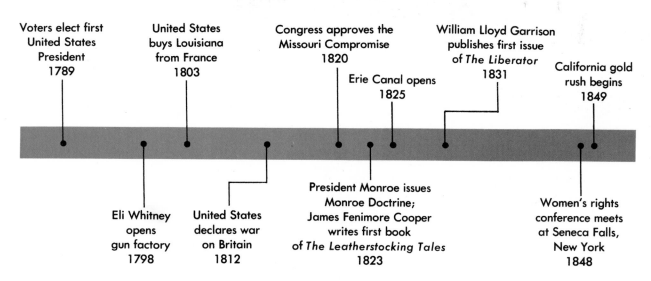

Voters elect first United States President 1789

United States buys Louisiana from France 1803

Congress approves the Missouri Compromise 1820

Erie Canal opens 1825

William Lloyd Garrison publishes first issue of *The Liberator* 1831

California gold rush begins 1849

Eli Whitney opens gun factory 1798

United States declares war on Britain 1812

President Monroe issues Monroe Doctrine; James Fenimore Cooper writes first book of *The Leatherstocking Tales* 1823

Women's rights conference meets at Seneca Falls, New York 1848

253

CHAPTER 14

Our Country Gets Started

1. Early developments at home
2. Early relations with other countries
3. Increasing the size of our country

Think of something that you have learned to do. You might have learned to play a musical instrument, or you might have learned a new sport. How did you feel the first time you tried to do what you had learned? Perhaps you felt a little worried about doing everything the right way. The leaders of our country felt somewhat that way in 1789. These leaders had worked in government before. But in 1789 they were just beginning their duties under our country's Constitution.

People in the United States and elsewhere were eager to see how our country's new government would work. In this chapter you will learn about the first years of our country's government under the Constitution.

Early developments at home

Getting off to a good start Our country's Constitution was a *plan* of government. But the government itself could not get started until leaders had been chosen. So early in 1789 the people voted for our country's leaders. They chose George Washington as our country's first President.

President Washington and other leaders knew that the first years under the Constitution would be very important. The things these leaders did during those years would help to guide our government for a long time. Why do you think this made the jobs of our first leaders very hard?

Congress created jobs for people who would help take care of the business of government. These people as a group became known as the **Cabinet.** Washington looked to the members of the Cabinet for their ideas and their feelings.

Compromising on a capital Alexander Hamilton was chosen to be in charge of government money matters. The states had borrowed money from many people during the War for Independence. Hamilton planned for the federal government to pay back money the states owed. The northern

President George Washington, at the far left, is shown here with his first Cabinet. The other people, from left to right, are Secretary of War Henry Knox, Secretary of the Treasury Alexander Hamilton, Secretary of State Thomas Jefferson, and Attorney General Edmund Randolph.

255

In 1794 an artist painted this view of the land on which our country's capital city was built. This land was partly in Virginia and partly in Maryland. How would you describe this land?

states agreed, but the southern states did not. Most southern states had already paid back the money they owed.

The best way to settle the matter seemed to be by a **compromise** [KAHM-pruh-MYZ]. A compromise is a plan by which each side gives up something it wants. The southern states agreed to vote for Hamilton's plan. In exchange, the northern states agreed to vote for building the country's capital city in the South. What did each side give up? What did each side gain?

President Washington chose land for the new capital. The picture on this page shows how this land looked. The work of measuring and planning the capital began in 1791.

The beginning of political parties
Our new government needed money. Hamilton wanted to raise money by placing taxes on certain goods. One of the highest taxes was placed on whiskey. Many backcountry farmers at that time used some of their corn to make whiskey. Whiskey was easier to store, to carry, and to sell than corn was. Some farmers in western Pennsylvania refused to pay the tax. They even attacked those who tried to collect the taxes. So President Washington sent soldiers there to back up the country's laws. Why do you think this was an important action by the President?

Thomas Jefferson, the Secretary of State, did not agree with Hamilton about taxes and many other things. People began to choose sides between Hamilton's ideas and Jefferson's ideas. These sides became **political parties,** or groups of people with certain ideas about how government should be run. These were the first political parties in our country.

The American Indians and the land Many people were moving west at the time our new government got started. As these people moved west, they settled on lands that belonged to the American Indians. The Indians fought to keep their lands. One of the biggest battles took place in 1794. The soldiers that the government had sent to protect the settlers defeated the Indians. Both sides signed a treaty that forced the Indians to move out of what is now Ohio.

People from the East soon settled the land that the Indians had given up. Then people began to push farther west onto American Indian lands. Once again the Indians fought for their lands. Soldiers led by William Henry Harrison defeated the Indians in what is now Indiana. The American Indians were forced to give up more land. How do you think this made the Indians feel about our country's government?

The Shawnee chief Tecumseh told William Henry Harrison and other government agents that the land belonged to all American Indians. Tecumseh then worked to unite many individual Indian tribes to fight for their land.

New ways of traveling As people went west, they needed better means of moving themselves and their goods. Many people traveled on rivers. But these people had a problem. Boats moved easily downstream, but they needed oars or sails to move upstream. In 1807 Robert Fulton built a boat powered by a steam engine. His steamboat, pictured on this page, moved easily both upstream and downstream. How do you think such a boat changed water transportation?

People also needed good roads. Private companies began building wide roads with hard, crushed-rock surfaces. The companies charged people for using these roads. But private companies did not want to build roads over the Appalachian Mountains. So the government began such a road in 1811. This road was called the National Road or the Cumberland Road. By 1818 it stretched from Maryland to the Ohio River. Why do you think this road was important to settlers?

Factories become important People in our country had been making goods by hand for many years. Then in the late 1700s a great change took place in the way people made goods. People began to use machines to make goods.

Samuel Slater was one of the first people in the United States to make goods by machine. In 1790 Slater built a mill that made thread and yarn. People used these goods for

Other inventors had built steamboats before Robert Fulton did, but Fulton's steamboat was the first to become a great success. What was the name of Fulton's steamboat?

weaving cloth in their homes. In 1814 Francis Lowell built a factory in which machines did the jobs of both spinning and weaving. How did such factories make it easier for people to make clothing at home?

Eli Whitney also helped make factories important. In 1798 Whitney began to use machines to make gun parts. Each machine made a different part. And the machines made the parts the same way every time. So the parts were **interchangeable**. This meant that the parts could be used in any gun made in Whitney's factory at that time. The use of such parts made the **assembly line** possible. This is a way of arranging parts and workers in a line for making goods. This way of making goods later led to **mass production**—the making of many goods of the same kind quickly. Why do you think Whitney's ideas came to be used in other factories?

Samuel Slater's mill was located in New England, as were the factories of Francis Lowell and of Eli Whitney. New England had many rivers that could be used for waterpower and many workers who were willing to work in mills and factories.

wrap ·up

- Why were our early leaders careful about what they did during the first years of government under the Constitution?
- Why did the American Indians fight against the settlers and against the soldiers sent by the government?
- How did ways of making goods change during the late 1700s?

A Biographical Sketch

Measuring for a new city

A lot of work must be done before a new city can be built. **Surveyors** do much of this work. They are people who measure land, make maps, and mark boundary lines. Benjamin Banneker was one of the surveyors who helped measure the land on which our country's capital city was built.

Benjamin Banneker made a living by farming. But he had many other interests. When Banneker was over fifty years old, he became interested in **astronomy**. This is the study of the sun, the moon, and the stars. Banneker borrowed books and tools from a neighbor. Before long Banneker was hard at work preparing astronomy charts for an almanac.

Banneker's new interest gave him the chance to work for his country. The surveyor of the new capital city needed the help of someone who knew astronomy. So Benjamin Banneker was chosen for the job.

Banneker was in charge of using certain tools and keeping records. Why do you think such work was important? Banneker had to camp in the woods and walk where there were no roads. That was hard work for an old man! But he enjoyed talking with people who had studied the same subjects he had.

It took several years to measure all the land for the new capital city. Benjamin Banneker worked for only part of that time. But he had helped to start the work of building our country's capital, which later was called Washington, D.C.

2

Early relations with other countries

Trying not to take sides In the 1790s the young United States had many matters to settle at home. But our country also had several matters to settle with other countries. Britain still had forts and trading posts in the Old Northwest. Many Americans thought that the British were helping the American Indians fight against the settlers.

The United States also had troubles with Spain. The western farmers and traders in our country needed a way to ship their goods to market. But Spain controlled the Mississippi River and the city of New Orleans, which was an important trading center. The Spanish would not allow Americans to ship goods on the Mississippi River. How do you think this affected American trade? Also, the United States and Spain did not agree on the boundary lines between our country and Spanish lands in America.

President Washington set guidelines for dealing with other countries. In 1793 Britain was at war with France. President Washington decided that our country should not take sides with either Britain or France. This was hard for Americans to do. The United States depended on trade with both countries. But British ships began stopping and holding American ships that were trading with France. How do you think this made some Americans feel?

Keeping the peace Some Americans wanted to go to war with Britain. But President Washington wanted peace. So he sent John Jay to Britain to arrange a treaty between the two countries. The British agreed to leave the Old Northwest and to pay for the ships they had taken. But they did not agree to leave other American ships alone. Why do you think some Americans were unhappy with Jay's Treaty?

Spain also wanted to settle its differences with the United States. So President Washington sent Thomas Pinckney to Spain to arrange a treaty. Spain agreed to let Americans ship goods on the Mississippi River and to store those goods at New Orleans. Spain also agreed with the United States over our country's southern and western boundaries. Why do you think many Americans were happier with Pinckney's Treaty than with Jay's Treaty?

Troubled times   Our country's second and third Presidents followed Washington's guidelines for dealing with other countries. Why do you think they did this? In 1797 President John Adams sent several people to France. These people felt that the French government insulted them. American and French ships attacked each other for the next two years. But President Adams kept us out of war with France.

Trouble with both France and Britain began again in 1803. These two countries were at war with each other. Both countries began attacking American ships. The British also began taking sailors from American ships and making them serve in the British Navy.

President Thomas Jefferson did not want war. So he asked Congress to pass an **embargo.** This is an order stopping ships or certain goods from leaving or entering a country. This embargo kept American ships at home. So it kept France and Britain from receiving American goods. But the embargo also hurt American businesspeople, farmers, sailors, and shipbuilders. Why do you think the embargo hurt such people?

The embargo was ended in 1809. But the British still stopped American ships. And many people still thought that the British were aiding the American Indians. President Madison tried to keep peace. But matters between the two countries did not improve. So in June of 1812, Madison asked

Congress to declare war. This war between Britain and the United States became known as the War of 1812.

The first months of war Our young country was not ready to go to war. Our country's army and navy were small. Our government needed money. And a number of our country's people were very much against this war.

The British Navy was much larger than the American Navy. Yet American ships defeated several British ships during the early months of the war. The American ship shown in the picture at the bottom of this page became well-known during this time. By 1813, however, British ships had sailed into many of our important harbors to keep American ships from sailing out. How do you think this hurt the American Navy and American trade? But some ships still sailed on the Great Lakes. Oliver Hazard Perry led the Americans to an important victory over the British Navy on Lake Erie in 1813.

Some American Indians in the Old Northwest joined the British to fight the Americans. After Perry's victory, William Henry Harrison was able to force the British and the Indians into Canada. Harrison won a victory that ended the power of the British and the Indians in the Old Northwest. Several months later, Andrew Jackson defeated the

The picture above shows British soldiers seizing an American sailor on board a captured ship. The ship shown below earned the name Old Ironsides *during the War of 1812. The ship is now in Boston Harbor, where visitors may tour it.*

Creek Indians in what is now Alabama. This victory ended the power of the American Indians in the Old Southwest.

Ending the war   In 1814 the British tried several things that they thought might end the war. First they attacked Washington, D.C. Why do you think the British thought that this might end the war? The British then attacked Fort McHenry. The picture on this page shows Francis Scott Key, an American who wrote a poem about this attack. Key wrote, "Oh! say, can you see, by the dawn's early light, . . . " Why is this poem important to Americans today?

Finally, the British attacked New Orleans. Andrew Jackson's army won this battle—our country's biggest victory of this war. But the battle need not have been fought. The United States and Britain had signed a peace treaty two weeks earlier. However, none of the leaders at the Battle of New Orleans knew this. What does this tell you about the speed with which messages traveled at that time?

The attack on Fort McHenry, outside Baltimore, lasted through the night. Francis Scott Key and other Americans awoke the next morning not knowing the outcome of the battle. How did Key and others know that the United States had held the fort?

Andrew Jackson did not have enough trained soldiers to defend New Orleans. Farmers, merchants, slaves, and other people joined the soldiers to fight the British troops.

The treaty that ended the War of 1812 was signed in 1814. By the terms of the treaty, neither side gained or lost any land. And neither side even agreed to stop holding the other's trading ships or sailors. But the treaty did bring an end to the fighting. The War of 1812 was important to our country. The war proved that the United States was a strong country that could defend itself. The war helped make many Americans proud of their country. And the United States gained the respect of many other countries. Why do you think this was important for a young country to do?

wrap·up

- What guidelines did our early Presidents follow in dealing with other countries?
- How was American Indian power ended in the Old Northwest and in the Old Southwest?
- How did the United States gain the respect of many other countries?

Increasing the size of our country

Doubling the land size of our country By 1800 many Americans had settled the land between the Appalachian Mountains and the Mississippi River. This was the western part of our country at that time. Many people who settled there depended on using the Mississippi River and the harbor at New Orleans for shipping goods. Pinckney's Treaty with Spain in 1795 had arranged this use.

In 1802 New Orleans was closed to American shipping. What do you think this did to our country's western trade? The United States learned that Spain no longer owned New Orleans or the Mississippi River. And Spain no longer owned the land between the Mississippi River and the Rocky Mountains. Spain had made a deal that gave all this to France.

Americans were angry about the closing of New Orleans. So President Jefferson asked France to sell New Orleans to the United States. France needed money for a war with Britain. So France sold all the land that it had received from

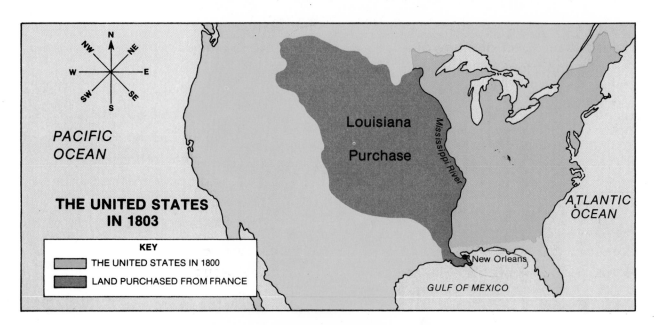

PACIFIC OCEAN

Louisiana

Purchase

Mississippi River

ATLANTIC OCEAN

THE UNITED STATES IN 1803

New Orleans

GULF OF MEXICO

KEY

THE UNITED STATES IN 1800

LAND PURCHASED FROM FRANCE

The land shown in this picture is much like the land Lewis and Clark crossed. What would make this land difficult to cross on foot and on horseback?

Spain to the United States in 1803. Look at the map on page 266. It shows the land that the United States bought from France. What was this land called? Notice that the purchase almost doubled the land size of the United States.

The Louisiana Purchase cost the United States just a few pennies an acre. An acre is about 0.4 hectares. By making this purchase, the United States became the owner of New Orleans and the Mississippi River. It also became the owner of much land west of the Mississippi River. Do you think this was a good deal for the United States? Why do you think so?

Beyond the Mississippi River President Jefferson was eager to learn more about the land west of the Mississippi River. So he sent a group of people to explore the Louisiana Purchase and lands further west. Jefferson wanted the group to gather facts about the land, the animals, and the plants that the members saw.

Meriwether Lewis and William Clark led the group of explorers. The group left St. Louis by boat in May of 1804. The members of the group followed the Missouri River until they could no longer travel by boat. By this time they had begun to cross the Rocky Mountains. An American Indian woman named Sacajawea [SAK-uh-juh-WEE-uh] had joined the group

The group led by Lewis and Clark met a large number of Shoshone Indians. What signs are there that this meeting was friendly? After exchanging greetings, Sacajawea recognized the Shoshone chief as her brother, whom she had not seen for many years.

along the way. She helped the group find a route through the mountains. Lewis and Clark reached the Pacific Ocean in November of 1805. How do you think the members of the group felt when they first saw the Pacific Ocean?

Lewis and Clark and several others kept daily records of their trip. They described meetings with many different American Indian tribes. The picture on this page shows how an artist thought one of these meetings might have looked. Lewis and Clark made maps of the land and drawings of the plants and the animals that they saw. How do you think such records helped people in the East learn about the lands west of the Mississippi River?

Lewis and Clark and most of the others returned to St. Louis in September of 1806. They had not found a good route to the Pacific Ocean. But they had explored lands all the way from the Mississippi River to the Pacific coast. And they had brought back valuable records of the lands, the American Indians, the plants, and the animals that they had seen. Do you think the journey of Lewis and Clark was a success? Why do you think so?

Adding new states to our country All the thirteen English colonies had become states by 1790. Before long these states were joined by new ones.

The first new state was Vermont. Even though New Englanders had lived in Vermont for many years, both New Hampshire and New York claimed that land. Then in 1791 they finally gave up their claims, and Vermont became a state.

A number of states were added to our country as more and more people moved west. Some of the first people who moved west followed the Cumberland River. By 1792 Kentucky had enough people to become a state. And in 1796 Tennessee also became a state. These two states were part of the Old Southwest. People who moved west also settled in the Old Northwest. In 1803 Ohio was the first state to come from this territory. Then in 1812 Louisiana became the first state to come from the Louisiana Purchase. And in 1816 Indiana became another state to come from the Old Northwest. Why do you think Ohio became a state before Indiana did?

The Gateway Arch stands on the banks of the Mississippi River in St. Louis, Missouri. The arch honors the Louisiana Purchase, Lewis and Clark, and the many people who passed through St. Louis on their way to the western parts of our country.

wrap·up

- Why was the Louisiana Purchase important to the United States?
- How did Lewis and Clark help people learn about lands west of the Mississippi River?
- How did the westward movement of settlers help to add new states to our country?

Using Your Skills

Reading a map

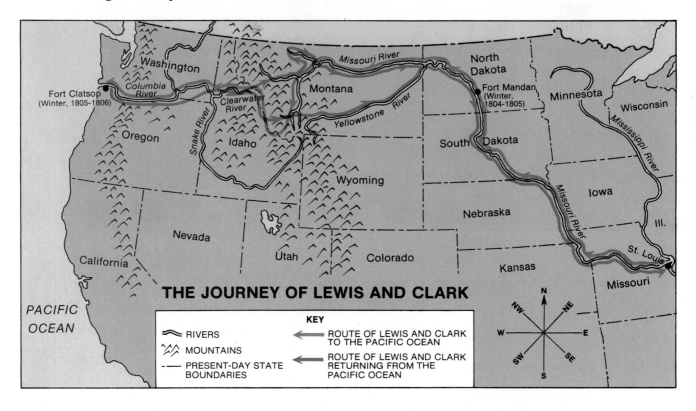

THE JOURNEY OF LEWIS AND CLARK

KEY

~~ RIVERS

ʌʌ MOUNTAINS

— · — PRESENT-DAY STATE BOUNDARIES

← ROUTE OF LEWIS AND CLARK TO THE PACIFIC OCEAN

← ROUTE OF LEWIS AND CLARK RETURNING FROM THE PACIFIC OCEAN

The land over which Lewis and Clark traveled had not been divided into states. This map shows the states as they exist today. Use the map to answer the following questions:

1. What does this map show?

2. Where did Lewis and Clark spend the winter of 1804–1805?

3. In what present-day states did Lewis and Clark see mountains?

4. On what rivers named on the map did Lewis and Clark travel?

5. During what part of the trip did the explorers split into two groups? How can you tell from this map?

Chapter-End Activities

The chapter-end activities may be done by writing the questions or statements and the answers on a separate sheet of paper or by writing just the answers on a separate sheet of paper, whichever your teacher desires.

Words and Terms

Louisiana Purchase   compromise
Cabinet   mass production
assembly line   embargo

_____ 1. A plan by which each side gives up something it wants

_____ 2. A way of arranging parts and workers in a line for making goods

_____ 3. The making of many goods of the same kind quickly

_____ 4. An order stopping ships or certain goods from leaving or entering a country

_____ 5. The land that the United States bought from France in 1803

Fact Recall

1. The United States government and the American Indians signed treaties that _____.
   a. forced settlers to give up land
   b. forced Indians to give up land

2. Robert Fulton's steamboat was different from most other boats because it could _____.
   a. move easily both upstream and downstream
   b. sail without power

3. One cause of the War of 1812 was Britain's practice of _____.
   a. trading only with France
   b. taking sailors from American ships to serve in the British Navy

4. The War of 1812 helped the United States gain _____.
   a. the respect of other countries
   b. a large amount of land

5. The group of explorers led by Lewis and Clark helped to _____.
   a. gather facts about the land west of the Mississippi River
   b. find an easy route by water to Canada

Concepts and Understandings

1. Why were early leaders of our country very careful about the things they did and about the guidelines they set up?

2. How did the United States grow in land size during the early years of our country's government?

271

CHAPTER 15

Our Country Grows Strong

1. A spirit of nationalism
2. Our country continues to grow
3. Telling other countries where we stand

Imagine yourself in the picture above. What would you be doing, or hearing, or seeing? After the War of 1812 ended, many Americans began moving farther westward. They followed roads and rivers in search of land or of jobs.

The years after the war also brought other changes. United States citizens began to have strong feelings for our country. Many more people received the right to vote than ever before. Congress tried to keep a balance between slave states and free states. And the United States government took a strong stand toward keeping European countries out of North America and South America. In this chapter you will learn about the changes in our country during the 1820s and 1830s.

1

A spirit of nationalism

Good feelings for our country   After the War of 1812, many Americans were proud of our country. They felt a growing love for and loyalty to the United States. People began to place the interests of our country as a whole above those of separate parts of our country. Such feelings are part of a spirit of **nationalism** [NASH-nuhl-IHZ-uhm]. Things our country's government did showed the spirit of nationalism. The United States government became stronger during this time.

Our country's government helped American factories become more important. After the War of 1812, Britain began to send large amounts of goods to our country. The British goods cost less than American goods. So people stopped buying American goods. This hurt the business of American factories. And it put many Americans out of work. So Congress placed a high tariff on certain goods brought in from

Fourth of July celebrations became very popular in the early 1800s. How does this celebration in Philadelphia in 1819 compare with Fourth of July celebrations today?

other countries. With the tariff, goods made in other countries cost more than American goods. How do you think this helped to protect American factories?

Henry Clay was an American leader who had a plan for the United States. Clay was in favor of the high tariff. But he also wanted the United States government to improve transportation throughout our country. Do you think Clay's plan showed signs of nationalism? Why or why not?

Building transportation links across the country The United States government, the state governments, and private companies all helped to improve transportation. Steamboats carried people and goods on the Mississippi River and the Ohio River. And the National Road stretched west into Illinois by 1838.

The use of canals became important in the United States during the 1820s and 1830s. Short canals had been used for several years in our country. Then in 1817 work began on the Erie Canal. This canal reached almost all the way across the state of New York. The canal was finally opened in 1825. The picture at the top of page 275 shows how the Erie Canal looked.

People could ship goods on the Hudson River from New York City to Albany. From there they could ship goods through the Erie Canal to the Great Lakes. Steamboats carried goods between cities on the Great Lakes. Later, the states of Ohio and Indiana built canals that connected the Great Lakes with the Ohio River. People could then ship goods between New York and New Orleans by means of inland waterways. Why do you think this was important to American trade?

In the 1820s a company in Britain started a railroad to carry people and goods. The railroad was powered by a steam locomotive. The idea soon spread to the United States. Before long, railroads became an important means of trans-

Canalboats, such as the ones shown above on the Erie Canal, were pulled by mules or horses. The animals walked on narrow towpaths along the sides of the canal. Curious crowds gathered to look over the early steam locomotives, such as the one shown at the right.

portation in our country. The Baltimore and Ohio Railroad was one of the first railroads in our country. It began in 1830 with 13 miles (20.9 km) of track. Soon other railroads were built. By 1836 the United States had more than 1,000 miles (1609.3 km) of railroad tracks. Notice the early train in the picture at the lower right on this page. How is this train different from trains that are used today?

Voting power for more Americans   Many changes had taken place in our country by the 1820s. One of the most important changes gave more American citizens a voice in government. In the early years of our country, only men who owned property could vote. So, many people had no voice in how our government was run.

Some new states that joined our country, however, allowed *all* free white men to vote. Other states soon accepted this idea. Blacks, women, and Indians did not receive the right to vote until many years later. But many more people were given the right to vote in the 1820s than ever before. And people who could vote could also run for public office. How do you think this gave Americans a greater voice in their government?

The people elect "Old Hickory"   By the 1820s, people who ran for public office found that they needed the support of many people to be elected. One of the first people to gain such support was Andrew Jackson. Jackson had narrowly missed being chosen as President in 1824. Soon after that, Jackson and his supporters began to work hard for the next election. They held meetings and talked with people throughout the United States. What things do people today do when they run for public office?

Many Americans already knew Jackson as Old Hickory— the hero of the Battle of New Orleans. Large numbers of these people eagerly voted for Jackson in 1828. This was the first time that many Americans had the chance to help choose a President.

President Jackson had many strong ideas about how government should be run. When Jackson took office, he decided to replace many of the people who had worked for the government for many years. Jackson chose people from his own political party to fill many of these jobs. He used the jobs to reward people who had helped him get elected. President Jackson also felt that many laws helped businesses and

Andrew Jackson was greeted by enthusiastic crowds as he traveled to Washington, D.C., to take office as President. What means of transportation did Jackson use on this journey?

wealthy people. Jackson did not believe that our country's government should help only these groups. So he worked to make the government more helpful to greater numbers of people. What groups of people do you think might have agreed with Jackson's ideas? What groups of people do you think might have been against Jackson's ideas?

wrap ·up

- How did our country's government help nationalism grow?
- How did transportation improve in the United States during the 1820s and 1830s?
- How did many citizens in our country gain a greater voice in government during the first part of the 1800s?

A Biographical Sketch

The Great Compromiser

Henry Clay went to school for only a few years. He earned his own living from the time he was fourteen years old. But between 1806 and 1852, Henry Clay was one of the most important people in American government.

Henry Clay was not quite thirty years old when he was chosen to represent Kentucky in the United States Senate. At that time, Clay was the youngest person there. Then in 1811, Henry Clay was elected to the United States House of Representatives. He was chosen to be the **speaker,** or leader, of the House on the very first day he was there!

Henry Clay wanted the United States to be a strong country. He worked for laws that would help our country's business and farms. Clay felt that all parts of our country had to work together. So Clay wanted to see transportation improved within the United States. How do you think good transportation helps to tie a country together?

There were many differences to settle within the United States, however. Many of these differences were between the northern and the southern parts of our country. Henry Clay worked hard to arrange compromises that would settle such differences. People throughout our country came to know Clay as The Great Compromiser.

Henry Clay ran for President three times. He was defeated each time. But during his many years in government, Clay helped our country in many ways.

2

Our country continues to grow

Problems with Spain The southern coast of the United States east of the Mississippi River was once part of Florida. Spain owned Florida, but Spain had little control over this land. Runaway slaves from our country escaped to Florida. And some American Indians in Florida stole goods from United States citizens who lived north of Florida. In 1810 and 1813 the United States took parts of western Florida from Spain.

Our country's government told Spain to keep order in the rest of Florida or give that land to the United States. Spain had little choice and so finally agreed to give Florida to the United States in 1819. The two countries also agreed on a boundary between United States lands and Spanish lands west of the Mississippi River. Why do you think this was important to our country?

Settlers on the move After the War of 1812, many people settled the land that American Indians had been forced to leave. Some people loaded their belongings on flatboats and floated down the Ohio River. What other kinds of transportation do you think people might have used for moving

Many flatboats were built with shelters for people, but they also had room aboard for animals. Why do you think this was important for settlers moving west?

279

west? Some settlers moved to the rich cotton-growing land of the Old Southwest. But American Indians still owned some of this land. In 1830 Congress passed a law that exchanged land the Indians then owned for land west of the Mississippi River. This law forced many Indians to move west.

The Cherokee had rights to land in Georgia. But in the 1830s, the Cherokee were forced to move to what is now Oklahoma. Thousands of them died on the way. The picture on this page shows how one artist thought this march, called the Trail of Tears, might have looked. How does this name help to show how the Cherokee felt about moving?

Adding new states People who moved west soon added new states to our country. Mississippi, settled by cotton growers, became a state in 1817. Illinois became a state in 1818. This state came from the Old Northwest. In 1819 Alabama became the last state to come from the Old Southwest.

Our country had the same number of **slave states** as free states in 1819. Slave states were those in which people could own slaves. What do you think free states were? In 1819 Missouri asked to become a state. Missouri would be a slave state. In that case the United States Senate would have more members from slave states than from free states. Why do you

The United States Supreme Court had ruled that the Cherokee had full rights to their land in Georgia. This ruling, however, was never carried out, and the Cherokee were forced to give up their land.

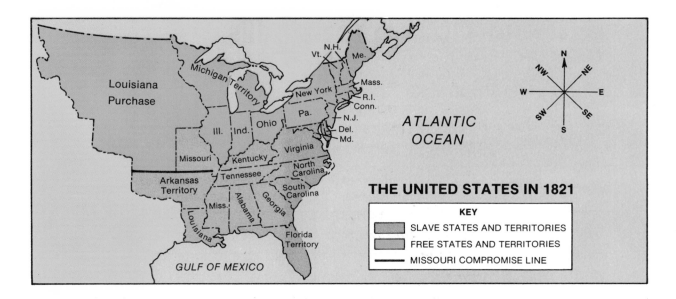

THE UNITED STATES IN 1821

KEY
SLAVE STATES AND TERRITORIES
FREE STATES AND TERRITORIES
MISSOURI COMPROMISE LINE

think the northern states were against accepting Missouri as a slave state? Congress settled the matter in 1820 by agreeing to a plan called the Missouri Compromise. By this plan Maine was accepted as a free state, and Missouri was accepted as a slave state.

The Missouri Compromise also set up a plan for deciding whether new states should be slave states or free states. Find the Missouri Compromise Line on the map on this page. Any new states formed north of this line would be free states. Any new states formed south of this line would be slave states. Arkansas became a state in 1836. Was it a slave state or a free state? How do you know?

wrap·up

- How did the United States grow in size following the War of 1812?
- Why were some American Indians forced to move west of the Mississippi River?
- How did the Missouri Compromise deal with the question of whether new states should be slave states or free states?

Using Your Skills

Reading a pictograph

UNITED STATES EASTERN AND WESTERN POPULATION, 1800–1840

Year	People Living in States East of the Appalachian Mountains	People Living in States or Territories West of the Appalachian Mountains
1800	𝟝	¼
1810	5½	1¼
1820	6½	2¼
1830	8	3½
1840	9½	6

Each 👤 = 1 Million People

1. About how many people lived east of the Appalachian Mountains in 1800? About how many people lived west of the Appalachian Mountains?

2. What was the total population of the United States in 1830?

3. About how many more people lived east of the Appalachian Mountains in 1840 than in 1800?

4. About how many more people lived west of the Appalachian Mountains in 1840 than in 1800?

5. Which increased more from 1800 to 1840—the population east of the Appalachian Mountains or the population west of the Appalachian Mountains?

3

Telling other countries where we stand

Improving relations with Britain
The years following the War of 1812 led to better relations between the governments of the United States and Britain. During and after the War of 1812, both countries kept warships on the Great Lakes. The Great Lakes are part of the boundary between the United States and Canada. Britain ruled Canada at that time. In 1817 the United States and Britain agreed to **disarm,** or remove the weapons from, their ships on the Great Lakes. This showed that both countries wanted a lasting peace.

In 1818 the United States and Britain agreed on the boundary between the United States and Canada from what is now Minnesota to the Rocky Mountains. Find this boundary on the map on this page. Then find the land called the Oregon Country. Both the United States and Britain wanted this land. The two countries settled the matter by agreeing to share this land. What does this tell you about relations between the two countries?

Wars for independence in Latin America The United States was the first country in the Americas to win its

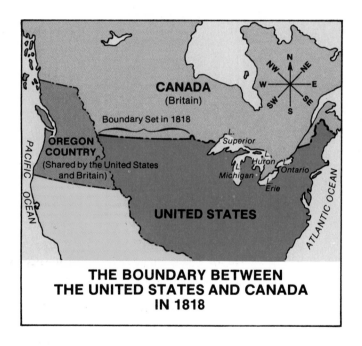

THE BOUNDARY BETWEEN THE UNITED STATES AND CANADA IN 1818

Father Miguel Hidalgo called on his followers to drive the Spanish rulers out of Mexico. He was called The Father of Mexican Independence.

independence. By 1810, however, people in **Latin America** began fighting for their freedom. Latin America is the land south of the United States where Spanish- and Portuguese-speaking people live. Father Hidalgo [ih-THAHL-goh] was a Mexican leader. The Spanish put him to death for leading the Mexican people in their fight for freedom from Spain. The fighting went on, however. Mexico became free of Spanish rule in 1821.

José de San Martín [hoh-ZAY-duh-SAN-mahr-TEEN] and Simón Bolívar [see-MOHN-buh-LEE-vahr] were two leaders who led the fight against Spain in other Latin American countries. San Martín led the fighting in Argentina, Chile, and Peru. Bolívar freed Venezuela, Colombia, and Ecuador from Spanish rule. Bolívar also helped defeat the Spanish in Peru. And his most able assistant freed Bolivia. Many people called Bolívar The Liberator of South America, or the person who set South America free. Why do you think Bolívar was given this name?

Our country's government did not take sides in the Latin American wars for independence. But many United States citizens were in favor of aiding the people who were fighting for their freedom. Why do you think many people in our country felt that way? In 1822 President James Monroe agreed to send representatives to five of the countries that had won their freedom. The United States was the first country to support the governments of these new countries. Do you think this was a bold move for our country? Why or why not?

Making our stand known By 1822 many parts of North America and South America were free of European rule. But Russia owned Alaska, and some Russians were moving south into the Oregon Country. At the same time, many people thought that several European countries were planning to help Spain gain back its Latin American colonies. Secretary of State John Quincy Adams urged the United States to take a strong stand.

President Monroe used some of Adams's ideas in a speech he gave to Congress in 1823. Monroe's message was for any European country that might have been planning to set up colonies in the Americas. He warned the European countries that the United States would view such a move as an act against our country. Monroe said that the Americas were for the people who were already here. He told the Europeans to stay out of American matters. And he promised that the United States would stay out of European matters. Why do you think this last promise was important?

In the picture above, José de San Martín is shown leading his troops from Argentina across the Andes Mountains into Chile. Simón Bolívar is shown below leading a charge against the Spanish.

President James Monroe and his Cabinet are shown here discussing the ideas that became part of the Monroe Doctrine. What details in the picture help show that this meeting took place in the 1820s?

The ideas stated by President Monroe became known as the Monroe Doctrine. The United States did not use the Monroe Doctrine right away. Because of problems at home, Russia soon withdrew its settlements from the Oregon Country. And Spain did not try to gain back its colonies. So the new countries in Latin America remained free. The Monroe Doctrine was important to the United States because it helped to guide our government in later years. It also showed that the United States was willing to take a strong stand in its dealings with other countries.

wrap·up

- What agreements between the United States and Britain after the War of 1812 showed improving relations between the two countries?
- What led the United States to issue the Monroe Doctrine?
- Why was the Monroe Doctrine important to the United States?

Chapter-End Activities

The chapter-end activities may be done by writing the questions or statements and the answers on a separate sheet of paper or by writing just the answers on a separate sheet of paper, whichever your teacher desires.

Words and Terms

Monroe Doctrine   slave states
disarm   Latin America
nationalism   Trail of Tears

1. People who feel love for and loyalty to their country and who are concerned about the interests of their country as a whole show a spirit of ____.

2. The westward march that the Cherokee were forced to make was called the ____.

3. To remove the weapons from a ship is to ____ it.

4. The land south of the United States where Spanish- and Portuguese-speaking people live is called ____.

5. The ____ warned European countries not to start any new colonies in the Americas.

Fact Recall

1. What did Congress do to help American factories after the War of 1812?

2. What kinds of transportation became important in our country in the 1820s and 1830s?

3. What right did many people gain in the 1820s that gave them a greater voice in government?

4. What plan provided a way for deciding whether new states would be slave states or free states?

5. What matters did the United States and Britain settle after the War of 1812?

Concepts and Understandings

1. What were some signs of nationalism in our country after the War of 1812?

2. How did the United States government help our country increase in land size, and how did the westward movement of settlers add new states after the War of 1812?

3. How did the United States show that it was growing stronger in its dealings with other countries?

CHAPTER 16

Our Country Continues to Develop

1. **Expanding to the Pacific**
2. **Developing an American style**
3. **Working for change**

An American writer of the 1800s gave some advice to the people of his day. ". . . Turn your face to the great West," he wrote, "and there build up a home and fortune." Many people of our country did just that. They packed up their family and their belongings. Then they headed for the land of the Far West. What form of transportation used by these people is shown above?

As more people moved west, other changes took place in our country. Americans changed their ideas about the arts. Americans also worked for changes that would make life better for people in our country. In this chapter you will learn about many changes that took place in the United States in the first half of the 1800s.

1

Expanding to the Pacific

From ocean to ocean   During the 1800s, many United States leaders had strong feelings about gaining more land for our country. These people felt that the United States should stretch west all the way to the Pacific Ocean. Do you think this goal was part of a spirit of nationalism? Why or why not?

In 1818, the United States and Britain had agreed to share the land called the Oregon Country. Yet few people from the United States lived there before 1840. Then people began to hear about the good land and the good climate of the Oregon Country. Soon thousands of settlers were on their way west.

As people settled the Oregon Country, the United States and Britain agreed to divide this land. They decided to extend the boundary that they had agreed upon in 1818. The United States **annexed,** or added, its part of the Oregon Country in 1846. For the first time, the United States owned land from the Atlantic Ocean to the Pacific Ocean.

Gaining land from Mexico   The United States also gained land from Mexico, which helped our country reach to the Pacific Ocean. Texas was part of Mexico when Mexico won its freedom from Spain. People from the United States soon began to settle in Texas. Before long there was trouble between these Texans and the Mexican government. One reason for the trouble was that some Texans paid little attention to Mexican laws. The Mexican government sent soldiers to keep order in Texas, but the Texans fought for their freedom. One well-known battle between the Texans and the Mexicans took place at the Alamo. Texas declared itself free from Mexico in 1836.

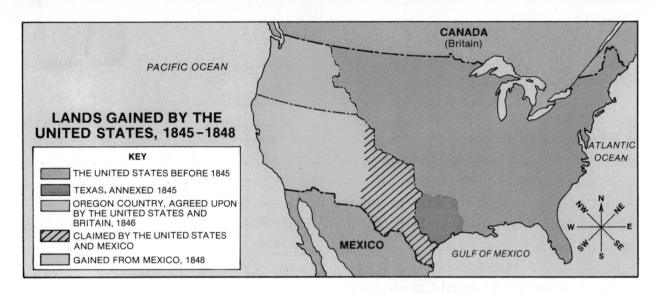

LANDS GAINED BY THE UNITED STATES, 1845–1848

KEY

- THE UNITED STATES BEFORE 1845
- TEXAS, ANNEXED 1845
- OREGON COUNTRY, AGREED UPON BY THE UNITED STATES AND BRITAIN, 1846
- CLAIMED BY THE UNITED STATES AND MEXICO
- GAINED FROM MEXICO, 1848

The leaders of Texas soon asked that Texas be annexed to the United States. Many United States citizens were in favor of this. But the use of slaves was allowed in Texas. For this reason some people in our country were against adding Texas to the United States. After a compromise, our country finally added Texas as a slave state in 1845.

The United States and Mexico did not agree about the boundary of Texas. Look at the map on this page. Find the land claimed by both the United States and Mexico. A fight between United States soldiers and Mexican soldiers on this land led to a war between the two countries. By the treaty that ended the fighting in 1848, the United States gained a large amount of land west of Texas.

Moving west   Oregon and the land gained from Mexico became known as the Far West. The people who moved to the Far West faced a long, dangerous journey. Most of these people traveled overland. They packed their belongings into covered wagons and followed one of the major routes that led west. However, these rough routes were little more than wagon tracks. They led across American Indian land, and they led through mountain passes that could not be used during the winter. A large number of families and wagons traveling together made up a **wagon train.** Why do you think many people chose to travel in wagon trains instead of on their own?

People who knew the routes well often served as guides for the wagon trains. Some guides had been fur trappers in the Rocky Mountains. These people, known as **mountain men,** had lived in the Far West long before any settlers came. They knew where to find food, and they knew the ways of the American Indians. Many of these people, such as Jedediah [JEHD-uh-DY-uh] Smith, James Beckwourth, and Jim Bridger, had discovered the mountain passes that the routes followed.

Overland travel was difficult for members of wagon trains, as shown above. Jedediah Smith, below left, explored much of the Far West. James Beckwourth, below right, was the best known of all black mountain men. He discovered a mountain pass that helped people reach California.

People moved west for different reasons. Some went west to look for good farmland, to seek their fortune, or to find adventure. But one group of people, the Mormons, moved west to be by themselves. The Mormons were a church group led by Brigham Young. Young took the Mormons to land near the Great Salt Lake. This was the beginning of settlements in what is now Utah.

Gold fever A discovery in California greatly aided the settlement of the Far West. California was part of the land the United States had gained from Mexico in 1848. In that same year, a California settler found tiny bits of gold in a riverbed.

By 1849, word of the discovery of gold reached other parts of our country. More than 80,000 people rushed to California that year, hoping to find gold. The picture on this page shows some miners at work. Some people who joined the California gold rush became rich. Others lost everything they had. Some

Gold miners rinsed soil and gravel in water. The water washed away the soil but did not wash away any small pieces of gold that might be present. What were some tools that gold miners used?

people took their riches and returned to their home. Others gave up and went home. But many people stayed in California and brought their families there to join them. Why do you think the California gold rush was one of the most important events in the settlement of the Far West?

New states for our country While some people moved to western territories, others helped form new states in the eastern half of our country. The Erie Canal had made it possible for many New Englanders to move west. These people helped Michigan become a state in 1837. Many people moved to Florida after the United States gained that land from Spain. Florida became a state in 1845. In that same year, Texas was annexed to our country.

The United States government had closed some parts of the Louisiana Purchase to settlement. Then in 1833, the government allowed settlers to move to a strip of land along the Mississippi River north of Missouri. Many people moved to settlements on the riverfront. What reasons can you think of that might make a riverfront a good place for a settlement? Some of these people later moved inland to settle the rich farmlands there. These people helped Iowa become a state in 1846. The lands across the river from the settlements in Iowa had rich deposits of lead ore. People moved to this area to mine lead, which was used for making paint. These people helped Wisconsin become a state in 1848.

wrap ·up

- Why did the United States want to gain land in the Far West?
- How did the United States gain land in the 1840s?
- Why did some people move to the Far West?

Using Your Skills

Reading a map

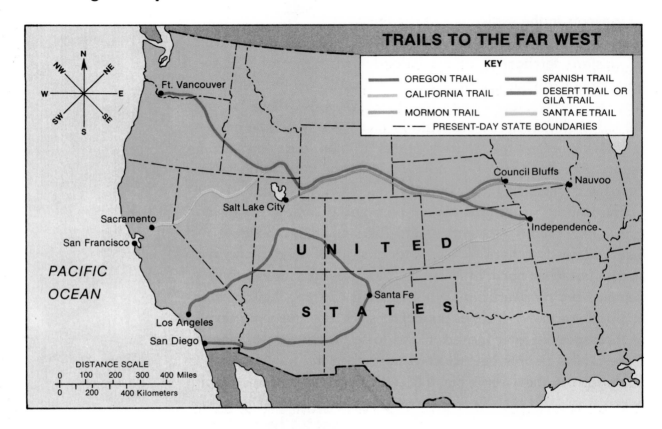

TRAILS TO THE FAR WEST

KEY
- OREGON TRAIL
- CALIFORNIA TRAIL
- MORMON TRAIL
- SPANISH TRAIL
- DESERT TRAIL OR GILA TRAIL
- SANTA FE TRAIL
- PRESENT-DAY STATE BOUNDARIES

Ft. Vancouver

Council Bluffs

Nauvoo

Salt Lake City

Sacramento

San Francisco

Independence

PACIFIC OCEAN

U N I T E D

S T A T E S

Santa Fe

Los Angeles

San Diego

DISTANCE SCALE
0   100   200   300   400 Miles
0   200   400 Kilometers

1. What does this map show?
2. Which trail started at two different cities?
3. Which trails would settlers have used to get from Independence to Los Angeles?
4. From the place where the Oregon Trail and the California Trail separated, what direction did the Oregon Trail take? What direction did the California Trail take?
5. About how far did the Mormons travel on the Mormon Trail from Nauvoo to Salt Lake City?

2

Developing an American style

Developing our own style   Our country grew in many ways during the early 1800s. Businesses and government became stronger and more important. Americans had more free time. People became interested in the arts, such as writing, music, and painting. In the early 1800s, most American arts followed the **style,** or manner, of European arts. But feelings of nationalism in our country helped lead to an American style in the arts.

Americans were proud of the United States. The American arts began to show how the people of our country felt and what they cared about. Some Americans began to write or paint about the **frontier,** or the land on which people were building new farms and settlements. Americans also used such subjects as the American Indians, the blacks, the Puritans, and the land. How might such subjects make American arts different from European arts?

The American style in writing   Many authors helped to develop an American style. The picture on this page is from one of Washington Irving's works. Irving wrote stories based

In one of Washington Irving's most-famous stories, a New Yorker named Rip Van Winkle fell asleep while out hunting. This picture shows Rip Van Winkle as he woke up from a twenty-year "nap."

Ralph Waldo Emerson, above, was known both for writings and for speeches. Many American writers of the 1800s based their works on Emerson's ideas. Nathaniel Hawthorne, below, based his writings on New England's Puritan past.

on the Dutch background of New York. James Fenimore Cooper wrote stories about frontier people. He also wrote about how the American Indians were being pushed off their land. The works of Irving and Cooper became well liked in our country. Their writings were some of the first works in the American style that were also well liked in other countries.

The works of some authors show how Americans felt about their life. Many Americans thought that life was good. Ralph Waldo Emerson and Henry David Thoreau based many of their writings on this idea. They also wrote that people should believe in themselves and depend on themselves to make their life worthwhile. Many people began to agree with the ideas of Emerson and Thoreau. Some Americans thought about the place of evil in their life. Several authors based stories on the workings of good and evil. Nathaniel Hawthorne, Herman Melville, and Edgar Allan Poe were well-known for such stories. Poe also wrote what some people think of as the first detective stories.

Some authors based their writings on everyday life. They wrote about people and places that they knew. But their works were enjoyed throughout our country. Some of these authors were poets. John Greenleaf Whittier wrote poems about life in New England. Henry Wadsworth Longfellow wrote several long poems based on events in American history, such as the ride of Paul Revere. Why do you think Americans enjoyed writings based on the history of our country?

Several black authors of the middle 1800s were poets. One of these people, George Moses Horton, was a slave. His first book of poems was called *The Hope of Liberty*. Frances E. W. Harper was a free person in the North. She wrote poems such as "The Slave Auction" and "Bury Me in a Free Land." How do the titles of Horton's and Harper's works show what the concerns of many Americans were at that time?

Music and drama in our country Many Americans enjoyed the music written by Europeans such as Beethoven, Schubert, and Mozart. Other Americans had brought their own kinds of music with them when they came to the United States. So, much of the music heard in our country came from other places. The Americans in the picture on this page are enjoying songs based on the music of Africa.

By the middle of the 1800s, some songs began to show the American style. Stephen Foster wrote more than 200 songs. Many of his songs were based on life in the South. Two of

The music of Africa was brought to our country by slaves. The banjolike instrument and the drum shown in this picture are based on musical instruments used in Africa. How are these people showing that they are enjoying the music?

Foster's well-known songs were "Oh! Susanna" and "Swanee River." Other songs that were well liked during the 1800s were "Jingle Bells," "Dixie," and "Home, Sweet Home."

Few Americans wrote plays during the first half of the 1800s. Some stories by authors such as Irving and Cooper were made into plays. And many plays by European authors were presented in theaters in our country. Groups of actors traveled throughout the United States presenting different plays. Several Americans became well-known for their parts in plays. Blacks were not allowed to act in many American theaters at that time. But at least one theater, the African Grove in New York City, gave black actors a chance to perform.

Painting American subjects Some painters in our country used American subjects in their works. Several painters belonged to the "Hudson River School." A school of painters is a group of painters whose works are somewhat

Thomas Doughty and Thomas Cole, the artists who painted these pictures, were both leaders of the "Hudson River School." According to these paintings, what did the land in the eastern United States look like in the 1800s?

alike. The artists of the "Hudson River School" all painted pictures of the land in our country.

George Caleb Bingham and George Catlin were frontier artists. Bingham painted pictures of everyday life in Missouri. Catlin painted the everyday life of the American Indians. John James Audubon based his works on nature. He is best known for his paintings of American birds. How did the works of these painters show the American style?

What season is shown in Thomas Cole's picture of northern New York? What feelings do you get from this picture?

wrap·up

- How did an American style in the arts begin to develop in the first half of the 1800s?
- How did the subjects used by American writers help to develop an American style?
- How did the works of American songwriters and painters of the 1800s help to show the interests of the American people?

A Biographical Sketch

Toward a new style of writing

Cooperstown, New York, was a frontier settlement when James Fenimore Cooper grew up there. The settlement had been named for Cooper's family. Many years later, Cooper used the land around Cooperstown as the setting for several of his stories. These and other writings made James Fenimore Cooper one of the best-known American authors of the 1800s.

Cooper first tried writing stories when he was about thirty years old. His first book wasn't very successful. However, Cooper's second book, *The Spy*, was well liked by people in our country. Many people read this book, and many others saw the story performed as a play.

Cooper's best-known works—*The Leatherstocking Tales*—are five separate books about the adventures of a frontier hero. The books describe the hero's love of the frontier and his friendship with the American Indians. But the hero did not feel free unless he lived far from the edge of any settled places. How do you think this feeling was like the ideas of many Americans of the 1800s?

Cooper wrote more than thirty books. Many of these books were stories about people who were somewhat alike. They were people who depended on themselves and often lived away from other people. They were honest and brave. Cooper was the first American author to write about life on the American frontier. He was also the first American to write about life at sea. His works were an important step toward an American style of writing.

3

Working for change

Making life better for others
During the years from the 1820s to the 1850s, many Americans became interested in **reform,** or the improving of things through change. These people began to work for changes that would make life better for others.

Some people in the 1800s worked for prison reform. Prisons at that time were crowded and dirty. People who were criminals, people who owed money, and people who were mentally disabled were all put in prison together. Often these people were crowded into one large room.

Some states began to improve their prisons. One person who worked for such changes was Dorothea Dix. She worked for better care of mentally disabled people. Because of Dix's work, many states built hospitals for these people instead of putting them in prison. How do you think Dix's work made life better for some people?

Changes in education Schools in our country were also in need of change. In many cases, there were no schools for children to attend. Some people had to pay to send their children to grade school. And most high schools were private schools that cost a

Dorothea Dix was shocked by the treatment of mentally disabled people in our country. What does this picture show about the manner in which such people were treated? Dix spent more than forty years working to improve these conditions.

Lucretia Mott, above, and Elizabeth Cady Stanton, below, were not allowed to take part in an abolitionist meeting in Britain, because they were women. This experience helped Mott and Stanton see the need for a women's rights meeting.

lot of money to attend. Teachers were not well trained for their jobs, and they received low pay.

Horace Mann was a leader who worked for changes in schools. Mann worked to have public schools built. These schools were supported with tax money. Teachers were better trained and better paid than before. Why do you think Mann's work helped provide schooling for more people than ever before?

Women take a stand In the early 1800s, women in our country had few rights. They couldn't attend college, because most colleges in our country were for white men only. Women couldn't vote or hold public office. However, they began to work for reforms.

Lucretia Mott, pictured at the top left, and Elizabeth Cady Stanton, pictured at the bottom left, worked for women's rights. In 1848 they held a meeting at Seneca Falls, New York, for women from all over the country. Those who attended the meeting listed some rights they thought women should have. They used some words from the Declaration of Independence. But the women at Seneca Falls stated that all men *and women* were created equal. How do you think this helped many people see that women were ready to stand up for their rights?

The movement against slavery The largest group of people working for reform in the 1800s worked to end slavery. These people were called **abolitionists** [AB-uh-LIHSH-(uh-)nuhsts]. Both blacks and whites had worked for change in the 1700s. But the work against the owning of slaves grew stronger in the 1830s.

The abolitionists used several ways to spread their ideas. William Lloyd Garrison and others wrote newspapers. Garrison's newspaper, *The Liberator*, was the best known. Abolitionists also held meetings and made speeches. Theodore Dwight Weld, Sojourner Truth, and Frederick Douglass made many speeches. Truth and Douglass had both been slaves. Why do you think their speeches were important to the work of ending slavery? Many white people fought the abolitionists, both in the North and in the South. Angry people broke up meetings and destroyed printing presses.

Theodore Dwight Weld, at the left, spoke at churches and colleges. Sojourner Truth, in the middle, bought her freedom from her owner. Frederick Douglass, at the right, wrote a newspaper plus several books about his life as a slave.

303

*This picture shows people at an Underground Railroad **station**, or safe hiding place. These stations were an important part of the system by which thousands of black people escaped from slavery. The people who helped slaves escape risked their own safety, because helping slaves escape was against the law.*

Slaves had their own ways of fighting for change. Some slaves joined uprisings. Many planned slave uprisings were stopped before they could even take place. But others, such as the one led by Nat Turner in 1831, took place as planned.

Many slaves escaped from the South. Slaves who stayed behind helped others to escape. When escaping slaves reached the North, they depended on people to feed them and to hide them. Such people then helped the slaves reach the next place where they would be safe. The picture on this page shows people helping escaping slaves. The secret routes and safe hiding places became known as the **Underground Railroad.** Harriet Tubman, who had escaped from slavery herself, helped others escape. She returned to the South nineteen times to bring slaves out by means of the Underground Railroad. Why do you think this was very dangerous? By joining uprisings or by escaping, many slaves showed that they were willing to fight for change.

wrap·up

- What reforms did Americans work for between the 1820s and the 1850s?
- How did changes in our country help make life better for some people?
- How did slaves fight for change?

Chapter-End Activities

The chapter-end activities may be done by writing the questions or statements and the answers on a separate sheet of paper or by writing just the answers on a separate sheet of paper, whichever your teacher desires.

Words and Terms

style   wagon trains
Underground Railroad   annexed
mountain men   reform

1. Land added to a country is ____.
2. The ____ were fur trappers in the Rocky Mountains.
3. In the 1800s people in our country began to develop an American ____ in the arts.
4. The improving of things through change is known as ____.
5. The secret routes and safe hiding places used by escaping slaves were known as the ____.

Fact Recall

1. In the 1840s the United States gained land in order to ____.
   a. expand to the Pacific Ocean
   b. provide land for American Indians

2. The California gold rush was important because it ____.
   a. made so many people rich
   b. aided the settlement of the Far West
3. Many American authors of the 1800s based their works on ____.
   a. subjects from our own country
   b. life in other countries
4. The Americans who worked for reform in our country ____.
   a. wanted to make life better for others
   b. wanted to become well-known
5. The largest group of people who worked for change in the early 1800s were ____.
   a. teachers
   b. abolitionists

Concepts and Understandings

1. How did the United States grow in land size during the 1840s?
2. Why did an American style in the arts begin to develop in the 1800s?
3. How did some Americans work for reform in our country during the 1800s?

Unit End

Main Ideas and Understandings

1. What were some things that happened during the first years under the Constitution that helped our government become strong? Why did the American Indians fight against settlers? How did the War of 1812 help the United States gain the respect of other countries? Why was the Louisiana Purchase important to the United States?

2. What is nationalism? How did nationalism begin to develop in the United States? How did transportation improve in the United States in the early 1800s? Why was the Monroe Doctrine important to our country?

3. For what reasons did Americans move to the Far West? How did an American style in the arts begin to develop? What were some of the important reforms that people in our country worked for during the first half of the 1800s?

Research Ideas

1. In 1791 President George Washington chose the site of our country's capital city. Find out about Washington, D.C. Who were the first people to live on the land that became our capital city? What states gave up land for the city? Who was Pierre Charles L'Enfant? Why is Washington, D.C., important to our country today? What might visitors today see in Washington, D.C.?

2. The flag of the United States has a star for each state in our country. Find out how our country's flag changed from 1789 to 1850 as new states joined the United States. Find out what the seal and the flag of each state that joined our country between 1789 and 1850 look like. What do the symbols on the seals and on the flags stand for? What do the seal and the flag of your state look like? What do the symbols used on the seal and the flag of your state stand for?

3. Some of the best-known American stories came from the frontier. These stories were not written down for many years. Instead, people told the stories to one another. Some of these stories are known as tall tales, and they are about such characters as Paul Bunyon, Pecos Bill, John Henry, Davy Crockett, and Mike Fink. Who were these characters? Where did they live? What kinds of adventures did they have?

Activities and Projects

1. Make a mural showing life in the United States during the late 1700s and the early 1800s. Show scenes of people working, traveling, having fun, going to school, and so on.

2. Imagine that you are a newspaper reporter or a television reporter. Write an article or present a newscast about a person or an event of the late 1700s or the early 1800s.

Unit 7

Our Country Faces Trouble and Change

In what ways is our country changing today? The United States changed in many ways between the middle 1800s and the early 1900s. It drifted apart and then grew back together again. It became a leading industrial country with many large cities. And it became a world power.

In this unit you will read about our country between the middle 1800s and the early 1900s. You will find answers to the following questions:

What caused our country to drift apart in the middle 1800s?

What changes took place during Reconstruction?

Why did businesses and cities grow rapidly during the late 1800s?

How did our country change during the early 1900s?

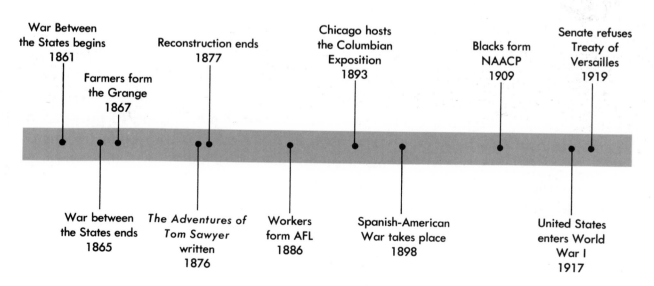

War Between the States begins 1861

Farmers form the Grange 1867

Reconstruction ends 1877

Chicago hosts the Columbian Exposition 1893

Blacks form NAACP 1909

Senate refuses Treaty of Versailles 1919

War between the States ends 1865

The Adventures of Tom Sawyer written 1876

Workers form AFL 1886

Spanish-American War takes place 1898

United States enters World War I 1917

CHAPTER 17

Our People Drift Apart

1. Different viewpoints
2. The westward movement continues
3. Slavery becomes a key issue

What are some of the questions facing our country's government today? How is our country's government trying to answer these questions?

Just as our country's government faces many questions today, so also did it face many questions during the 1850s. Some of the questions during the 1850s had to do with the tariff. Others had to do with the price of land in the West and with better means of transportation. Still others had to do with slavery. In this chapter you will learn how these questions caused our country's people to drift apart. And you will learn how the West kept growing.

Different viewpoints

The industrial North By the middle 1800s three major **sections,** or parts, had developed in the United States. These were the North, the South, and the West. These three parts together made up our country, yet each was growing in a different way.

The North was becoming the industrial section of our country. Here many factories, such as the one in the picture on this page, could be found. These factories made many kinds of goods. Some made cloth out of cotton. Some made goods such as wagon wheels, guns, and tools out of iron. And some made other kinds of goods.

Factories needed many workers. Some people left farming to work in the factories. Many people from Europe also came to the United States to work in the factories. Most of the factory workers lived near the factories. Why do you think the workers did this? Before long cities began to grow near the factories. By the middle 1800s most of the large cities in our country were located in the North.

Many people living in the northern section of our country during the middle 1800s worked in factories. The workers in this factory are making iron. What are some of the activities taking place in this factory?

King Cotton The South was becoming the cotton-growing section of our country. By the middle 1800s cotton had become the major money crop of the South. People who grew cotton came to depend more and more on it for their living. So also did those who bought and sold and shipped cotton.

Much cotton grown in the South was used by factories in the North and in Britain to make cloth. This, in turn, was made into many kinds of clothing. "Cotton is king!" someone in the South said in the middle 1800s. What do you think this saying meant?

It took a lot of land to grow cotton. So most of the cotton was raised on plantations. It also took a lot of slaves to clear and plant the land and to harvest the cotton. As the desire for cotton grew, the need for land also grew. And the need for more slaves grew. Soon cotton plantations could be found from North Carolina to Texas. But few large cities could be found in the South. Why do you think this was so?

The developing West By the middle 1800s many people in our country had moved to the West. At that time the West included the lands between the Appalachian Mountains and the Mississippi River. Today the West is thought of as the lands around the Rocky Mountains and the Pacific Coast.

The West was growing rapidly in the 1800s. It was becoming the major farming section of our country. New machines such as steel plows and **reapers**—machines for cutting grain—were helping farmers to grow more food. Some of this food remained in the West to feed its own people. But most of the food was sent to the North and to the South. Why do you think the North and the South needed food from the West?

An important difference Each section of our country continued to grow in its own way. As each part grew, it began to have different needs and wants. People began to give more thought to their own section than they did to the country as a whole. This was **sectionalism**.

The Currier and Ives picture above shows slaves harvesting cotton on a southern plantation in the middle 1800s. The picture on the left shows a reaper invented by Cyrus McCormick. What is furnishing the power to run this machine?

After a while each section of the country began to want different things from our country's government. The North wanted a high tariff to protect the price of the goods made in its factories. This was because the North was afraid goods made in Britain and other countries might sell at a cheaper price. What do you think this might do to the sale of American-made goods? What do you think might happen to American factories and to workers' jobs?

The South depended upon cotton growing, not factories, for making a living. So people in the South had to buy factory-made goods from the North or from outside our

313

country. But a high tariff would cause the price of the factory-made goods to be high. Do you think the South wanted a high tariff or a low tariff? Why?

The West was divided on the tariff question. The West, like the South, wanted to keep the price of factory-made goods low. But the West also wanted a tariff to protect the price of its own farm goods.

Other important differences The West wanted more people to come to its section. So the West wanted our country's government to pass a law to lower the price of land in the West. Do you think cheap land would help to get more people to settle in the West? Why do you think so?

The South favored high prices for land in the West. The South wanted our country's government to get money from the sale of land rather than from a high tariff. The North also favored high prices for land in the West, but for a different reason. What do you think the northern factory owners feared might happen if the price of western land was low?

The West wanted our country's government to spend money to help pay for better roads and canals. Why do you think the West wanted these things? The North also favored government spending for better roads and canals, but the South didn't. The South feared that the government might pass high tariffs to pay for such things.

The North, the South, and the West continued to grow apart. Do you think this caused problems for our country? Why do you think so?

wrap ·up

- What three major sections had developed in the United States by the middle 1800s?
- How did each section grow in its own way?
- Why did each section want different things from our country's government?

2

The westward movement continues

The West grows   People began to move farther and farther west during the 1850s. Some of these people came from the eastern part of the United States. Others came from countries in Europe such as Ireland, Germany, Norway, Sweden, and Denmark. These people moved to the West for different reasons. Some went to look for gold, which had been discovered in present-day Oregon and Colorado. These people started many mining towns, like the one in the picture on this page. Life in such towns was often very exciting. Why do you think this was so?

Some people moved to the West to be with relatives and friends. Others went to find work in the new towns that were being started. Still others went for the adventure that places in the West offered.

"Go west, young man, go west" was a saying often heard during the 1850s. It was used in several newspaper stories. Do you think this saying might have caused some people to go west? Why do you think so?

Transportation expands   The western movement of people brought about a growing need for more and better

This picture shows Central City, Colorado, in the 1860s. Many of the people living in Central City in the 1860s worked in gold mines. What kinds of work might other people living in Central City in the 1860s have done?

transportation. Some roads stretched as far west as the Mississippi River by the late 1850s. And canals could be found in many large cities as far west as Chicago, Illinois.

A greater number of steamboats began taking the place of smaller boats during the 1850s. Steamboats carried many goods and people up and down the Mississippi River. And they carried many goods and people east and west to towns or rivers that flow into the Mississippi River.

More and more railroads were being built in our country during the 1850s. Look at the map on this page. Many railroads connected the East and the West as far as the Mississippi River and a little farther. Were there more railroads in the northwestern or in the southwestern part of our country in 1860? Why do you think this was so?

Railroads helped our country grow and improve. They helped the North send factory-made goods to the West in greater amounts. They also helped the West send more farm goods to the North and the South. And the railroads helped to make it easier for people to go west.

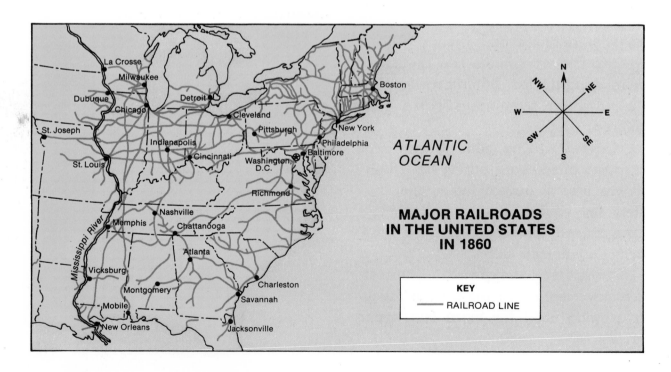

MAJOR RAILROADS IN THE UNITED STATES IN 1860

KEY
—— RAILROAD LINE

Which means of transportation do you think was the most important during the 1850s? Why do you think so?

Communication improves Communication also helped to connect the different parts of our country during the 1850s. An early mail service between New York and California was by sea. The mail was carried by steamship to Panama, where it was carried across the land. Then the mail was carried to California by another steamship. People in the West were not pleased with the mail service by sea. The cost was high, and the journey was long.

By the late 1850s a new mail service was being used. Railroads carried mail and people from the East coast to Missouri. Then overland stagecoaches carried the mail and people from Missouri to California in about twenty-four days. By 1860 the **pony express** had cut the time of the trip from Missouri to California to about nine days. The pony express was a means by which mail was carried across the West by riders on fast horses. A rider would ride one horse to a station along a set route. There the rider would mount a fresh horse and ride to the next station. At certain stations a new rider would take over.

The pony express lasted only eighteen months. It stopped in 1861 when

The picture above shows an overland stagecoach traveling along a scenic route from Missouri to California. The picture below was painted by Frederic Remington. It shows a pony-express rider quickly leaving a station on a fresh horse.

317

This picture shows Astoria, Oregon, during the middle 1800s. What natural resource shown here attracted people to this part of the West?

the **telegraph** reached from the East coast to California. The telegraph is a means of sending messages by code over an electric wire. Why do you think this means of sending messages put an end to the pony express?

More land and more states In 1853 the United States agreed to pay Mexico $10 million for a small piece of land. This was a piece of land that made up the southern part of present-day Arizona and New Mexico. It was needed for building a railroad across the southern part of our country. James Gadsden helped to make the deal with Mexico for this land. So it was called the Gadsden Purchase.

During the 1850s three states were added to the United States. These new states were California, Minnesota, and Oregon. So by 1860 our country had thirty-three states. By adding California and Oregon, our country had states along the Pacific coast. How do you think this affected our country? Why do you think so?

wrap·up

- Why did people move to the West during the 1850s?
- How did the growth of transportation during the 1850s help our country?
- How did different methods of communication during the 1850s help our country?

Using Your Skills

Reading a map

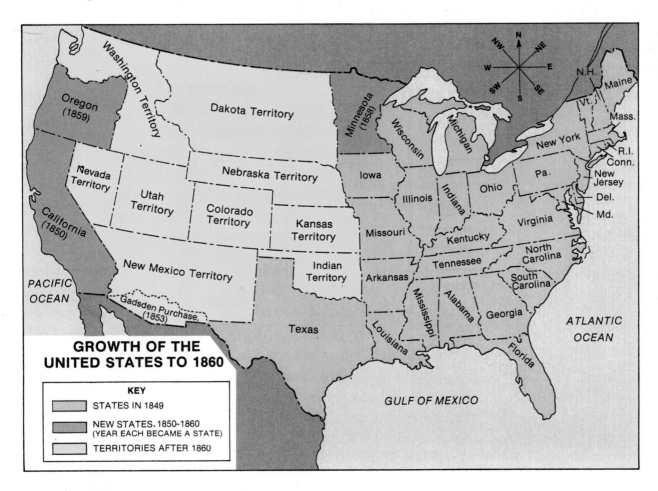

GROWTH OF THE UNITED STATES TO 1860

KEY

STATES IN 1849

NEW STATES, 1850-1860 (YEAR EACH BECAME A STATE)

TERRITORIES AFTER 1860

Use the map to answer these questions.

1. What does the map show?

2. Were most of the states in 1849 located in the eastern half of the United States or in the western half of the United States?

3. Which states were admitted to the United States between 1850 and 1860? In which year was each of these new states admitted?

4. In which part of the United States was the Gadsden Purchase located?

5. To which territory was the Gadsden Purchase added?

3

Slavery becomes a key issue

An important compromise   Should people be allowed to own slaves in the lands that had been gained from Mexico? This was one of the major questions facing our country during the 1850s. Many people from the North believed that slaves should not be allowed in the new lands. But many people from the South believed that slaves should be allowed in the new lands. Why do you think many people from these two parts of our country had different views? Still others believed in **popular sovereignty** [SAHV-(uh-)ruhn-tee]. This was a plan that let those living in new lands decide if slaves should be allowed or not.

In 1850 California asked to become a free state, where slaves were not allowed. But if a free state were added, the number of free states and slave states would no longer be equal. Congress could not agree on what to do with California. Then Senator Henry Clay of Kentucky spoke up. He set forth some ideas that he hoped would be accepted by everyone. These ideas became law as the Compromise of 1850. It allowed California to enter as a free state. And it

Senator Henry Clay rose on the floor of the United States Senate to present the ideas that became the Compromise of 1850. Clay hoped these ideas might hold the Union together.

divided the land gained from Mexico into territories. Look at the map on this page. Which territories were formed by the Compromise of 1850? States formed from these lands could be slave or free, depending upon what the people in the states wanted. The compromise also agreed that a stronger Fugitive Slave Law was needed. Such a law would order the return of all runaway slaves to their owner.

Two more territories Life was quieter for several years after the Compromise of 1850. People kept moving west. More railroads were built. Some people even began talking about building a railroad across our country from east to west. Senator Stephen A. Douglas of Illinois wanted Chicago to be the starting point for such a railroad. Before this could happen, the land west of the states of Iowa and Missouri had to be formed into territories. To do this, Douglas got Congress to pass the Kansas-Nebraska Act in 1854.

Look at the map on this page. Which two new territories were formed by this act? At one time these lands were not allowed to have slaves. Look at the map again. How did the Kansas-Nebraska Act intend to have the slavery question settled in the two new territories it formed?

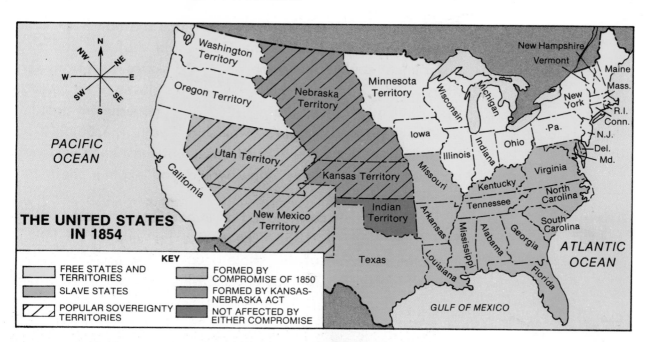

THE UNITED STATES IN 1854

KEY

- FREE STATES AND TERRITORIES
- SLAVE STATES
- POPULAR SOVEREIGNTY TERRITORIES
- FORMED BY COMPROMISE OF 1850
- FORMED BY KANSAS-NEBRASKA ACT
- NOT AFFECTED BY EITHER COMPROMISE

This is one of several debates Abraham Lincoln and Stephen A. Douglas had in their attempt to become senator of Illinois. Lincoln is standing, and Douglas is seated beside the speaker's table.

An influential decision   The North and the South kept growing further and further apart. Then in 1857 the case of Dred Scott, a slave, came before the United States Supreme Court.

The Supreme Court said that Dred Scott was not a citizen of Missouri or of the United States. Since Scott was not a citizen, he couldn't bring a case before our country's courts. The Court also said that living in a free place did not make Dred Scott a free person. And the Court said that our country's government couldn't keep the owning of slaves out of any territory. The Court said this was because slaves were owned. And the Court added that our country's government couldn't pass laws to take people's ownership away. The South liked the outcome of the *Dred Scott* case. But the North was very upset over the outcome. How would you explain these different views?

The *Dred Scott* case played an important part in the voting that took place in 1858. The choice for senator of Illinois drew the attention of the whole country. The choice was between Stephen A. Douglas and Abraham Lincoln. Lincoln and

Douglas made many speeches dealing with the spread of slavery. Lincoln was against owning slaves in the territories. Douglas was in favor of popular sovereignty. Which person held views that went against the *Dred Scott* ruling? Lincoln lost the vote for senator but became a leading spokesperson for the newly formed Republican party.

Growing further apart   In 1859 John Brown became interested in an idea to help the slaves. He led a small group of people to a building in Harpers Ferry, Virginia, where guns were stored. Brown wanted to get the guns to give to the slaves. Then he wanted to lead them in a fight for their freedom. But Brown and those with him at Harpers Ferry were forced to give up. Later, Brown and some of the others were hanged for their acts. Both what John Brown did and what happened to him further divided our country.

Another thing that further divided our country happened in 1860. This was the choice of Abraham Lincoln as President of the United States. Many people were pleased with the choice of Lincoln. But many others, mostly in the South, were very upset. These people did not like the way Lincoln and other Republicans felt about slavery and other matters facing our country. Some people in South Carolina held a meeting to decide what to do. They decided to **secede,** or withdraw, from the Union. Soon some of the other southern states did the same thing. Our country was rapidly becoming two separate parts.

wrap·up

- How did the issue of slavery play an important part in the development of our country during the 1850s?
- How did the Supreme Court rule on the slavery question in the *Dred Scott* case?
- How did the election of President Lincoln in 1860 affect our country?

A Biographical Sketch

An attempt to be free

Dred Scott's early years as a slave were spent in Virginia and in Missouri. While in Missouri, Scott was bought by John Emerson, a doctor in the United States Army. Scott spent three years with Emerson in Illinois, a free state. And Scott and Emerson spent two years in the Wisconsin Territory, a free territory. Then Scott returned with Emerson to Missouri. Following Emerson's death, Scott was owned by Mrs. Emerson.

In 1846 Mrs. Emerson was sued in order to gain Scott's freedom. The suit stated that a slave who had lived in free places should be free upon returning to a slave state. Since the suit was such an important one, it kept appearing before a higher and higher court. Finally, the *Dred Scott* suit reached the United States Supreme Court. By this time Scott had a new owner.

In 1857 the Supreme Court ruled against Scott. It said that Scott was not a citizen and so could not bring a suit in our country's courts. The Supreme Court also ruled that Scott was not free, even though he had lived in free places.

The Supreme Court did not give Scott his freedom, but Scott became a free person anyhow. Shortly after the Court's ruling, Scott was sold once again. Two months later the new owner gave Scott his freedom. Scott spent the rest of his life in Missouri enjoying this freedom.

Chapter-End Activities

The chapter-end activities may be done by writing the questions or statements and the answers on a separate sheet of paper or by writing just the answers on a separate sheet of paper, whichever your teacher desires.

Words and Terms

popular sovereignty   secede
reapers   telegraph
pony express   sections

_____ 1. Machines that were used for cutting grain and that made it possible for farmers to grow more food

_____ 2. A means by which mail was carried across the West by riders on fast horses

_____ 3. A means of sending messages by code over an electric wire

_____ 4. A plan letting people living in new lands decide if they would allow slavery or not

_____ 5. To withdraw from the Union, as South Carolina and some other southern states did in the early 1860s

Fact Recall

1. By the middle 1800s the North was becoming the (farming, industrial) section of our country.

2. By the middle 1800s the South was becoming the (industrial, cotton-growing) section of our country.

3. (Railroads, Steamboats) were the most important means of transportation during the 1850s.

4. The Compromise of 1850 and the Kansas-Nebraska Act favored (no slavery, slavery, popular sovereignty) in the new territories they formed.

5. (Dred Scott, John Brown) tried to take guns from a building in Harpers Ferry and give them to the slaves.

Concepts and Understandings

1. How did the growth of transportation and communication during the 1850s help our country?

2. How did the issue of slavery play a major role in the development of sectionalism in our country during the 1850s?

CHAPTER 18

Fighting a War and Rebuilding Our Country

1. **Fighting the war**
2. **Rebuilding the South**
3. **Our country develops more**

The picture on this page shows part of Gettysburg, Pennsylvania. How would you describe this picture? More than a hundred years ago an important battle took place on the land shown in this picture. This battle was fought during the War Between the States.

In this chapter you will learn more about the War Between the States. And you will learn how our country tried to rebuild itself after the war. You will also learn about different ways in which our country developed both during and after the war.

Fighting the war

Choosing sides President Lincoln had not been in office long when trouble broke out between the North and the South. This happened at Fort Sumter, which was on the harbor of Charleston, South Carolina. A southern army officer asked the North to give up the fort. The North refused, and the South fired on the fort for two days. Then the North gave up the fort. This was on April 14, 1861. This happening was the start of the War Between the States.

The fall of Fort Sumter brought about a time for choosing sides. One side was the United States of America. This side was also known as the Union and as the North. Its leader was

Although there were many fires and explosions during the southern bombardment on Fort Sumter, no one on either side was killed.

Abraham Lincoln. Look at the map on this page. Which states made up the Union? The other side was the Confederate States of America. This side was also known as the Confederacy and as the South. Its leader was Jefferson Davis. Which states made up the Confederacy before the fall of Fort Sumter?

After Fort Sumter fell, other southern states decided to join the Confederacy. Which states were these? Some southern states decided to remain in the Union. These states were slave states. But these states lay between other slave states and northern free states. So these states were called **border states.** Which states were border states?

Union and Confederate advantages   Each side had its advantages in the War Between the States. The North had more people and more factories. And the North had a long-standing government. The North also had an army and a navy.

The South would be fighting on home soil. People in the South would be fighting for their homes and their families. The South had the ablest officers. And the South had people who were used to handling firearms and horses. The South also believed that some European countries would help the South because they depended on the South's cotton. But this never happened.

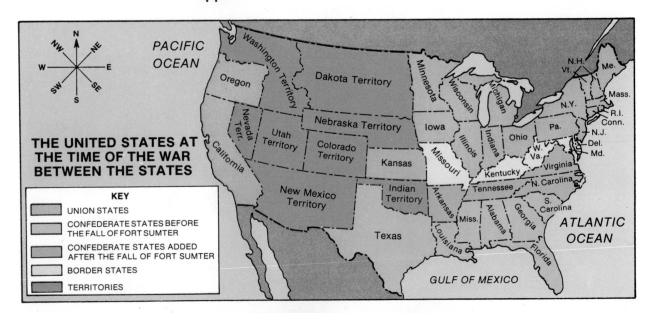

THE UNITED STATES AT THE TIME OF THE WAR BETWEEN THE STATES

KEY
UNION STATES
CONFEDERATE STATES BEFORE THE FALL OF FORT SUMTER
CONFEDERATE STATES ADDED AFTER THE FALL OF FORT SUMTER
BORDER STATES
TERRITORIES

Using Your Skills

Reading a pictograph

THE COMPARATIVE STRENGTHS OF THE UNION AND THE CONFEDERACY IN 1861

	Population	Factories	Factory Workers	Railroad Lines	Food Products	Gold
NORTH						
SOUTH						

Use the pictograph to answer these questions.

1. What does the pictograph show?

2. Which side had the greatest number of people?

3. Which side had more factories and workers?

4. Which side had the lesser number of railroad lines to move soldiers and supplies?

5. Which side had a greater amount of food products?

6. How many times greater was the amount of gold that the North had compared with the amount of gold that the South had?

7. Based on the pictograph, which side appeared to have the most advantages? Why do you think so?

The first attempt by the North to capture Richmond, Virginia, led to the first Battle of Bull Run. The North was defeated in this battle, which took place on July 21, 1861.

The goal and the plans of each side   The goal of the South in the War Between the States was to win its freedom from the Union. The South planned mostly to fight a war of defense. It planned to cause huge losses to the North each time that the North attacked the South. The South thought that the North would tire of the war and give up. However, the South did plan to attack Maryland and Pennsylvania. The South hoped this would divide the Union into two parts. Do you think this was a good idea? Why or why not?

The major goal of the North was to save the Union. The North planned to fight a war of offense. The North would have to attack and beat the South in the South. The plan of the North had many parts. One part was to take Richmond, Virginia—the Confederate capital. Another part was to use warships to **blockade** the southern coastline. This meant that the North's warships were to keep ships from entering or leaving southern harbors. The North was able to blockade much of the southern coast. How do you think this hurt the South? Still another part of the North's plan was to take charge of the Mississippi River and its branches. This would divide the South into two parts. Then, the North planned to march east from the Mississippi River to the Atlantic Ocean. This would further divide the Confederacy.

The North was fighting to save the Union, not to free the slaves. But after a while, President Lincoln decided that freeing the slaves might help win the war. So Lincoln set forth the Emancipation Proclamation, which freed the slaves in the Confederate states as of January 1, 1863.

Some major battles In June of 1863, General Robert E. Lee of the South crossed Maryland and marched into Pennsylvania. On July 3 Lee's army was defeated by the North at Gettysburg, Pennsylvania. One day later, on July 4, the South suffered another major loss. The North, under General Ulysses S. Grant, captured Vicksburg, Mississippi. This victory made it possible for the North to take charge of the Mississippi River. The Union victories at Gettysburg and Vicksburg marked a turning point in the war. Southern losses were so great that the southern army was never able to fight again at full power.

Later in 1864, General William Tecumseh Sherman took over Atlanta, Georgia, for the North. Atlanta was one of the South's chief railroad

Women helped in different ways during the War Between the States. Clara Barton, shown in the circular picture, began helping shortly after the war started. Among other things, she worked in a hospital like the one shown here. What are some of the activities taking place in this hospital? Later, Clara Barton founded the American Red Cross Society.

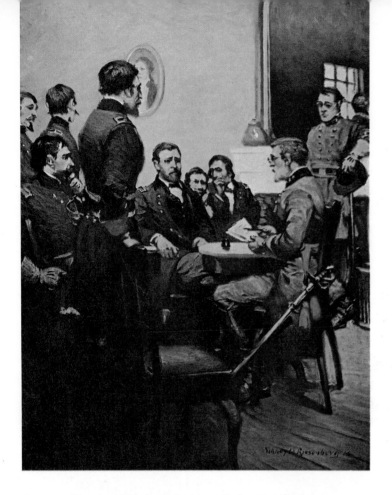

General Robert E. Lee of the Confederacy surrendered to General Ulysses S. Grant of the Union on April 9, 1865. Their meeting took place at the McLean House in the village of Appomattox Court House in Virginia. Lee is seated at the right side of the table, and Grant is seated at the left side of the table. What is Lee doing?

centers. It also had most of the South's factories. Do you think taking over Atlanta was important to the North? Why do you think so?

The end of the war Another major battle of the war took place near Richmond, Virginia. The fight for Richmond was long and hard. But finally Grant forced Lee out of Richmond. Shortly after leaving Richmond, Lee knew he had no place to go. So Lee decided to **surrender,** or give up. The picture on this page shows the meeting that took place between Lee and Grant. This meeting, held on April 9, 1865, ended the War Between the States.

President Lincoln was happy when the war ended. He began at once to make plans for northerners and southerners to get together again and to rebuild our country. But Lincoln never got to carry out any of his plans. On April 14, 1865, Lincoln was **assassinated,** or suddenly murdered, by John Wilkes Booth. His death was a great loss to our country—both to the North and to the South. Why do you think this was so?

wrap·up

- What were some of the advantages of each side in the War Between the States?
- How did each side plan to win the war?
- Why did Lee surrender to Grant?

2

Rebuilding the South

The need for rebuilding Much damage had been done during the War Between the States. Most of this damage had been done in the South. Why was this so? **Reconstruction** means rebuilding. And that is what the years after the war were used for. Many things in the South needed rebuilding. Look at the picture on this page. Many cities like this one needed rebuilding. So, too, did many towns. Plantations, farms, and railroads also needed rebuilding. State and local governments had to be set up again. And a new way of life both for blacks and for whites had to be brought about.

Two chief matters were part of rebuilding. One matter had to do with the return of the Confederate states to the United States. The other matter had to do with the life of the **freedmen**—those who had been slaves.

This picture shows the damage done in Charleston, South Carolina, during the War Between the States. What things in Charleston needed rebuilding?

Plans for rebuilding Our country's government made plans to aid in rebuilding. President Lincoln made a plan. He wanted Confederates to swear to be true to the Union and to the United States Constitution. And they had to agree to the Emancipation Proclamation. After a certain number of people in a southern state had done these things, they could set up a state government. Later that state would be allowed to enter the Union again. Only four states formed new state governments under Lincoln's plan.

Some members of Congress thought Lincoln's plan was too easy on the South. These members were known as Radical Republicans. After President Lincoln's death, Andrew Johnson became our country's leader. Johnson's plan was quite a bit like Lincoln's plan. By the end of 1865 all states except Texas had formed new state governments under Johnson's plan.

Congress gets into the act Several months after the war ended, our country's government passed the Thirteenth Amendment. This law freed the slaves. Why was this an important law for the blacks? Congress also set up the Freedmen's Bureau to help those in need. This office set up housing, like the housing pictured at the top of page 335. It also gave food, clothing, and medicine to blacks and whites in need.

Congress wanted to be in charge of the rebuilding of the South. So in 1867 it passed some laws cutting down on the power of President Johnson. When Johnson acted against these new laws, Congress tried to get him out of office, but failed to do so.

Many people in our country's government became upset when they heard of the **black codes** in the South. These were laws saying what blacks could and could not do. These laws allowed blacks to go to school, to marry, and to own some things. Blacks could also take cases to court. But blacks could not vote or hold public office. They could not sell or exchange goods without the word of .the person for whom they

Our country's government set up many villages for people in need during the Reconstruction years. The village shown here was located near Hampton, Virginia.

worked. And they could not be out at night without a pass from the person for whom they worked.

In 1868 our country's government passed the Fourteenth Amendment. This law states that all persons born in the United States are citizens. How do you think this law helped the blacks in our country? Tennessee was the first Confederate state to accept Congress's plan by agreeing to this amendment. So Tennessee was the first to enter the United States again.

Congress next divided the ten remaining Confederate states into five parts. Soldiers from our country's army were sent to keep order in these five parts of the South. Then our country's government passed the Fifteenth Amendment. This law gave black men the right to vote. Why do you think this was an important law for the blacks? By 1870 the remaining southern states had accepted Congress's plan by agreeing to the Fifteenth Amendment. These states were then allowed to enter the United States again.

In the early part of 1868, charges were brought against President Andrew Johnson by the House of Representatives. His trial before the United States Senate lasted about two months. The Senate failed by one vote to remove Johnson from office.

These are the first black members of the United States Congress. Each represented a southern state during Reconstruction. The man at the left is Senator H. R. Revels. The others were in the House of Representatives.

Republican governments   It was not long before Republicans took over the new state governments in the South. The leaders for these new governments came from three different groups. One group was the **scalawags**. These were people in the South who had remained true to the United States and who worked with the new governments. Another group was the **carpetbaggers**. These were people from the North who went to the South to seek new fortunes. The third group was the blacks. Blacks became leaders at all levels of government.

The Republican state governments were both bad and good. Sometimes these governments were not honest. Sometimes they wasted money. And sometimes the leaders were weak. But these governments helped the South in many ways. They helped to rebuild and repair buildings, roads, and bridges. They started many schools and improved prisons and hospitals. They helped to gain more rights for women. And they helped to make the courts fairer for everyone.

The end of Reconstruction Those who had been Confederates made up the Democratic party in the South. They wanted to gain power in their own state governments. So they tried to take the black vote away from the Republicans. When the Democrats failed to do this, they sometimes made life hard for blacks. Some landowners refused to rent land to blacks. And some storeowners made blacks pay for things as soon as they bought them. Sometimes secret groups of southern whites used rough means to keep blacks from voting and from holding office.

After a time the Republican state governments began to break down, and the Democrats began to gain power. One reason for this was the smaller part that blacks began to play in the government. Another reason was the greater number of southern whites who could vote. These people added to the power of the Democratic party. Also, many people in the North slowly began to lose interest in the South.

Reconstruction came to an end in 1877. In that year President Hayes ordered our country's soldiers to leave the South. Then the southern whites took charge of state governments throughout the South. This was the beginning of many, many years of the South's remaining strongly Democratic. Why do you think this was so?

wrap ·up

- What were the two chief matters that were part of Reconstruction?
- What were three amendments passed during Reconstruction that helped the blacks?
- How were the Republican state governments in the South both bad and good?

3

Our country develops more

Under the Homestead Act of 1862, our country's government gave free land to some 15,000 settlers. These homesteaders generally plowed their land and planted their crops before building a permanent home. What are these farmers using to plow their land?

Land for farmers Our country's government wanted to help the farmers. So it passed the Homestead Act of 1862. This act gave a person 160 acres (64 hectares) of government land free. The person had to pay only a small sum of money to record the land. The person had to build a home and raise some crops on the new land. If these things were done within five years, then the land belonged to that person.

The Homestead Act did not work out as well as those who planned it had hoped it would. The amount of land given to each person was too small for a farmer to make a good living. And some people who were given land did not want to farm. These people wanted only to sell the land after it belonged to them. The Homestead Act did help our country to grow, though. It helped people to settle in the West.

Adding more land and states In 1867 Secretary of State Seward agreed to pay Russia $7,200,000 for Alaska. Many Americans knew little about Alaska and saw no value in buying it. Some called Alaska "Seward's Icebox." Why do you think they called it that? The United States Senate finally accepted the deal, and our country bought Alaska.

Several states were added to our country in the 1860s and the 1870s. Kansas was added before the War Between the States. West Virginia and Nevada were added during the war. Nebraska and Colorado were added during Reconstruction.

Communication and transportation During the 1860s and the 1870s communication in our country kept improving. The first transatlantic telegraph cable was laid in 1866. It went under the Atlantic Ocean from North America to Europe. This cable helped our country send messages to countries in Europe. Do you think this was important? Why or why not? Ten years later, in 1876, the telephone was **invented,** or made for the first time. How do you think the telephone helped our country?

People had long talked about building a **transcontinental railroad.** This was to be a railroad that went from the East coast to the West coast. Such a railroad was finally built by two companies. The Central Pacific started in California and worked east. The Union Pacific started in Nebraska and worked west. Many Chinese workers and Irish workers helped to build this railroad. Look at the picture on this page. It shows the day when the two railroads met in 1869 in present-day Utah. How do you think this first transcontinental railroad was important?

The Central Pacific and Union Pacific railroads met on May 10, 1869, at Promontory, Utah. This meeting marked the completion of the first transcontinental railroad in our country. How are these people celebrating this occasion?

On December 10, 1869, the same year that the National Woman Suffrage Association was formed, a law was passed in the territory of Wyoming granting women the right to vote. This law was the first of its kind in our country. How is the way these women are voting different from the way people in our country vote today?

Getting organized   Several groups in our country were formed during the 1860s. One of these groups was known as the Grange. It got farm families to work together. It also got state governments to pass laws that set railroad rates that the farmers thought were fair. And it helped farmers get better prices for their crops.

The Knights of Labor was another group formed in the 1860s. It was open to all workers over eighteen years of age. The group favored an eight-hour day for workers. It favored equal pay for men and women. And it favored keeping young children from working.

The National Woman Suffrage Association was also formed in the 1860s. It was formed by Susan B. Anthony and Elizabeth Cady Stanton. This group did not favor the Fifteenth Amendment because it gave only black men the right to vote. This group favored a law giving women the right to vote.

Baseball likely started in the East in the middle 1800s. Baseball spread rapidly. In 1876 the National League was formed. It was made up of eight baseball teams. These were professional teams, because the players got paid. The picture on page 341 shows an early baseball team. How are the player's uniforms different from the uniforms worn by baseball players today?

Chapter-End Activities

The chapter-end activities may be done by writing the questions or statements and the answers on a separate sheet of paper or by writing just the answers on a separate sheet of paper, whichever your teacher desires.

Words and Terms

freedmen	surrender
assassinated	scalawags
carpetbaggers	blockade

Last week I read a book about the War Between the States. It told how the North used warships to __(1)__ much of the southern coastline to keep ships from entering or leaving southern harbors. It also told what happened when Lee decided to __(2)__, or give up, to Grant. And it told how Lincoln was __(3)__, or suddenly murdered.

Now I'm reading a book about Reconstruction. So far I've read about the __(4)__, or those who had been slaves. I'm about to read about the __(5)__, or people from the North who went to the South to seek new fortunes.

Fact Recall

1. What was the main difference between the plan of the South and the plan of the North for winning the War Between the States?

2. Which two Union victories marked a turning point in the War Between the States?

3. What are some of the ways in which Congress tried to help the blacks during Reconstruction?

4. What piece of land did the United States buy from Russia?

5. What organizations were formed in the 1860s, and which organization helped what group of people?

Concepts and Understandings

1. Why did the Union win the War Between the States?

2. How was Reconstruction an important time in our country's history?

3. How did our country continue to grow during the 1860s and the 1870s?

343

CHAPTER 19

Our Reunited Country Forges Ahead

1. An expanding economy
2. Important groups of Americans
3. Growth of our country and of cities

The years between the 1870s and 1900 saw many changes take place in the United States. The picture on this page shows one of those changes. Cities in our country grew rapidly during the late 1800s. What things in this picture do you especially notice?

In this chapter you will learn about some of the changes that happened in our country during the late 1800s. You will learn about some of the major businesses that developed. You will learn how Americans formed different groups to gain the things they thought they should have. And you will learn about the growth of our country and its cities.

An expanding economy

The West   Mining played an important part in the growth of the West. Valuable metals such as gold, silver, and copper were sought after by the miners. Mining was first done by a person working alone or by small groups of people. Later, mining companies were formed. They were able to buy tools and machines and to hire many miners.

Cattle raising also played an important part in the growth of the West. Cattle could be raised easily and cheaply in the West and could then be sold for high prices in the East. The picture on this page shows a **long drive**. That was an early means of getting cattle from Texas to railroads in Kansas and Nebraska. The railroads then carried the cattle to markets in the East. By the late 1880s railroads reached most of the cattle country, and the long drive ended.

Mining and cattle raising both helped the West to grow. They caused many towns to be started in the West. People who put on shows, people in business, and others moved to these western towns. Why do you suppose they did that?

These cowhands are driving a herd of Texas longhorn cattle along a trail to either Kansas or Nebraska. How were the cowhands able to keep the cattle on the trail?

A rapid growth Businesses in the United States grew rapidly following the War Between the States. This rapid growth was caused by a number of things. Our country had many important natural resources, such as coal, iron ore, and oil. It had good means of transportation. Our country had much money for starting businesses and for helping them to grow. And it had a large number of people who were willing to work in factories. Some of these people were immigrants. Others were people who wanted to leave farming for a different way of life. Our country also had strong and able leaders to take charge of its growing businesses. Do you think it is important for businesses to have strong and able leaders? Why do you think so?

In some ways governments helped businesses to grow. Our country's government passed a high tariff that protected some businesses. Local governments sometimes offered free land on which to build factories. They also often helped businesses by giving them low tax rates. How do you think this helped? Finally, all levels of government let our country's businesses carry on with few laws to govern them. What difference do you think this made to businesses?

Some major industries The railroads were one of the major businesses that grew in our country during the late 1800s. Our country's government helped the railroad companies by giving them public land. The companies sold the land to help pay for building railroads to nearly all parts of the United States.

Another major business in our country was the making of steel goods, such as tools and machines. Andrew Carnegie was a leader of our country's steel business. Carnegie made his fortune by owning or controlling each step in the steel-making business. Carnegie's steel company owned or controlled iron-ore mines, railroads and ships, and steel mills. How do you think owning or controlling all these things might help a business grow?

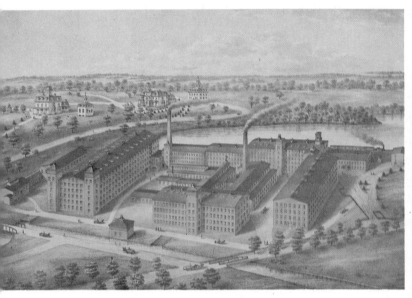

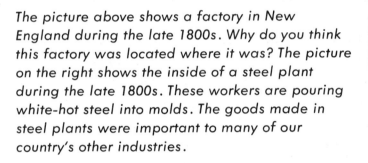

The picture above shows a factory in New England during the late 1800s. Why do you think this factory was located where it was? The picture on the right shows the inside of a steel plant during the late 1800s. These workers are pouring white-hot steel into molds. The goods made in steel plants were important to many of our country's other industries.

The oil business was another major American business. Oil was important for its use in machines and in lamps. John D. Rockefeller was a leader in our country's oil business. He made his fortune by owning or controlling each step in the business. Rockefeller formed the Standard Oil Company, which owned oil fields, buildings where oil was refined, and oil pipelines. Rockefeller also set up the means for **marketing,** or selling, oil both within our country and to other countries. How do you think a good means for marketing goods might help a business grow?

Other important industries The food business was one of our country's most important businesses during the late 1800s. The picture on this page shows meat-packing. It made up a large part of the food business. Flour milling and sugar refining also made up a large part of the food business. So, too, did the processing of dairy goods and the canning of many kinds of fruits and vegetables. How do you think being able to buy such goods in stores helped to change people's way of life?

Another important business in our country during the late 1800s was that of making **textiles,** or cloth. Much of the cloth was used in making clothing. Among other important businesses in the late 1800s were those that made lumber products. Businesses that made paper and printing materials were also important.

The workers in this meat-packing house of the 1880s are preparing beef carcasses for market. What are some of the activities taking place in this picture?

wrap·up

- What were two ways of making a living that were important to the growth of the West?
- What things helped businesses in our country to grow rapidly in the late 1800s?
- How were the railroads, the steel business, and the oil business able to grow so well in the late 1800s?

2

Important groups of Americans

A large work force Our country had a large number of workers during the late 1800s. Most of the workers were men. But many women and children also worked in factories such as the one pictured on this page.

Workers generally worked long hours for low pay during those times. Most businesses had no plans that made money payments to their workers in case they got sick or hurt. Businesses also had no plans that made money payments to workers after they became old and quit working. Do you think workers need such plans? Why or why not? Places where people worked were generally not very safe during the late 1800s. Because of this, accidents often happened.

Workers join together In the late 1800s many workers began to form **unions.** These are groups of workers who join together to gain the things they think they should have. Workers wanted shorter hours, higher pay, and safer places in which to work.

One of the first large unions was the Knights of Labor. Different groups of workers had different ideas about what the goals of this union should be. These

These people are working in a textile factory during the late 1800s. They are operating looms that weave threads into cloth.

This picture is of Samuel Gompers. In 1886 he led a group of cigar makers out of the Knights of Labor to form the American Federation of Labor (AFL). Gompers was president of the AFL from 1886 to 1924 (except for one year, 1895).

differences finally led to a breakup among the members. In 1886 the American Federation of Labor (AFL) was formed. It was made up of workers who had training for the jobs they did. The AFL became one of the largest unions in our country.

Workers had a hard time forming unions. Some business owners kept a list of known union members. Members on the list were not hired. And some businesses made workers sign a promise that they would never join a union. Why do you think businesses took such steps against unions?

Workers sometimes became angry at the way that businesses treated them. Sometimes workers called a **strike**. This means that they refused to work. Sometimes things got pretty rough. In 1892 the Carnegie steel plant at Homestead, Pennsylvania, cut workers' pay. So the workers called a strike. Fighting broke out between the workers and the soldiers that the state sent to keep order. In 1894 a strike took place in Chicago, Illinois. It started when the Pullman Company, which made railroad cars, cut the pay of its workers. The strike spread until workers refused to run the trains. The picture on page 351 shows soldiers sent by President Cleveland to keep order at Pullman. The soldiers were also sent to make sure that the mail got moved.

When strikers at the Pullman Company stopped trains carrying the mail, President Cleveland sent troops to Chicago. The soldiers quickly restored order. How were the soldiers able to get trains moving again?

Farmers join together   By 1890 nearly 3 million farmers were connected with a farm group. One such group was the National Farmers' Alliance. Another was the Colored Farmers' Alliance. These and other farm groups had certain goals. They wanted our country's government to own the railroads. They wanted banks to lend money at lower rates. And they wanted our government to have a plan for storing crops until their prices went up. How do you think these things would help the farmers?

Before long, farm groups began to gain power. So farmers decided to join with other groups to form a new political party to fight for their goals. This new party was known as the People's party or the Populist party. The People's party made a strong showing in the voting that took place in 1892. But the party lost power after making a poor showing in the election of 1896.

Our country's dealings with the American Indians For many, many years our country's government had made treaties with the American Indians. By these treaties, the Indians had been made to give up more and more of their land. The American Indians fought to keep their lands. But they were few in numbers, and their weapons were less powerful than those of the United States soldiers. In time, the Indians

This painting, "Attack at Dawn," by Charles Schreyvogel, shows the United States Army trying to make some American Indians move to reservations. How are these soldiers trying to make these Indians move? How are the Indians defending themselves?

were defeated. Different groups of American Indians agreed to move onto **reservations,** or government-owned lands set aside for them. Then in 1871 our country's government stopped making treaties. Instead our government made the Indians move onto reservations. Those who refused to move were hunted down by the United States Army.

The American Indians had always had their own way of life. They lived in groups, and their land belonged to the group rather than to individuals. In 1887 Congress passed the Dawes Severalty Act. This law said that Indian groups could no longer own land. Only individual Indians could own land. Do you think this law was trying to make the American Indians be more like other Americans? Why or why not? The Dawes Severalty Act lasted about fifty years. It did not work very well. Why do you suppose this was so? Finally, a new act was passed that allowed Indian groups to own land again.

wrap •up

- Why did workers form unions during the late 1800s?
- Why did farmers form the People's party?
- How did Congress try to change the way of life of the American Indians in the late 1800s?

A Biographical Sketch

A concern for the American Indians

Helen Fiske grew up in Amherst, Massachusetts. In 1852 she and Edward Hunt were married. After the death of her first husband, Helen Hunt took a trip to California. Because of poor health, she went to Colorado Springs, Colorado. There she met and married William Jackson. And there she saw how the American Indians were treated by our country's government and people.

Helen Hunt Jackson had long been a writer. So she decided to write a book about how the American Indians were treated. In 1881 she wrote *A Century of Dishonor*. This book told about the dealings of our country's government with the Indians. It showed how the American Indians had been treated unfairly. This book was widely read.

Jackson sent a copy of her book to each member of the United States Congress. The following year she was chosen by our country's government to be a special commissioner of Indian affairs. She and Abbot Kinney were to study the needs of the Mission Indians of southern California. Then Jackson

again wrote books about the American Indians. Her best-known book was *Ramona*. It's a story that points out some of the wrongs the Indians of southern California suffered.

Helen Hunt Jackson is remembered for her many writings. But she is especially remembered for the work she did to help gain rights for the American Indians. Other people are carrying on this kind of work today. Helen once wrote that "nothing looks to me of any value except the words I have spoken for the Indians." Why do you suppose she said that?

3

Growth of our country and of cities

Interest in the Pacific During the late 1800s many United States citizens became interested in having lands in other parts of the world. Business people saw other parts of the world as markets for selling United States goods. Military people saw other parts of the world as bases for the United States Navy.

One of the first United States colonies was the Samoa Islands in the Pacific Ocean. The United States, Britain, and Germany were all interested in the Samoa Islands. They agreed to a plan whereby no one of them would take over the islands. But the plan finally fell apart, and in 1899 Britain pulled out. Then the United States and Germany divided the Samoa Islands.

Another United States colony in the Pacific was the Hawaiian Islands. The picture on this page shows a sugar plantation in Hawaii in the late 1800s. Some United States business people had put a lot of money into the sugar business in Hawaii. Queen Liliuokalani [lih-LEE-uh-woh-kuh-LAHN-ee]

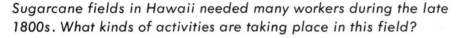

Sugarcane fields in Hawaii needed many workers during the late 1800s. What kinds of activities are taking place in this field?

of the Hawaiian Islands was against these United States citizens. She wanted Hawaii to be for Hawaiians. The business people from the United States wanted to protect their business. So they led a plan to remove the queen from office. They also sent a group of people to ask our country's government to annex Hawaii to our country. Several years later, in 1898, Hawaii was made a United States colony.

For many years a number of countries in Europe tried to get trading rights in China. Business leaders in our country were afraid that they might be left out of the trading market in China. So Secretary of State John Hay set up talks among the interested countries. These talks led to what became known as the *open-door note*. This note gave the European countries and the United States control over trade in parts of China. Do you think this was a good way to settle the matter? Why or why not? Later, the United States sent a second note. It said our country would protect both the right of free trade and the land rights of the Chinese.

A short war   In the late 1800s, the Philippine Islands, Puerto Rico, and Cuba belonged to Spain. But the Cubans wanted their freedom. President McKinley did not want our country to take part in the Cuban matter. But two things took place that changed McKinley's mind. First, a letter written by the person who spoke for the Spanish government in the United States was made public. The letter said that McKinley was a weak leader. Second, the United States received news that the battleship *Maine* had been blown up in a Cuban harbor. About 260 United States sailors were killed. These events led our country's government to declare war on Spain in 1898.

The Spanish-American War only lasted about four months. After the war ended, a peace settlement was agreed upon between the United States and Spain. Spain freed Cuba with the understanding that our country had no plans to keep

Cuba. Spain accepted our country's offer of $20 million for the Philippines. Spain also gave our country Puerto Rico and several small islands in the Pacific. Look at the map on this page. What were some of the small Pacific islands that belonged to our country after the Spanish-American War?

The rise of cities Cities in our country grew rapidly during the late 1800s. This happened for a number of reasons. Business people built factories in or near cities. They did this to make use of the large numbers of workers that could be found in cities. In turn, workers moved to cities to find jobs. Many of these workers were immigrants. Many farmers also moved to cities in search of work.

Large and costly houses could be found in cities. **Slums** could also be found in cities. These are parts of a city or town that are crowded and dirty and that generally have poor housing. Little by little those who had money moved to clean, safe, and quiet neighborhoods. The large homes they left behind were often divided into small apartments. **Tenements—**

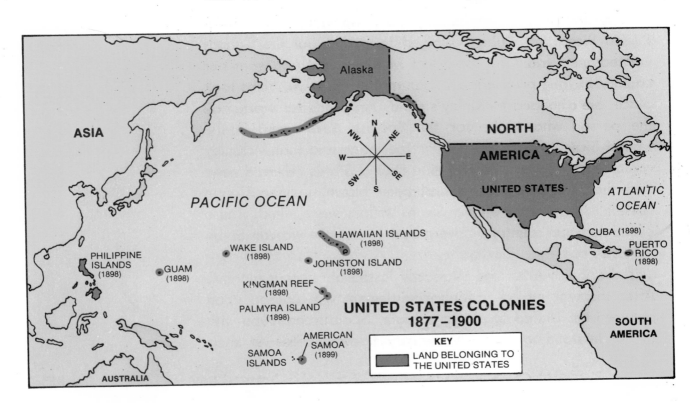

UNITED STATES COLONIES
1877–1900

KEY
LAND BELONGING TO THE UNITED STATES

This painting, "Cliff Dwellers," by George Bellows, shows the slums of New York City's Lower East Side around 1900. How would you describe conditions in this slum?

cheaply and poorly built housing units—were also built. Such housing was often very crowded.

Cities were crowded and were growing too fast. Yet many parts of city life were improved. Transportation was improved by the use of electric-powered trolleys, elevated railways, and electric underground railways. Cities began to be lighted by electric streetlights. Ways of getting better water and getting rid of wastes were improved. Police and fire departments were improved. And laws calling for better housing were passed.

A large number of immigrants Almost 15 million immigrants came to our country between 1860 and 1900. Before 1880 most of these people came from western and northern Europe. After 1880 more people from other parts of Europe began coming to our country. To many people in the United States these newer immigrants seemed like strange

Immigrants arrived in the United States in large numbers during the late 1800s. How would you describe the immigrants pictured here?

people. Few of them spoke English. Most of them had little schooling. And they had many different ways of doing things.

Most immigrants came to our country hoping to find a better way of life. But they generally had to settle for low-paying jobs. Those who tried to rent or buy housing in some parts of cities were often not welcome. So these people generally had to live in the poorest parts of cities. Even those who found better housing generally lived in the same neighborhoods as others who had come from the same country. Why do you suppose this was so?

For years people in the United States had accepted people from other countries. But this idea began to change in the late 1800s. Business leaders began to blame immigrants for troubles in factories. Workers began to fear that immigrants might take their jobs. Some people joined with others to form groups to keep immigrants out of our country. These groups wanted our country's government to allow only a certain number of immigrants to enter our country each year. They also wanted immigrants to have to take a reading and writing test. Those who could not read or write in their own language would not be able to enter our country. In 1882 our government passed the Chinese Exclusion Act. This law stopped Chinese immigrants from coming into our country for ten years. In the early 1900s our country limited the number of immigrants who could enter the United States from each country. And our country began to make those who came pass a reading and writing test.

New states More states were added to our country during the late 1800s. North Dakota, South Dakota, Montana, and Washington were added during the 1880s. Look at the map on this page. Which of these states got all or part of its land from the Louisiana Purchase? Which got all or part of its land from the Oregon Country?

Idaho, Wyoming, and Utah were added to our country during the 1890s. Which of these states got all of its land from the Oregon Country? Which of these states came entirely from land that our country got from Mexico? Where did the land for Wyoming come from?

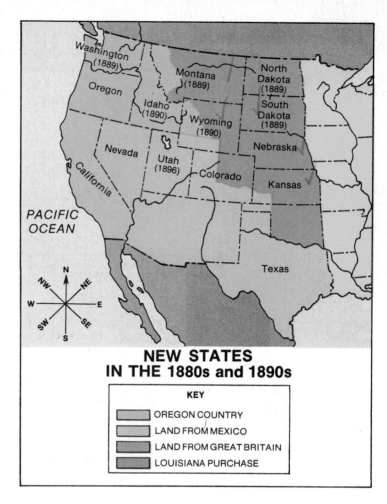

**NEW STATES
IN THE 1880s and 1890s**

KEY
OREGON COUNTRY
LAND FROM MEXICO
LAND FROM GREAT BRITAIN
LOUISIANA PURCHASE

wrap·up

- What were some of the overseas colonies that belonged to our country by 1900?
- Why did United States cities grow rapidly during the late 1800s?
- Why did people in the United States change their attitude toward immigrants?

Using Your Skills

Reading a bar graph

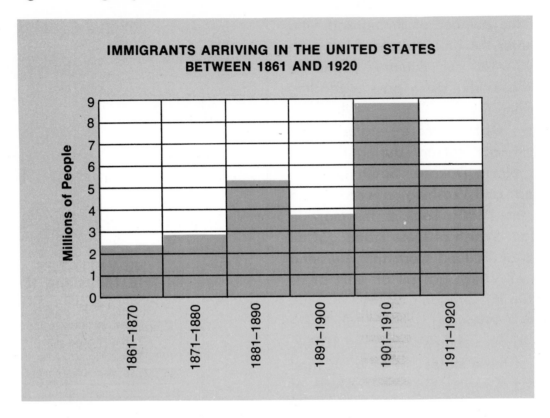

IMMIGRANTS ARRIVING IN THE UNITED STATES BETWEEN 1861 AND 1920

Use the bar graph to answer these questions.

1. What does the bar graph show?

2. During which years did the least number of immigrants arrive in the United States?

3. During which years did the greatest number of immigrants arrive in the United States?

4. Did more or fewer immigrants arrive between 1871–1880 than between 1881–1890?

5. About how many more immigrants arrived between 1911–1920 than between 1871–1880?

Chapter-End Activities

The chapter-end activities may be done by writing the questions or statements and the answers on a separate sheet of paper or by writing just the answers on a separate sheet of paper, whichever your teacher desires.

Words and Terms

strike	reservations
tenements	slums
textiles	unions

1. The making of _____, or cloth, was an important business in our country during the late 1800s.

2. In the late 1800s many workers began to form _____, or groups, to gain the things they did not have but thought they should have.

3. Sometimes workers called a _____, which means they refused to work.

4. Government-owned lands that have been set aside for the American Indians are called _____.

5. Parts of a city or town that are crowded, dirty, and generally have poor housing are called _____.

Fact Recall

1. Andrew Carnegie was a leader of this major business in our country.
   a. steel
   b. oil

2. The People's party, or Populist party, was formed by this group.
   a. farmers
   b. factory workers

3. The Dawes Severalty Act tried to change the way of life of these people.
   a. workers
   b. American Indians

4. Spain gave our country these islands after the Spanish-American War.
   a. Hawaiian Islands
   b. Philippine Islands

5. An act of 1882 stopped these immigrants from coming into our country for ten years.
   a. Chinese
   b. Spanish

Concepts and Understandings

1. Why did businesses in our country grow rapidly during the late 1800s?

2. Why did our country's cities grow rapidly during the late 1800s?

CHAPTER 20

Our Country Experiences Many Changes

1. An age of reform
2. Our country as a world power
3. The life and culture of a growing country

The person pictured on this page is President Theodore Roosevelt. He was one of our country's leaders during the early 1900s. What is President Roosevelt doing in this picture?

In this chapter you will learn about the United States during the early 1900s. You will learn about some of the ways in which our country changed. You will learn about some of the ways in which our country took part in happenings around the world. And you will learn about some of the changes in American life and culture.

1

An age of reform

Changes in government During the early 1900s a large number of Americans wanted to make changes in our country. Most of these people were known as Progressives. They did not think that a few people should control government. They wanted to put the control of all levels of government in the hands of more people. They also wanted government to better serve the needs of all people.

The Progressives were able to get a number of changes in city and town governments. They helped to set up different plans of government for cities. One plan places the powers of city government in the hands of a small group of people. Another plan calls for a highly trained person to be hired to run a city. In general, Progressives helped to get more able people into city, town, and village governments.

The Progressives also helped to get a number of changes in state governments. The changes described here helped to give more power to the people. The **initiative** allows people to vote directly for a law that they want passed. The **referendum** allows people to vote to get rid of a law that a state lawmaking-body has already passed. The **recall** allows people to remove a leader from office. Do you think it is important for people to be able to remove a leader from office? Why or why not? The **direct primary** allows people to vote to select citizens to run for office in a general election. The **secret ballot** allows people to vote in a place where others cannot see how they vote. Do you think these changes are important? Why or why not?

The Progressives also helped bring about changes in our country's government. Most United States senators were chosen by a state lawmaking-body. But in 1913 the Seventeenth Amendment was passed. This law states that United

The efforts of these women in 1912 helped women in New York gain the right to vote in 1917. Such efforts also helped all women in our country gain the right to vote in 1920.

States senators are to be chosen by the people in each state. In the early 1900s only a few states allowed women to vote. Look at the picture on this page. How are these women trying to win the right for women to vote? With the help of the Progressives, women were finally given the right to vote in 1920.

Changes in businesses   In the early 1900s a few big companies had control of making and pricing certain goods. Other businesses had control of pricing certain services. Such companies could raise prices whenever they wanted. Or they could lower prices in order to cause smaller companies to go out of business. Do you think it was good or bad that businesses could do these things? Why do you think so? The Progressives and many other people wanted these business ways changed. They wanted our country's government to break up the big companies.

During the early 1900s our country's government did order the breakup of several big companies. Then in 1914 the Federal Trade Commission (FTC) was set up. The FTC has the power to order businesses to stop doing certain unfair things. And it has the power to take companies to court. Do you think the FTC is important? Why or why not?

The Progressives also worked for laws that would help workers. Some of these laws called for an age limit for working children. Others called for shorter hours and more pay. Still others called for making the places where people worked safer. Also, in 1913 a separate group within our government was set up to look after the well-being of workers.

Other changes in our country For a number of years many Americans had wanted our country's government to pass laws to protect **consumers.** These are people who use goods and services. However, little was done to protect these people until stories telling about the bad conditions in some businesses were written. Then in 1906 our government passed both the Meat Inspection Act and the Pure Food and Drug Act. These laws help to protect Americans from the careless handling and making of foods and drugs.

The picture above shows young boys working in a mill in Georgia during the early 1900s. In what kind of mill are they working? The picture below shows federal inspectors checking a beef carcass. What might they be looking for?

Since the War Between the States, business leaders had wanted to keep tariff rates high. But in the early 1900s our country's government passed a new bill calling for a lower tariff. Our government expected to lose some income because of this lower tariff. So in 1913 it passed the Sixteenth Amendment. This law states that our government can tax the incomes of people and of businesses. This income tax called for people with higher incomes to pay a higher tax rate. Do you think this is a fair way to tax people? Why or why not?

In the early 1900s a report was made telling how a few powerful bankers had money in most American businesses. The report pointed out that these bankers were able to direct much of our country's money matters. So in 1913 our country's government passed the Federal Reserve Act. This law set up a new banking plan that cut back the power of some large banks. This new plan also gave our government more power over our country's money.

Concern for natural resources Americans had long been careless with our country's natural resources. This bothered President Theodore Roosevelt. So he helped protect these resources. He set aside millions of acres (hectares) of forestland so it would be protected. And he set aside land for five national parks. In 1903 Roosevelt helped get the Newlands Act passed. This law gave our country's government power to build dams, such as the one pictured on page 367. It gave our government power to form lakes from dams. And the Newlands Act gave our government power to build ways to bring water to dry lands.

In 1908 Roosevelt held a meeting on **conservation**—a means of protecting and wisely using the world around you. This meeting helped people by giving them a better understanding of the need for conservation. Within a short time, most state governments had conservation groups of their own.

Theodore Roosevelt Dam is located on the Salt River near Phoenix, Arizona. It was completed in 1911. The water in the background is Roosevelt Lake. How is the water level of the lake controlled?

Three more states   Three more states were added to our country during the early 1900s. Oklahoma was added in 1907. It was the last state to be formed from the Louisiana Purchase.

New Mexico and Arizona were both added to our country in 1912. Each of these states came from land that our country had received from Mexico. These two states were the last ones formed from our country's land that lies between Canada and Mexico.

wrap ·up

- What changes did the Progressives make at each level of government?
- What changes took place in our country during the early 1900s that affected businesses, workers, and consumers?
- How did President Roosevelt help protect our country's natural resources?

Using Your Skills

Reading a map

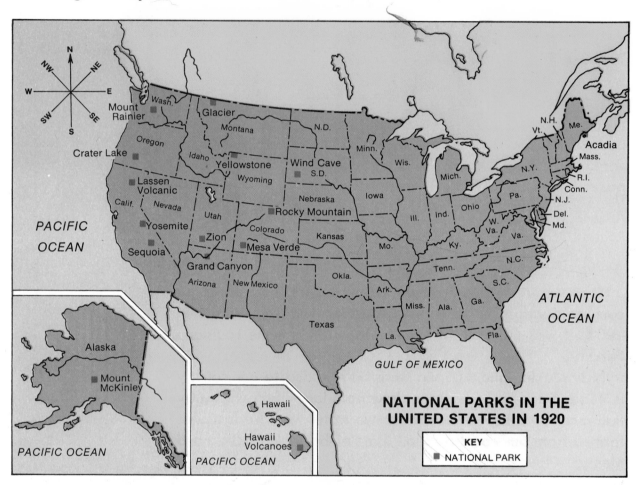

NATIONAL PARKS IN THE UNITED STATES IN 1920

KEY
■ NATIONAL PARK

Use the map to answer these questions.

1. What does the map show?

2. What national park is located in Alaska?

3. In which state is the Grand Canyon National Park located?

4. Which national park is located in the northeastern part of the United States? In which state is this national park located?

5. Which state has the greatest number of national parks? What are the names of these national parks?

2

Our country as a world power

The Panama Canal President Theodore Roosevelt wanted a canal built across Panama. He believed that it would be a step toward United States power in the Caribbean. Military people and business people also favored a canal. Look at the map on this page. Why do you think both of these groups of people favored building a canal across Panama?

Panama belonged to the South American country of Colombia. In 1901 our country offered Colombia $10 million and a yearly payment of $250,000 for the right to build a canal across Panama. Colombia refused our country's offer. At that time the people of Panama were seeking their freedom. President Roosevelt supported them in their attempt to overthrow the Colombian government in Panama. He sent United States ships and troops to keep Colombian soldiers from ending the uprising. In the end, Panama became a free country.

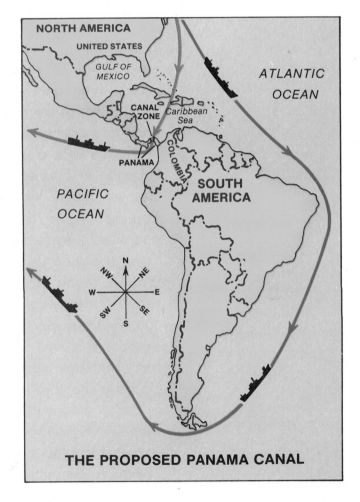

THE PROPOSED PANAMA CANAL

Water-filled chambers that raise and lower ships from one level to another are called locks. This ship is passing through the Miraflores Locks in the Panama Canal.

In 1903 our country and Panama signed a treaty. It gave our country the right to build a canal. Panama received $10 million then and a yearly rent of $250,000 for the land through which the canal was built. The Panama Canal was finished and opened to ships in 1914.

Drawn into a war   In 1914 a war, known as World War I, began in Europe. The countries that fought on the side of Germany and Austria-Hungary were called the **Central Powers.** Those that fought on the side of Britain, France, and Russia were called the **Allied Powers,** or the **Allies.**

Americans found it hard not to take sides over the war in Europe. Many Americans or their parents had come from Europe. These people generally favored the side on which the country from which they had come was fighting. Why do you suppose this was so? The use of **propaganda** also made it hard for Americans not to take sides over the war. Propaganda is the spreading of ideas to further one's own cause or to hurt someone else's cause. Both sides used it often to try to shape American thoughts about the war.

A British blockade caused American trade with the Central Powers to become less. It also caused American trade with the

Allies to grow. Germany tried to end the British blockade by using submarines to attack ships. Many American lives were lost in German attacks on ships. In February of 1917 the British discovered a note from a German leader to the Mexican government. The note asked Mexico to join Germany in a war against the United States. The German attacks on ships and the note to Mexico greatly angered our country. So in April of 1917 our country declared war on Germany.

The war effort The United States had a small army when it entered the war. So a law was passed stating that all men between certain ages had to sign up for the army. The new soldiers had to be trained. So training camps were quickly set up. Many things such as weapons, uniforms, ships, and airplanes were needed for fighting the war. How do you think these needs affected our country's businesses? American soldiers and sailors went overseas to help the Allies. They served well, and a number of them received medals.

Americans who stayed at home also helped. They saved food by going certain days without wheat or meat. So our country had more food to send overseas. Americans worked in factories to make war goods. And they bought bonds to help pay for the war.

Many men were called into the army during World War I. This greatly lowered the work force in our country. So large numbers of women were hired for the first time. Some worked in factories. Others took jobs as auto mechanics, ice deliverers, and traffic officers. What job did the woman pictured here take?

The signing of the Treaty of Versailles took place in the Hall of Mirrors on June 28, 1919. President Wilson, holding some papers, is seated near the center.

The League of Nations World War I ended on November 11, 1918. The Allies won. Their leaders met at Versailles [vur-SY], near Paris, France. There they worked out the Treaty of Versailles, which had many parts. Among other things, Germany had to give up some of its land. And it had to agree to pay for war damages. Several new countries in Europe were also formed. And there were plans for forming the League of Nations to help settle differences among countries. This part was President Wilson's major goal. Do you think this was an important goal? Why or why not?

Wilson returned from France to present the Treaty of Versailles to the United States Senate. The Senate did not favor the League of Nations. The Senate felt that it might cause our country to take part in world matters again. So the Senate refused to accept the Treaty of Versailles.

wrap·up

- Why did our country want to build the Panama Canal?
- How did our country help the Allies in World War I?
- Why was the Treaty of Versailles refused by the Senate?

The life and culture of a growing country

Some important changes Our country's schools changed greatly during the late 1800s and the early 1900s. More kindergartens were started. High schools began to offer more courses. Many teachers colleges were set up. And our country's government gave states land on which to build colleges. At first few colleges accepted women. But by 1900 many colleges did so. Blacks found most colleges closed to them. There were, however, a number of all-black colleges, such as Tuskegee Institute and Howard University.

Changes also took place in our country's cities during the late 1800s and the early 1900s. In 1890 Jacob Riis [REES] wrote a book about life in many slums. People who read his book became very upset. They demanded that something be done to get rid of slums. During the early 1900s many states passed new housing laws. These laws set up tight rules for the building of better tenements in slums.

Jacob Riis told how children living in slums had no place to play other than in dirty streets and alleys. During the early 1900s public playgrounds began to appear in many cities. What are some of the activities taking place on this playground?

The picture above shows one of the many different activities provided at Hull House during the early 1900s. What activity does it show? The picture below shows how some blacks in Cincinnati, Ohio, lived in the early 1900s. How would you describe these living conditions?

During the late 1800s Jane Addams became interested in the city poor. In 1889 she opened Hull House in Chicago, Illinois. This was a **settlement house**—a place where people are able to form a neighborhood center. Programs in sports, music, acting, cooking, and sewing were offered. Classes to teach people to speak English and to become American citizens were also offered. Soon settlement houses were started in other cities in our country. Do you think settlement houses were a good way of helping the city poor? Why or why not?

The fight for equal rights The role of blacks in American society in the late 1800s and the early 1900s was a hard one. Black children attended the most-run-down schools. Many stores and eating places refused to serve blacks. And landlords and homeowners generally would not rent or sell to blacks. In which parts of cities do you think most blacks ended up living? Why do you think so?

Booker T. Washington was a well-known black leader. In 1881 he became the head of a black college in Tuskegee, Alabama. He believed that once blacks had learned useful skills, whites would allow them their full rights. William E. B. Du Bois [d(y)oo-BOYS], another black leader, did not agree with Washington. Du Bois felt that as free citizens blacks did not have to earn their rights. He believed that blacks had to have political power to help them get ahead. In 1909 the National Association for the Advancement of Colored People (NAACP) was formed. Du Bois was chosen as a leader of this group. This group worked for better schooling and equal rights for blacks. Do you think this was an important group? Why or why not?

Blacks made some gains during the early 1900s. Many blacks went into business. A few, such as Madame C. J. Walker, became rich. Some banks and several newspapers were owned and run by blacks. But most blacks had little chance to get good jobs.

Reading becomes popular Large numbers of Americans began to enjoy reading more during the late 1800s and the early 1900s. Improved ways of printing and less-costly paper made newspapers and magazines cheaper. Photographs and certain features, such as sports pages, comics, puzzles, and household hints, were added to most newspapers. Two widely read magazines were the *Ladies' Home Journal* and the *Saturday Evening Post*. Look at the pictures on this page. What other magazines were widely read during the early 1900s?

What is the cost of each of these magazines? Low-cost magazines were very popular during the early 1900s. Which of these magazines might have been popular with young people?

Many different kinds of books were also widely read during the late 1800s and the early 1900s. One group of American authors tried to write honestly about our growing country. These people were called **realists**. Realists are people who present things as they really are. Stephen Crane wrote about the evils of city life. Hamlin Garland wrote about the problems of farmers. After 1900 another group of American authors appeared. These authors wrote very strongly about many wrongs in our country. Lincoln Steffens wrote about people in government who were not always honest. Ida Tarbell wrote about the dealings of John D. Rockefeller. And Upton Sinclair, in *The Jungle*, wrote about the dirty conditions in the meat-packing business.

Many American authors wrote about the part of our country where they lived. Sarah Orne Jewett and Edith Wharton wrote about life in the East. Louisa May Alcott also wrote about the East in *Little Women* and in *Little Men*. Mark Twain wrote about the Mississippi River valley in *The Adventures of Tom Sawyer* and *The Adventures of Huckleberry Finn*. George W. Cable and Charles Waddell Chesnutt wrote about life in the South. And Bret Harte and Charles A. Eastman wrote about life in the West.

Some American poets also wrote about our country and its people. Two of these were Walt Whitman and Carl Sandburg. Paul Laurence Dunbar wrote poems about the life of blacks. Other American poets, such as Emily Dickinson, Amy Lowell, and Sara Teasdale, wrote about feelings, beauty, and life in general.

The arts During the late 1800s and the early 1900s Americans wrote many different kinds of music. John Philip Sousa wrote marches, such as "The Stars and Stripes Forever." Charles Ives wrote marches and other kinds of songs. George M. Cohan gave people many popular songs, such as "You're a Grand Old Flag." Such songs were part of the mus-

Mary Cassatt often painted pictures of mothers and children in everyday settings. The picture on the left, "The Bath," was painted by Mary Cassatt around 1892. What is happening in this painting? Winslow Homer often painted pictures of people who made their living by working at sea. The picture below, "The Fog Warning," was painted by Winslow Homer in 1885. What is happening in this painting?

ical plays that he wrote. James Bland wrote folk songs, such as "Carry Me Back to Old Virginia."

American artists of the late 1800s and the early 1900s generally made their paintings look very real. Winslow Homer painted pictures of New England life, especially the sea. Frederic Remington became a well-known painter of the West. Mary Cassatt and Thomas Eakins painted people in everyday settings. Some artists painted pictures of American city life. And Henry O. Tanner showed the life of blacks in his paintings.

An **architect** is a person who plans buildings. Louis Sullivan was a well-known American architect in the early 1900s. He helped plan **skyscrapers,** or many-storied buildings. Such tall buildings were needed in cities to save space. New building materials, such as steel, helped make tall buildings possible. The electric elevator also helped make tall buildings possible. Why do you suppose this was so?

Leisure time   Americans had more leisure time during the late 1800s and the early 1900s than they ever had before. So, many Americans became interested in sports. Baseball games, college football games, boxing matches, and automobile races were enjoyed by many people. People also enjoyed golf and tennis. And they enjoyed basketball, which was started in our country by James Naismith in 1891. But the sport that was perhaps enjoyed most of all was bicycling. Why do you suppose this was so?

Many Americans also turned their attention to music and other forms of entertainment. A large number of people owned record players. Many enjoyed band shows. People

Many people in New York City rode bicycles during the 1900s. How do these bicycles compare with bicycles today?

also enjoyed **silent movies**—moving pictures without sound. And they enjoyed wild-West shows, circuses, fairs, and traveling shows that offered speakers, music, and plays. The picture on this page shows one of the wonders of the world's fair held in Chicago in 1893. This fair was called the Columbian Exposition because it was held to honor the discovery of the Americas by Columbus.

The automobile became a source of pleasure for Americans during the early 1900s. The first American gasoline-powered car was built in 1893. Three years later Henry Ford built his first car. Then in 1908 the Ford Motor Company made the *Model T*. This was a simple, well-built car that did not cost a lot of money. It became one of the most popular cars of the early 1900s. Why do you suppose this was so?

This Ferris wheel, built for the Chicago World's Fair in 1893, could carry 2,160 passengers. Each trip lasted 20 minutes.

wrap ·up

- What were some of the things done in the late 1800s and the early 1900s to try to improve schools, life for the city poor, and life for blacks?
- What were some of the things American authors wrote about during the late 1800s and the early 1900s?
- How did Americans spend some of their leisure time during the late 1800s and the early 1900s?

A Biographical Sketch

An all-around athlete

James Thorpe, who was part American Indian, grew up in present-day Oklahoma. He attended Carlisle Indian School in Pennsylvania. There he helped the football team have several winning seasons. And he won all-American honors in football. Thorpe also joined the track team and the baseball team at Carlisle Indian School.

In 1912 Thorpe took part in the Olympic Games held in Sweden. He entered the **pentathlon**—a five-part contest. And he entered the **decathlon** —a ten-part contest. James Thorpe became the first person to win both these contests. When he returned to our country, he was honored by President Taft and others.

In time, it was learned that Thorpe had received pay for playing baseball during the summers. This meant he was a professional player. But the Olympics are for amateurs only. So Thorpe had to return his medals. Americans still thought highly of Thorpe. They understood that he had not meant to do anything wrong.

James Thorpe later became a professional baseball player. He also became

a professional football player. And he helped start a football club for paid football players. This club later became the National Football League. Later, Thorpe was selected as a member of a football Hall of Fame.

James Thorpe is thought to be one of the greatest all-around sports figures in the first half of the 1900s. Do you think Thorpe was a great all-around sports figure? Why or why not?

Chapter-End Activities

The chapter-end activities may be done by writing the questions or statements and the answers on a separate sheet of paper or by writing just the answers on a separate sheet of paper, whichever your teacher desires.

Words and Terms

consumers   skyscrapers
initiative   recall
conservation   propaganda

_____ 1. A means of allowing people to remove a leader from office

_____ 2. People who use goods and services

_____ 3. A means of protecting and wisely using the world around you

_____ 4. The spreading of ideas to further one's own cause or to hurt someone else's cause

_____ 5. Many-storied buildings

Fact Recall

1. The (Progressives, Allies) helped to get a number of changes in each level of government during the early 1900s.

2. President Theodore Roosevelt helped protect our country's (natural resources, large banks).

3. The United States Senate refused to accept the (Panama Canal, Treaty of Versailles) following World War I.

4. The (FTC, NAACP) was formed to work for better schooling and equal rights for blacks.

5. Large numbers of Americans began to read (more, less) during the late 1800s and the early 1900s.

Concepts and Understandings

1. How did changes made in our country in the early 1900s affect governments, businesses, and natural resources?

2. Why did our country become involved in Panama and in World War I?

3. How did improvements made in our country in the late 1800s and the early 1900s affect schools, the city poor, and blacks?

Unit End

Main Ideas and Understandings

1. What three major sections developed in our country during the 1850s? What role did slavery play in sectionalism? Why did the North win the War Between the States? What were some of the results of Reconstruction?

2. Why did United States businesses grow rapidly in the late 1800s? Why did workers form unions and farmers form the People's party during the late 1800s? What were some of the overseas colonies that belonged to the United States by the end of the 1800s? Why did cities in our country grow rapidly during the late 1800s?

3. How did changes made in our country during the early 1900s affect governments and businesses? Why did our country build the Panama Canal? Why did the Senate refuse the Treaty of Versailles at the end of World War I? How did people spend their leisure time in the late 1800s and the early 1900s?

Research Ideas

1. Some people played important roles in the War Between the States. Find out what each of the following people did: Clara Barton, Mary Bickerdyke, Belle Boyd, Stonewall Jackson, George B. McClellan, Hiram Revels, and Robert Smalls. Which side of the war did each of these people help? What did each of these people do during the war?

2. Many people made important achievements between the middle 1800s and the early 1900s. Find out what each of the following people did: Elizabeth Blackwell, George Washington Carver, Thomas Edison, Jan Matzeliger, Walter Reed, Kate Douglas Wiggin, and Orville and Wilbur Wright. Which of these people made achievements in the field of science? Which of these people made achievements in the field of education? In what field did Gifford Pinchot make important achievements?

3. Conservation has continued to be a matter of concern in our country since the early 1900s. Find out about some of the different kinds of conservation. And find out about some of the different groups that are interested in conservation. What are some jobs in the field of conservation?

Activities and Projects

1. Make a diorama showing some part of our country's history between the middle 1800s and the early 1900s. You might show a war, a development in transportation, a development in communication, a business, or a city. Make your diorama in a box from which the top has been removed.

2. Prepare a television program reviewing life in our country between the middle 1800s and the early 1900s. Include short plays and interviews. What else might you include in your program?

Chicago Daily Tribune
THE WORLD'S GREATEST NEWSPAPER

** FINAL

THREE CENTS—PAY NO MORE

WEDNESDAY, AUGUST 15, 1945—34 PAGES

VOLUME CIV—NO. 195 C

GREAT WAR ENDS!

Japs Will Surrender to Gen. M'Ar...

**STOCK PRICES SLUMP $14,000,000,000
IN NATION-WIDE STAMPEDE TO UNLOAD;
BANKERS TO SUPPORT MARKET TODA...**

Sixteen Leading Issues Down $2,893,520,108;
Tel. & Tel. and Steel Among Heaviest Losers

PREMIER ISSUES HARD

The New York Times

NEW YORK, MONDAY, JULY 21, 1969

MEN WALK ON MOO...

ASTRONAUTS LAND ON PLA...
COLLECT ROCKS, PLANT FL...

Voice From Moon:
'Eagle Has Landed'

A Powdery
Is Closely

The New York Times

"All the News That's Fit to Print"

LATE CITY EDITION

VOL. CXXII..No. 42,904

NEW YORK, WEDNESDAY, JANUARY 24, 1973

15 CENTS

VIETNAM ACCORD IS REACHED;
CEASE-FIRE BEGINS SATURDAY;
P.O.W.'S TO BE FREE IN 60 DAYS

THE SITUATION IN INDOCHINA

THIEU IS CAUTIOUS

Says the Agreement Doesn't Guarantee Lasting Peace

By SYLVAN FOX

Transcript of the Speech by President on Vietnam

SPORTS ON PAGE 17

THE CHICAGO DAILY NEWS.
TWO CENTS—45TH YEAR—198.

FINAL EDITION

WEDNESDAY, AUGUST 18, 1920.

HOME EDITION

WOMEN WIN FULL U. S. VOTE

TO-DAY'S BASEBALL GAMES

THOMPSON'S LEGION SPONSORS ROLL POST

ENVY FOR 'HEAVEN FLAT'

DRIVE RUSS 9 MILES; CLEAR DANZIG LANE

YOUTH FROM GOAT GLAND

TENNESSEE RATIFIES VOTES FOR WOMEN; REJOICE IN CHICAGO

VICTORY AGAINST POLIO!
SALK'S VACCINE WORKS

A vial of Salk vaccine

CHICAGO DAILY NEWS
An Independent Newspaper

FINAL MARKETS
RED STREAK

5¢

80TH YEAR—86   Tel. DEarborn 2-1111   TUESDAY, APRIL 12, 1955.

CUBS WHIP ...

2d Bli-
W...

The New York Times.

"All the News That's Fit to Print"

VOL. LXXXII...No. 27,318.

NEW YORK, WEDNESDAY, NOVEMBER 9, 1932.

TWO CENTS

ROOSEVELT WINNER IN LANDSLI...
DEMOCRATS CONTROL WET CONGRE...
LEHMAN GOVERNOR, O'BRIEN MA...

BIG VOTE FOR M'KEE

O'Brien Is 245,464 Behind Ticket as Protests Rise

BUT FINAL LEAD IS 616,736

THE GOVERNOR-ELECT

STATE VICTORY SOLID

Lehman Gets Record Party Plurality of 887,000.

WAGNER CLOSE TO HIM

National Ticket Has Mar...

The President's Message To the President-Elect

OVERTURN IN SENATE

Bingham, Watson, Moses and Smoot Are Defeated.

DEMOCRATIC MAJORITY 12

Party Adds to Control in House—May Rule Both Branches This Winter.

THE PRESIDENT-ELECT

Unit 8

384

Our Country in a Rapidly Changing World

Much has happened in our country since the early 1900s. Look at the newspaper headlines on page 384. What were some of the important events that took place during those years? However, these headlines give only a few of the important happenings in the United States.

In this unit you will learn about our country and its people since the early 1900s. You will also learn about our country's relations with other countries since this time. And you will find answers to the following questions:

What are some of the problems our country has faced since the early 1900s?

How did our country become a world leader in the mid-1900s?

How have our country and its people changed since the early 1900s?

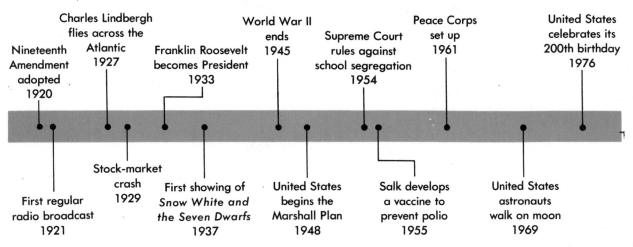

Nineteenth Amendment adopted 1920

Charles Lindbergh flies across the Atlantic 1927

Franklin Roosevelt becomes President 1933

World War II ends 1945

Supreme Court rules against school segregation 1954

Peace Corps set up 1961

United States celebrates its 200th birthday 1976

First regular radio broadcast 1921

Stock-market crash 1929

First showing of Snow White and the Seven Dwarfs 1937

United States begins the Marshall Plan 1948

Salk develops a vaccine to prevent polio 1955

United States astronauts walk on moon 1969

A Poor Fish Out of Water

CHAPTER 21

Our Country During Prosperity and Hard Times

1. **Attempting to withdraw from the world**
2. **Prosperity ends with a crash**
3. **Good times and bad times**

The years after World War I brought about many changes in the American way of life. Many Americans had more money to spend and more goods to buy than ever before. Automobiles, radios, and motion pictures became part of the American way of life. And women enjoyed a freedom they had never had before. These years are called the Golden Twenties or the Roaring Twenties. Why do you think this is so?

All Americans, however, did not share in the good times of the 1920s. And by the end of the 1920s, the entire country faced hard times. In this chapter you will learn how the United States felt about dealings with other countries after World War I. You will learn how businesses grew in the United States during the 1920s. You will learn about changes in the American way of life. And you will learn what happened when people in our country had to face hard times.

1

Attempting to withdraw from the world

Refusal to join the World Court After World War I the United States tried to withdraw from dealings with other countries. Many Americans believed that such dealings might lead to another war. And many Americans were more concerned with matters at home. Even so, the United States found it impossible to stay out of matters that had to do with other countries. Why do you think this was so?

The League of Nations set up the World Court in 1920. The purpose of this court was to settle problems between countries. For a time it looked as if the United States would join the World Court. But the United States Senate agreed to join only on its own terms. Other countries would not agree to these terms, so the United States did not join.

Attempts to build world peace In 1921 the United States invited eight countries to a meeting in Washington, D.C. This meeting was called to try to limit the number of warships and weapons that certain countries could own. How do you think this might help to lead to world peace? This meeting

At the Washington Conference of 1921–1922, several important agreements were reached between the major countries of the world. Most Americans hoped that these agreements would prevent another world war from taking place. How can you tell from this picture how many countries were represented at the Washington Conference?

Frank Kellogg, the United States Secretary of State, and Aristide Briand, the French foreign minister, proposed a plan to outlaw war. Other countries were invited to sign the Kellogg-Briand Pact. This picture shows Kellogg signing the agreement.

was known as the Washington Conference. Among those who attended were representatives from Britain, France, Italy, Belgium, China, and Japan.

At the Washington Conference, the United States offered a plan whereby countries would agree not to build any warships for ten years. The plan also called for the United States, Britain, and Japan to destroy some of their warships. This was to help keep these countries from becoming too powerful. The United States, Britain, France, Italy, and Japan accepted the plan. Why do you think many people looked upon this meeting as a major step toward world peace?

The picture on this page shows the signing of the Kellogg-Briand Pact. In 1928 sixty-two countries signed this agreement to outlaw war. Each of these countries agreed not to go to war except in self-defense. And these countries agreed to settle problems with one another by peaceful means.

Many people looked upon this pact as another major step toward world peace. But there was no way to make certain that the countries would carry out what they had agreed upon. And nearly every country that goes to war says it is doing so for self-defense.

The League of Nations loses strength During the 1920s the League of Nations was able to settle some problems between weak countries. But it was not able to settle problems between more powerful countries.

By the end of the 1930s the League of Nations had lost much of its strength. Two of the strongest countries in the League—France and Britain—often did not agree about important matters. And by 1939 Japan, Germany, Italy, and the Soviet Union had left the League of Nations. What effect do you think this had on the League?

The League of Nations might have been stronger if the United States had been a member. The League might also have been stronger if its members had worked together. But as it was, the League of Nations could do very little toward keeping world peace.

The picture below shows the Palace of Nations building in Geneva, Switzerland. This building served as the headquarters of the League of Nations until the League ended in 1946.

wrap·up

- Why did the United States try to withdraw from dealings with other countries after World War I?
- How did the United States try to work for world peace during the 1920s?
- Why did the League of Nations lose much of its strength during the 1930s?

2

Prosperity ends with a crash

After the war   During World War I our government had placed many businesses in the service of our country. When the war was over, the government removed all wartime controls. It also cut back on the money it was spending to help business. This caused a business slowdown. However, by the spring of 1919 business began to boom. People were eager to get goods that they had not been able to get before.

This boom in business, however, did not last. Our country suffered a **depression** that started in 1920 and lasted until 1922. During a depression many businesses fail, and many people lose their jobs. So people do not have the money to buy the things they need. Thus many factories and stores are forced to close. The depression of 1921 likely came about for a number of reasons. Other countries stopped buying as many goods as they had been buying. Our own government began to spend less money. And there was a steep drop in farm income.

By 1922, though, things were looking better. Businesses began to recover. And many new businesses were started. People who had been out of work began to find jobs. This meant that people once again had money to spend for things they had not been able to buy before. Many people began to buy goods on the **installment plan.** This meant that people could buy goods by making small monthly payments over a long time.

As the demand for goods became greater, factories increased their production. This meant that more people were needed to work in the factories. Between 1922 and 1929 many Americans earned more money to spend for goods and services than ever before.

Businesses grow During the 1920s the automobile industry became our country's biggest business. People no longer thought of the automobile as something they would like to have. They thought of it as something they *had* to have.

The making of automobiles led to the growth of many other businesses. Steel, glass, and rubber were needed for making automobiles. Gasoline and oil were needed for running automobiles. There was also a rising need for new businesses such as garages and service stations. And more cars and trucks meant a need for more roads and highways. How do you think these businesses helped our country?

Other kinds of businesses also grew rapidly during the 1920s. The need for new homes and factories caused the **construction,** or building, business to grow. Gas companies, electric companies, and telephone companies also grew. The making of household goods, such as refrigerators, irons, toasters, and electric stoves, became an important business. And during the 1920s radios and motion pictures became very popular with the American people. These industries provided jobs for thousands of workers.

Not as good as it seemed A number of major industries, however,

From 1920 to 1930, the number of automobiles in our country nearly tripled. Automobile companies constantly increased production to keep up with demand. The picture above shows an assembly line during the 1920s. How would such a method of production have helped workers assemble an automobile in less than two hours?

did not share in the business **prosperity,** or well-being, of the 1920s. Many of these businesses suffered because of the sale of new goods. Companies that made cotton and woolen goods were among these businesses. Why do you think this was so? As the use of gas and electricity became greater, some coal mines were forced to shut down. Between 1923 and 1929 nearly 200,000 coal miners lost their jobs. And most of the country's railroads suffered heavy losses during this time.

Farmers were another group that did not share in the well-being of the 1920s. During World War I there had been a great demand for farm goods. So American farmers had planted large crops. But after the war, the demand for farm goods was not as great. Farmers found that they could not sell all the crops that they had grown. And they could get only very low prices for the crops they could sell. Many farmers lost their farms. Why do you think this happened?

The stock-market crash By the end of the 1920s there were signs that our country was headed for trouble. Much of the country's wealth was in the hands of a few people. And many people did not have money to buy the goods being produced. This caused factories to cut back on production. What do you think this did to workers?

Throughout the 1920s many people had bought **stock,** or shares, in different companies. When business is good, the price of stock in many companies goes up, and people make money. When business is bad, the price of stock in many companies goes down. What do you think happens to people's money then?

In October of 1929 stock prices began falling. Many people started selling their stocks. This caused stock prices to drop even more. This was known as the stock-market crash. Thousands of people who owned stocks lost large amounts of money. Many banks had also bought stock. When the stock market crashed, such banks lost so much money that in time

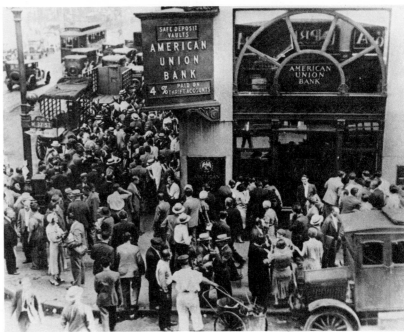

The picture on the left shows coal miners out of work in 1925. The picture on the right shows people outside the American Union Bank in New York City after the bank was ordered to close.

some of them had to close. Look at the picture at the upper right of this page. How did people who had placed their savings in these banks react? How do you think these people felt?

The prosperity that many Americans had enjoyed was over. All over our country, people were without jobs and homes. This was the beginning of the Great Depression. And unlike the earlier depression of the 1920s, this one would last much longer and would cause much greater suffering.

wrap ·up

- What were some of the reasons for the depression of 1921?
- What were some businesses that grew during the 1920s?
- Why did the prosperity of the 1920s turn into the Great Depression?

Reading a bar graph

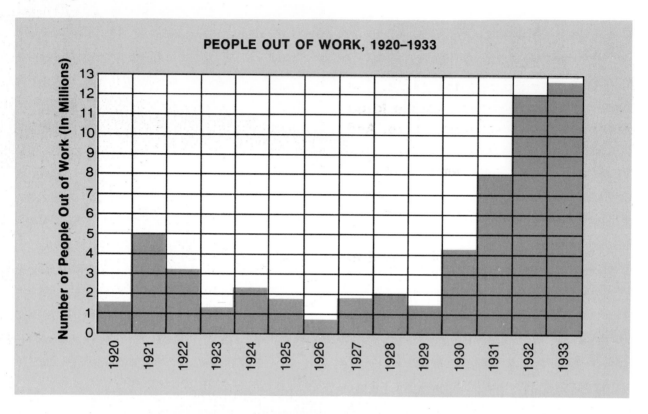

PEOPLE OUT OF WORK, 1920–1933

Use the graph to answer the following questions:

1. What does the graph show?

2. In what year was the number of people out of work the lowest?

3. In what year was the number of people out of work the highest?

4. According to the graph, about how many more people were out of work in 1933 than in 1926?

5. Between which years shown on the graph did the number of people out of work increase the most?

3

Good times and bad times

Americans on the move The automobile changed not only American business life but also the way many Americans lived during the 1920s. The automobile allowed more people to go places they had never been before. And it allowed more people to do things they had never done before. Do you think the automobile gave Americans a new sense of freedom? Why or why not?

The use of the automobile helped to bring people in urban places and people in rural places closer together. People who lived on farms or in small towns could drive to cities for shopping and entertainment. **Suburbs,** or small communities on the outskirts of cities, began to grow. How do you think the use of automobiles and buses led to the growth of such communities?

In 1920, for the first time in the history of our country, more people lived in cities than on farms. People went to the cities in search of jobs. Rapidly growing cities began to change in many ways. Huge apartment buildings were built for housing. And skyscrapers were built to provide office space for the many growing businesses in our

This picture, taken in 1926, shows the crowded streets of New York City during that time. Notice the traffic tower in the middle of the street. What problems did these New Yorkers face during the 1920s that New Yorkers still face today?

country. Some parts of cities became overcrowded. And many people in cities lived in poor housing. What problems do you think this might have caused?

The new woman   The 1920s also brought about many changes for women in the United States. In 1920 the Nineteenth Amendment gave women the right to vote. This meant that women were able to take an active part in the running of our country's government. During the 1920s more women also worked outside the home than ever before. World War I had opened up many new jobs for women. Millions of women went to work in factories and in offices. Many women worked at jobs that had once been held only by men.

The use of electricity also changed the way of life for American women. Electric washing machines, stoves, irons, and vacuum cleaners helped women have time for things other than cooking and cleaning. Women of the 1920s wore short hair and short skirts, both of which were thought to be quite daring. How do these things show that women were enjoying a new-found freedom during the 1920s?

A time of fear and distrust   The 1920s were years of fear and distrust for many people. Some Americans did not accept people whose backgrounds, beliefs, or ideas were different from their own. Americans feared that some groups of people were planning to overthrow the United States government. Because of this fear, thousands of immigrants were arrested. Many were sent back to where they had come from. But most of these people had done nothing against the United States.

The United States had always welcomed immigrants from western and northern Europe. After World War I many people came to the United States from eastern and southern Europe. These people had different languages and different ways of life from people who already lived in our country. And these European immigrants were willing to work for lower

A new way of life was enjoyed by many American women during the 1920s. Some women became an important part of the American work force. What kind of work are the women on the left doing? Some women, like the ones pictured below, showed their independence with new dress styles. Such women were known as flappers.

pay than some Americans were willing to work for. So in 1921 our government passed a law that cut down on the number of immigrants who could come to the United States. How did this law show that many Americans had strong feelings against people they thought were different?

Prohibition In January of 1920 the Eighteenth Amendment put a stop to the making and selling of alcohol in our country. This is called **prohibition**. Prohibition in the United States lasted fourteen years. But many Americans did not obey this law.

Some people made alcohol in their basements or backyards. And alcohol was brought into the United States from Canada and the West Indies. People sold alcohol in bars called speakeasies.

Gangs made hugh amounts of money and became very powerful from making and selling alcohol. By the end of the 1920s, it was clear that prohibition had not worked. So it was ended in 1933 by the Twenty-first Amendment.

Entertainment and heroes   During the 1920s Americans wanted to have fun and enjoy life. They learned new dances called the Charleston and the Black Bottom. They listened to a kind of music called jazz. And they enjoyed sports, such as baseball, football, boxing, tennis, and golf. How do such activities show that Americans had much free time?

The 1920s were also a time of heroes. Millions of Americans became interested in the lives of great sports figures and famous movie stars. But one of the greatest heroes of the time was neither a sports figure nor a movie star. On May 20, 1927, Charles Lindbergh became the first person to fly nonstop from New York City, New York, to Paris, France. Look at the picture on this page. How did the people of New York City greet Lindbergh when he returned home after his famous flight?

After Charles Lindbergh's flight across the Atlantic, he was a hero to millions of people. Huge crowds greeted him wherever he went. And he received medals and honors from leaders throughout the world.

Depression grips our country
After the stock-market crash of 1929, many factories, mines, mills, banks, stores, and businesses shut down. By 1932 about 12 million Americans were out of work. Some people sold apples for pennies on street corners. Other people stood in long lines to get free bread and soup.

Between 1929 and 1934, thousands of Americans lost their homes. About half the farmers in our country lost their farms. Many people packed up all their belongings in old trucks and cars and headed for California. Thousands of black families left the South and moved north looking for jobs. Many of these families were forced to live in shack towns on the edge of large cities.

Conditions throughout the country were getting worse. Something had to be done. In 1932 Franklin Roosevelt was elected President of the United States. Americans looked to President Roosevelt to give them hope for the future.

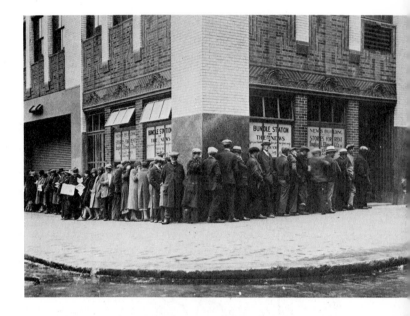

During the Great Depression, scenes such as this were common. Thousands stood in lines waiting to receive free food or clothing. At no other time in our country's history was there so much human suffering.

wrap·up
- How did the automobile and electric machines change the way of life for many Americans?
- How were fear and distrust of some groups of people shown during the 1920s?
- How did the depression affect the lives of Americans throughout our country?

A Biographical Sketch

One of the greats

A new kind of music was played in the United States toward the end of the 1800s. It was called jazz. This kind of music had its beginnings in the American South. But between 1910 and 1920 it began to spread throughout our country.

The 1920s are often called the golden age of jazz. During this time there were many great stars of jazz. One of these greats was Duke Ellington.

Ellington was born in 1899 in Washington, D.C. He had a happy childhood

and loved baseball, football, and going to the movies. By the time Ellington finished high school, music had become an important part of his life. He formed a jazz band along with five other musicians.

In 1922 Ellington and the other members of the band went to New York City. After a while Ellington became leader of the band. At first life in New York City was hard for this new jazz band. But by late 1927 Ellington and his band began playing at a well-known club. They played there for nearly five years. During this time they made recordings of their music. How do you think this helped Ellington and his band become well-known throughout the United States and Europe?

Duke Ellington did much for American music. He was a piano player, a bandleader, and a writer of music. He gave of his time and talent so others could enjoy and learn from his music.

Throughout his career, Ellington helped many new musicians get started. And he received many honors for his work. Duke Ellington died in 1974. But he is not forgotten. He is remembered by those who continue to listen to and to enjoy his music.

Chapter-End Activities

The chapter-end activities may be done by writing the questions or statements and the answers on a separate sheet of paper or by writing just the answers on a separate sheet of paper, whichever your teacher desires.

Words and Terms

prohibition   installment plan
prosperity   Kellogg-Briand Pact
World Court   stock
depression   suburbs

1. In 1920 the _____ was set up to settle problems between countries.
2. The countries that signed the _____ agreed not to go to war except in self-defense.
3. During a _____ businesses fail, and many people are out of work.
4. People who buy goods on the _____ make small monthly payments over a long time.
5. When business is good, the price of _____ in many companies goes up, and people make money.
6. _____, or small communities on the outskirts of cities, grew during the 1920s.
7. During _____ it was against the law to make or sell alcohol.

Fact Recall

1. In what ways did the United States work for world peace in the 1920s?
2. What industry had become our country's biggest business by the end of the 1920s?
3. What were some results of the stock-market crash of 1929?
4. In what ways were the 1920s years of fear and distrust for many people?
5. What did Charles Lindbergh do to become a hero in the 1920s?

Concepts and Understandings

1. Why did the United States try to withdraw from the world in the early 1920s?
2. Why was the United States plunged into the Great Depression?
3. How did the way of life change for many Americans during the 1920s?

Franklin Roosevelt became President of the United States on March 4, 1933. On that day he told the American people, "The only thing we have to fear is fear itself." What do you think President Roosevelt meant by this? During the 1930s President Roosevelt led the American people in the battle against the Great Depression. Much was done to help Americans throughout our country.

By 1940 most Americans became concerned about the threat of war in Europe and in the Far East. And in 1941 the United States became involved in another world war. This war was fought not only on the battlefront but also on the home front. In this chapter you will learn how President Roosevelt worked to try to bring our country out of the Great Depression. You will also learn why the United States became involved in World War II. And you will learn how Americans helped our country during the war.

1

A time of government programs

Relief, recovery, and reform When Franklin Roosevelt became President, millions of people in our country were out of work. Thousands were homeless. And many Americans had lost all faith in their government. Roosevelt believed that the United States government should play a major part in bringing our country out of its hard times. So President Roosevelt and his advisers set up a new government program to deal with the problems of the Great Depression. This program was called the **New Deal.**

The New Deal had three major goals. The first goal was to offer relief right away to those Americans in need. The second goal was to help American businesses recover. And the third goal was to make reforms so that hard times would not come to our country again. Do you think the goals of the New Deal helped Americans have faith in the United States government once again? Why or why not?

Our country's money problems Between 1929 and 1933 nearly 5,000 banks had failed. People no longer trusted banks. Many people were withdrawing all their savings. So President

Frances Perkins, shown here meeting with steelworkers in Pittsburgh, Pennsylvania, was President Roosevelt's secretary of labor from 1933 to 1945. She was the first woman in our country's history to serve as a member of a President's Cabinet.

Roosevelt ordered all banks in the United States closed. He then ordered government officials to check and see which banks were strong. Only these banks were allowed to open again.

A short time later an act was passed that set up the Federal Deposit Insurance Corporation (FDIC). This program protects people's savings up to a certain amount. President Roosevelt also called upon the government to place certain safeguards on the stock market. All these things helped Americans begin to have faith in banks and in the stock market once again.

Dealing with workers and business President Roosevelt felt it was not enough just to give people handouts. He felt that what people really needed was work. So he asked the government to set up programs that made work for people without jobs. The Civilian Conservation Corps (CCC) put many young people to work. Look at the picture at the left of page 405. Young people such as these planted trees, built dams, cleared streams, and fought forest fires. The Works Progress Administration (WPA) also put people to work. Workers built such things as bridges, highways, streets, parks, and airports.

Some people did not think it was right that the government was paying people for jobs such as these. But President Roosevelt defended these programs. He said that these jobs raised the spirit of people in our country. And he said that these jobs gave people money with which to buy things. How would this be of help to businesses in the United States?

The National Industrial Recovery Act (NIRA) was passed in 1933 to aid businesses in the United States. All businesses were asked to draw up a set of rules. These rules covered such things as prices, working conditions, and the amount of goods factories could make.

Later, the Wagner Act was passed. This act gave workers the right to join unions. And it set up the National Labor Relations Board (NLRB) to make certain that workers were treated

The picture on the left shows CCC workers planting trees in Massachusetts. How would planting trees improve the land in this picture? The picture above shows Illinois farmers destroying milk during the early 1930s. They did this in hopes of raising milk prices.

fairly. The Fair Labor Standards Act, passed in 1938, put an end to working long hours for low pay. This act stated that workers must receive no less than a certain hourly pay. And it stated that people could not work more than a certain number of hours during a week. Why would these things be important to workers?

Helping farmers and homeowners Many of the problems our country's farmers faced during the 1920s and early 1930s were brought about because of too many crops. So the goal of one of the New Deal measures was to have farmers grow less crops. The Agricultural Adjustment Administration (AAA) asked farmers not to grow crops on some of their land. If a farmer agreed, the government paid the farmer. This cut down on farm output and caused farm prices to go up.

The highest dam built by the Tennessee Valley Authority was Fontana Dam, pictured below. This dam, built on the Little Tennessee River in North Carolina, is 480 feet (146 meters) high. Besides providing power for electricity, such dams also provided means for flood control.

Other New Deal measures also helped farmers in the United States. Loans were given to farmers so that they could buy back the farms they had lost. Loans were also given to farm workers so that those who wished to buy farms could do so. A plan was set up to bring electricity to many farms throughout the United States. How do you think these things would be of help to farmers?

In 1933 the Home Owners Loan Corporation (HOLC) was set up. It loaned money to homeowners so they could pay what they owed on their homes. And the Federal Housing Administration (FHA) was set up to help banks make such loans. It also made loans for building, repairing, and improving homes or farm buildings. Do you think these were important New Deal measures? Why do you think so?

Other New Deal programs In 1933 the Tennessee Valley Authority (TVA) was set up. The TVA built a number of dams on the Tennessee River. These dams brought electricity to millions of people for the first time. The TVA improved life for many people in the Tennessee Valley.

In 1935 the Social Security Act was passed. President Roosevelt believed that this was the most important measure of the New Deal. This act provides a monthly income for retired people and for people who are not able to work. It also gives aid to other people in our country who are in need of help.

Another New Deal measure was the Indian Reorganization Act. This act once again gave American Indians the right to tribal ownership of land. It also helped Indian children learn about the history and the way of life of their people. Do you think this was an important act for the Indians in our country? Why or why not?

More government programs were set up during the New Deal than at any other time in our country's history. Some New Deal measures have been done away with. But some still exist today. Not all Americans agreed with the New Deal. Some said the government had done too much. Others said the government had not done enough. But the New Deal had brought aid to millions of Americans when they needed it the most.

John Collier, commissioner of Indian affairs from 1933 to 1945, was largely responsible for the passage of the Indian Reorganization Act. This picture shows Commissioner Collier with two American Indians in 1939. What are the Indians showing Collier?

wrap ·up

- What were the three major goals of the New Deal?
- What were some New Deal programs that put people to work?
- How did the New Deal come to the aid of many needy Americans?

A Biographical Sketch

First Lady of the World

Eleanor Roosevelt was born on October 11, 1884. Her parents died when she was quite young, so she and her brother were raised by their grandmother. When Eleanor was fifteen, she went to Britain to attend school. After three years, she returned to the United States. On March 17, 1905, Eleanor married her distant cousin Franklin Delano Roosevelt.

In 1921 Franklin Roosevelt became ill with polio. For the rest of his life Franklin was not able to use his legs. Eleanor encouraged her husband never to give up. With her help, he became President of the United States.

As First Lady, Mrs. Roosevelt served our country in many ways. She traveled throughout our country talking with people and letting them know she cared. She visited slums, coal mines, prisons, factories, schools, and hospitals. When the United States went to war, she visited the soldiers overseas.

After President Roosevelt died, Eleanor Roosevelt continued to serve our country. She also fought for the rights and freedom of people throughout the world. She was no longer the First Lady of the United

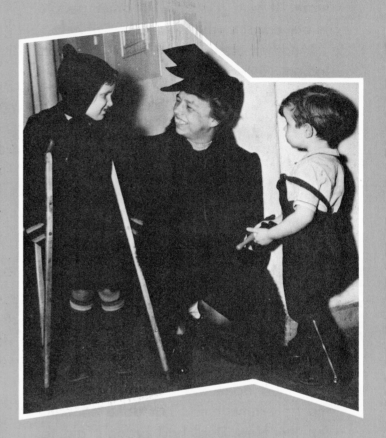

States, but she was thought of as the First Lady of the World. Do you think this is a good name for Eleanor Roosevelt? Why or why not?

Eleanor Roosevelt died at the age of seventy-eight. She had done much good in her lifetime. She had loved and cared for all people no matter who they were or where they were from. She is remembered by many people as one of the greatest women in the history of our country.

2

Relations with others and World War II

Being a good neighbor and granting independence
President Roosevelt continued the work of earlier Presidents to
stay on good terms with Latin American countries. Roosevelt's
Good-Neighbor Policy, as it was called, led to a number of
meetings between the United States and Latin America. At
these meetings it was agreed that no American country had
the right to interfere in the matters of any other American
country. It was also agreed that problems between American
countries would be settled peacefully. Do you think these
things were important to the United States? Why or why not?

Since 1898 the Philippine Islands had been under the control of the United States. But in 1934 the Tydings-McDuffie
Act was passed. This act stated that the Philippines would
become a free country ten years after they had drawn up a
constitution. So on July 4, 1946, the United States granted
full independence to the Philippines.

Another world war After World War I, some countries
in Europe and in Asia came under the rule of **dictators.** Dictators are leaders who have complete power over the country
in which they rule. Benito Mussolini of Italy, Adolf Hitler of
Germany, and Hideki Tojo of Japan were three such leaders.
The people of these countries did not have a say in their government. How is this different from the rights United States
citizens have?

During the 1930s Italy, Germany, and Japan were a threat
to world peace. They built up large armies and large supplies
of weapons. In 1931 they began attacking and taking over
other countries. In 1936 Germany and Italy formed an alliance. They were called the **Axis Powers.** Within three years

Germany had taken over much of Europe. Britain and France knew that Hitler had to be stopped. So on September 3, 1939, these two countries declared war on Germany. World War II had begun.

The United States helps   During the middle 1930s our government passed a number of laws to keep the United States out of the troubles in Europe. In 1939, though, these laws were changed. The **Allied Powers,** or those countries who fought against the Axis Powers, were in need of help. The United States came to their aid in a number of ways.

In 1940 President Roosevelt met with Winston Churchill, the government leader of Britain. The United States gave fifty warships to Britain. And in 1941 the United States passed the Lend-Lease Act. This act stated that the United States could lend or lease such things as weapons, airplanes, and warships

Adolf Hitler, pictured on the left, was dictator of Germany from 1933 to 1945. He organized a group called the Nazi party to help him gain power. The picture below shows Franklin Roosevelt and Winston Churchill meeting together in 1941. At this meeting, plans for stopping Hitler were discussed.

Battleship Row—a line of battleships in port—was a major target of the Japanese attack on Pearl Harbor. Of the eight battleships that were sunk, five were repaired and put to use again.

to any country whose defense was important to the United States. Many Americans believed that by helping the Allied Powers the United States could stay out of the war. But some Americans did not agree. They were afraid this act would bring the United States into the war.

The United States declares war   In September of 1940 Japan joined the Axis Powers. The Japanese knew that the United States was the only country that could stop them in the Pacific. So they planned attacks to weaken American power in the Pacific. At dawn on December 7, 1941, about 360 Japanese planes attacked the American naval base at Pearl Harbor, Hawaii. Look at the picture on this page. Eight American battleships were sunk, many American planes were destroyed, and more than 2,300 Americans were killed. That same day the Japanese also attacked other American bases in the Pacific.

The next day President Roosevelt asked Congress to declare war on Japan. On December 11, Germany and Italy declared war on the United States. The United States then declared war on these two countries.

The war in Europe When the United States entered the war, Hitler and Mussolini controlled most of Europe, northern Africa, and parts of the Soviet Union. But toward the end of 1942, the Allied Powers began to stop the Germans and Italians. In northern Africa, British soldiers defeated the Germans at the Battle of El Alamein [EHL-AL-uh-MAYN]. And in the Soviet Union, the Germans were defeated at Stalingrad. These two battles were important turning points of the war.

On June 6, 1944, the Allied armies landed on the coast of Normandy in France. They were led by General Dwight Eisenhower. By May 8, 1945, the German Army had been defeated, and Germany surrendered. The world then learned of the deaths of both Hitler and Mussolini. And the world learned of the terrible happenings in concentration camps throughout central and eastern Europe. More than 6 million people, mostly Jews, had died horrible deaths in such camps.

The war in the Pacific After winning the victory in Europe, the Allied Powers turned their full attention to the war in the Pacific. President Roosevelt had died one month be-

In April of 1945, American troops set free about 21,000 survivors of Buchenwald [BOO-kuhn-WAWLD] concentration camp in Germany. More than 100,000 people had died at the camp during the war.

fore the war ended in Europe. So it was up to President Truman to bring the war with Japan to an end.

The Battle of Midway Island in 1942 was a turning point in the war in the Pacific. This battle was important to the Allied Powers because it ended Japanese threats to Hawaii and to the United States. During 1943 and 1944 Allied land, sea, and air forces attacked major islands in the Pacific. By 1945 war factories and important harbors in Japan were being bombed. President Truman ordered the Japanese to give up, but they refused.

President Truman then decided to use the atomic bomb. He believed it would end the war and save lives. So he gave the order for an atomic bomb to be dropped on Hiroshima [HIHR-uh-SHEE-muh], Japan. Two days later another atomic bomb was dropped. On September 2, 1945, Japan signed the terms of surrender. World War II was over.

The picture at the upper right shows the mushroom cloud of an atomic bomb. Moments after such a bomb was dropped on Hiroshima, Japan, the city was in ruins. What kinds of destruction were caused by the bomb?

wrap ·up

- How did the United States show it wanted to be a good neighbor during the 1930s?
- How did the United States help the Allied Powers before our country entered World War II?
- Why did the United States enter World War II in 1941?

Using Your Skills

Reading a map

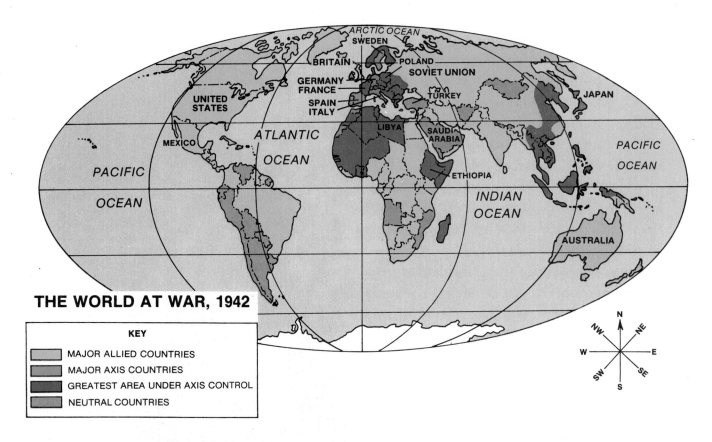

THE WORLD AT WAR, 1942

KEY	
	MAJOR ALLIED COUNTRIES
	MAJOR AXIS COUNTRIES
	GREATEST AREA UNDER AXIS CONTROL
	NEUTRAL COUNTRIES

Use the map to answer the following questions:

1. What does the map show?

2. What were three major Allied countries during World War II?

3. What were three major Axis countries during World War II?

4. What were three countries under Axis control in 1942?

5. What were three neutral countries in 1942?

6. Why do you think this war was called a world war?

3

Our country's people pull together

Building up our forces When the United States entered World War II, many Americans were needed to build up our country's armed forces. During the war, as many as 10 million men were drafted. Thousands of men joined the armed services on their own. And over 250,000 women joined different branches of the armed services. Some women drove jeeps and trucks during the war. Others repaired machinery and operated radios.

More than 15 million Americans served in our country's armed forces during World War II. People from different backgrounds did their part to help. American Indians helped our country during the war by breaking enemy codes. More than a half million blacks were sent overseas during the war. And many Mexican Americans also fought for our country. Several black companies and Mexican-American companies received special honors for their part in the war.

Treatment of Japanese Americans After the attack on Pearl Harbor, many people in our country did not trust Japanese Americans. It was feared that these people would be more

During World War II members of the 92nd Division were awarded special honors for their part in the war effort. This picture shows the 92nd Division during a battle in Italy. How are these soldiers showing their bravery?

This picture shows Japanese Americans on their way to relocation camps during World War II. Most of the camps were located in undesirable parts of our country. How can you tell from this picture that these people were treated as prisoners?

loyal to Japan than to the United States. Early in 1942, around 117,000 Japanese Americans were taken from their homes and moved to camps throughout our country. They lost much of what they owned, and they were treated as prisoners.

Japanese Americans were angry and hurt because of the way they were treated. A few gave up their American citizenship because of it. But most remained loyal to the United States throughout the war. Many of them joined the armed forces. Like other Americans, they fought bravely to help bring peace to our country again.

From peacetime to wartime production When the United States entered World War II, it did not have nearly enough war materials to fight a major war. So President Roosevelt set up the War Production Board. The goal of this board was to change our country's industries from peacetime to wartime production. Factories that once made such things as washing machines and automobiles began making tanks, airplanes, and guns instead. Many mines, steel mills, and factories throughout the country were kept open twenty-four hours a day. And over 5 million new workers were hired. Young people and older people all did their part. Almost every person who could work did so. Women, such as those pictured on this page, worked in factories making such things as ships, weapons, ammunition, and airplanes. By 1944 the United States was producing more war goods than all the Axis Powers put together. How do you think this helped the Allied Powers in the war?

Farmers also played an important part in the war effort. From 1941 to 1945 American farmers raised greater amounts of crops and livestock than ever before. They helped to meet the needs of our country's people at home and in the armed services. They also helped to meet the needs of people in other Allied countries.

Paying for the war The cost of World War II was the highest of any war in our country's history. Between 1940 and 1946 the United States government spent more than $350 billion on the war. Much of this money came from taxes, which were raised to high levels during the war.

The United States government also sold war bonds. This was a way by which the government could borrow money to help pay for the war. United States citizens and businesses bought billions of dollars worth of bonds. This was still another way in which many Americans helped our country during the war.

During World War II women played a very important part in our country's production of war materials. By 1943 more than 2 million women were working in America's war industries. The women in the picture below are working on a transport plane.

During World War II posters such as this urged Americans to cut back their use of certain goods so that the goods could be used for the war effort. What does this poster urge Americans to do?

Everyone helps During the war Americans at home learned to do without many things. Many goods and raw materials were hard to get. Some goods were needed for the war. And the major source of other goods, such as rubber, was cut off during the war. So the government **rationed** these goods. This meant that the government allowed people to buy only certain amounts of these goods. Meat, sugar, butter, coffee, canned goods, shoes, gasoline, tires, and fuel oil were rationed. Why do you think this was so?

Nearly every American did something to help in the war effort. Many people planted vegetable gardens so food that farmers grew could be used for the armed services. People gathered scrap metal, old tires, paper, and even empty toothpaste tubes to be used to make war goods. Many Americans also willingly gave blood to the Red Cross Blood Bank to help save the lives of those wounded in battle.

wrap ·up

- How did Americans help build up our country's armed forces during World War II?
- How did the United States increase its production to meet the needs of the war?
- How did Americans at home help in the war effort?

Chapter-End Activities

The chapter-end activities may be done by writing the questions or statements and the answers on a separate sheet of paper or by writing just the answers on a separate sheet of paper, whichever your teacher desires.

Words and Terms

Social Security Act   rationed
War Production Board   New Deal
Allied Powers   dictators
Axis Powers   war bonds
Fair Labor Standards Act

In 1934 President Roosevelt began a program called the __(1)__ to bring our country out of the Great Depression. Under this program the __(2)__ was passed to help workers. And the __(3)__ was passed to help retired people or people who were not able to work.

After World War I __(4)__, or leaders with complete power, ruled Germany, Italy, and Japan. These countries were called the __(5)__. The countries that fought against Germany, Italy, and Japan were called the __(6)__.

During World War II, our government sold __(7)__ to help pay for the war. It also __(8)__ goods that were hard to get, such as shoes and gasoline.

Fact Recall

1. What were some New Deal programs that made work for people?

2. What did the Indian Reorganization Act provide for?

3. What was the policy of the United States toward Latin America during the 1930s called?

4. Who was the leader of Germany during World War II?

5. What happened to Japanese Americans in the United States during World War II?

Concepts and Understandings

1. How did the New Deal help millions of needy Americans?

2. How did the United States become involved in World War II?

3. How did Americans help our country during World War II?

CHAPTER 23

Our Country and Unsettled Times

Throughout many years of United States history, our country tried to mind its own business. During many periods of its history, the United States tried to withdraw from world affairs. But World War II was a turning point for our country. When the fighting stopped in 1945, our country was one of the two most powerful countries in the world. Many people in other countries turned to the United States for help after the war. Why do you think these things helped the United States take its place as a world leader after World War II?

The war also brought about changes within our country. Changes took place in our businesses and in our way of life. In this chapter you will learn about many changes in our country and in the world between 1945 and 1960.

1

The government and the economy

Changing to a peacetime economy While our country was still fighting World War II, government leaders began to make plans for a peacetime **economy**. An economy is the way people make, get, and use goods and services. Government leaders knew that after the war, many Americans who were in the armed services would need jobs.

In 1944 Congress passed the GI Bill of Rights. This bill set aside money for people returning from the armed services. Much of this money could be used for schooling. So when the war was over, many people attended college instead of taking jobs. How do you think this bill helped make sure that many people could find jobs?

After the war, government-run factories were sold to private companies. Many factories that had made goods for the war began to make goods for citizens. These factories began to make such things as cars and household goods. Many Americans had money that they had saved during the war. They were eager to buy goods they had not been able to get during the war. What do you think this did for business in our country after the war?

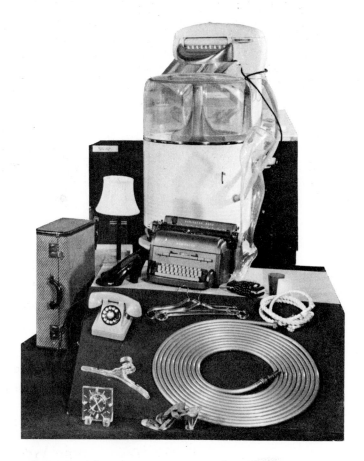

After World War II, American factories began to make more household goods from plastics. This picture shows some of the goods that were made from plastics at that time. What were some of these goods?

421

Taking an active role   In 1946 Congress passed the Full Employment Act. This act made the United States government responsible for our country's economy. The act gave our government certain powers to deal with business and money problems.

Our government had to deal with two major problems during the late 1940s and the 1950s. These were business slowdowns and rising prices. The government generally spent more money during business slowdowns. The government also cut taxes during such times. This meant that Americans had more money to spend on goods. How do you think this helped get business moving again? During times of rapidly rising prices, the government generally spent less money and raised taxes. Americans had less money to spend. So they stopped buying certain high-priced goods. This helped cause prices to drop. How do these things show that our government was active in our country's economy?

Our country's government also aided companies whose business helped the public. One such business was that of putting atomic power to peaceful use. An atomic power plant is pictured on this page. This plant was built to produce electricity. How do you think such plants helped supply needed power?

This private atomic power plant in Connecticut supplies electricity for homes and for businesses. Such plants were first built during the 1950s.

The government also tried to help farmers. Farmers generally shared less in the prosperity of our country than other people did. This was because of too many crops and falling farm prices. The government aided farmers by helping to keep the price they got for certain farm goods from becoming too low. And the government paid farmers for not growing crops on some of their land. How do you think this helped farmers?

Working people and union power Rapidly rising prices caused problems for working people. Workers found that they had to earn more money just to keep up with rising prices. Many unions called strikes in order to get higher pay for their members. In one year, more than 4 million workers, like those pictured on this page, went on strike.

Many Americans began to think that unions were too powerful. This was because they could upset many of our country's important businesses. So Congress passed the Taft-Hartley Act in 1947. This act outlawed some things that unions had done in the past. The act also gave the President the power to stop strikes that put people's health or safety in danger. Do you think union leaders agreed with the Taft-Hartley Act? Why or why not?

These telephone workers went on strike in 1947. It was the first time workers in this industry went on strike throughout the United States. About 250,000 workers were involved in this strike. What were some of the things these workers wanted?

The growth of big businesses   During the 1950s, big businesses grew even bigger. Some of the biggest companies were worth many billions of dollars. Companies of this size often bought smaller businesses. In this way, huge companies that made many different kinds of goods began to grow.

As huge companies began to grow, small companies found it hard to stay in business. Big companies had more money to spend for making and selling goods. And many big companies could sell goods for lower prices than small companies could. Why do you think this hurt the business of small companies? The government tried to help small companies by setting up the Small Business Administration (SBA). The SBA loaned money to small companies.

Changes in American industries   Between 1945 and 1960, many kinds of goods became more widely used than they had been before. The making of cars and trucks became a bigger business than ever before. As the number of cars and trucks in our country grew, people needed more gasoline and better highways. How do you think this helped other businesses become important?

Companies began making jet airplanes during the 1950s. Electronic goods, such as telephones and television, also

Television became widely available to American families after World War II. During the 1950s television changed the way many people used their free time. What does this picture show about the popularity of television in an American home?

became more widely used than they had been. Some companies began to make new kinds of goods. And it became more important for companies to **advertise,** or to tell the public about their goods. Why do you think this was so?

During the 1950s, many companies began to make goods through **automation.** This is the use of machines to run other machines. Through automation, companies made more and better goods at a lower cost than before. But the use of machines put many people out of work. Why do you think this happened? Why do you think many people were needed for new jobs, such as planning or repairing machines?

Our country became interested in outer space during the 1950s. The picture on this page shows *Explorer I.* This was our country's first **satellite,** or human-made object that circles the earth.

Explorer I *was attached to the top of a Jupiter-C rocket. The rocket provided the great power needed to send the satellite into outer space.*

wrap ·up

- How did our country change from a wartime economy to a peacetime economy?
- How did the United States government take an active role in our country's economy between 1945 and 1960?
- How did American industries change after World War II?

Using Your Skills

Reading a line graph

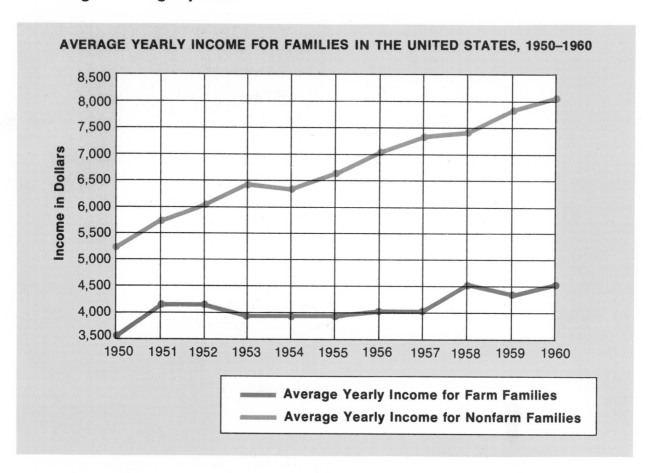

AVERAGE YEARLY INCOME FOR FAMILIES IN THE UNITED STATES, 1950–1960

Income in Dollars

— Average Yearly Income for Farm Families
— Average Yearly Income for Nonfarm Families

Use this graph to answer the following questions:

1. What was the average yearly income for farm families in 1950? What was the average yearly income for nonfarm families?

2. In 1953, did the average yearly income for farm families increase or decrease? Did the average yearly income for nonfarm families increase or decrease?

3. In 1957, about how much less was the average yearly income for farm families than for nonfarm families?

4. Which increased more from 1950 to 1960—the average yearly income for farm families or the average yearly income for nonfarm families?

2

Changing American patterns

A time of suspicion After World War II, **communism** began to spread through parts of Europe. Communism is a form of government that is generally ruled by a committee that has complete power over a country and its people. Those who favor this form of government are known as **Communists.** Many Americans feared that Communists in the United States might try to overthrow our country's government.

Congress began to look into the matter in the late 1940s. Then during the early 1950s, Senator Joseph McCarthy of Wisconsin charged that there were Communists in government offices. The picture on this page shows McCarthy asking questions about the Communists in our country. McCarthy made charges against many Americans whom he thought were or had once been Communists. Many of those charges turned out to be false. But a number of people had their good name destroyed. This happened even though charges were proved false or were never proved at all.

During the years that McCarthy was making charges, many Americans became worried. They were afraid that Americans

*Senator Joseph McCarthy, standing to the left of the chart, led a series of **hearings**, or meetings at which people were questioned, about Communist activities. In 1954 the Senate openly found fault with McCarthy for his actions at those meetings.*

The Supreme Court ruling that allowed black students to enter public schools was not quickly accepted in some parts of our country. In 1957, three years after the ruling had been made, President Eisenhower sent soldiers to Little Rock, Arkansas, so that black students could enter this high school.

were losing the right to have their own ideas. Why do you think some people felt this way? By 1954 many people had stopped believing McCarthy's charges. And many people felt that the government should not try to control what people thought or said.

Working for civil rights Many black Americans began to work for their **civil rights**—their rights as United States citizens—during the 1950s. Black Americans had joined the armed services during World War II. They also held jobs in government and in many industries. But blacks did not enjoy the same rights that whites did. And in many places, black people were **segregated** [SEHG-rih-GAYT-uhd], or separated, from white people.

In 1954 the Supreme Court ruled that black children must be allowed to attend public schools with white children. In some places this happened quickly. But in other places, soldiers were needed to protect black children who entered all-white schools. In still other places schools would remain segregated for years.

Black people began to work to change laws that they thought were unfair. One such law made blacks sit at the back of public buses. Some black people of Montgomery, Alabama, refused to ride the buses. For more than a year, the buses in Montgomery were nearly empty. Why do you think this caused the bus company to lose money? Dr. Martin Luther King, Jr., and other black leaders in Montgomery were arrested for working against the bus company. But by 1956, black people were no longer segregated on Montgomery buses.

The Civil Rights Act of 1957 also helped black Americans. This law was passed to protect voting rights. It set up a group to find out why blacks and certain other people were not allowed to vote in some places. During the 1950s, black Americans and others who had not been treated equally gained some of their civil rights. But these people knew that they still had a long way to go.

Americans on the move After World War II, Americans moved more often than ever before. This was partly because many people had more money. Transportation had improved. And people were willing to move to take different jobs.

Large numbers of Americans moved to suburbs. Between 1950 and 1960, suburbs grew more than four times faster than cities did. The picture on this page shows new houses in a suburb in the 1950s. Some people moved from one part of

In some suburbs that grew rapidly after World War II, the houses were built close together and looked very much alike. How is this community in New Jersey like the community in which you live? How is it different?

the country to another. The southern and western parts of our country grew rapidly during the 1950s. New jobs were opening in such places. And many people liked the climate of such states as Texas, Florida, and California.

Even though large numbers of people moved to the suburbs, other people moved to cities. Most of these people were looking for jobs. Many of these people were Puerto Ricans, Mexican Americans, and southern blacks. These people often came from poor, rural areas. How do you think their lives changed when they moved to urban settings? Why do you think many American cities had rapidly growing numbers of poor people?

The poor people in American cities could afford to live only in run-down neighborhoods. They had trouble finding jobs and often received poor health care. Their children had to attend run-down and highly crowded schools. The United States government tried to help such people by finding them jobs and by giving them money. The government also tore down slums to build new, low-rent housing. Some people felt that this kind of government aid did not work very well. They felt that poor people were being made to depend on the government. Some of those who received aid weren't so sure it was a good thing either. They thought government workers were looking into their private life to see if they deserved aid.

Advances in medicine   American doctors and scientists made many discoveries during the late 1940s and the 1950s. They found many things that helped people live longer. Some doctors found ways to keep people from getting certain diseases, such as polio. Doctors also discovered many new drugs with which to treat sicknesses.

During the 1950s, doctors found new ways to help people with heart diseases. The picture on page 431 shows a machine that takes over for a person's heart. The machine helps make it possible for a person's heart to stop beating while a doctor operates on it. The first such machine was used in 1953. How do you think such machines help to save people's lives?

Adding new states Our country added two new states in the 1950s. Alaska had belonged to our country since 1867. Many United States citizens had moved there during a gold rush around 1900. People in Alaska had wanted to join the United States for a long time. Alaska was finally made a state in 1959.

Hawaii became a state later that same year. The United States had annexed Hawaii in 1898. During World War II, Hawaii was the headquarters for our country's war against Japan. Why do you think this helped Hawaii become more important to our country?

Heart-lung machines, such as the one shown here, have made it possible for doctors to save the lives of many people with heart diseases.

wrap·up

- How did a fear of communism affect our country in the late 1940s and in the early 1950s?
- What happened during the 1950s to help black Americans gain some of their civil rights?
- How did some patterns of the American way of life change between 1945 and 1960?

A Biographical Sketch

Leading the fight against polio

Every year as summer began, people started to worry. This was because every summer thousands of people, mostly children, became ill with polio. This sickness sometimes kept people in bed for weeks. Many of these people lost the use of part of their body. And many others died.

Dr. Jonas Salk knew that very tiny living bodies called **viruses** [VY-ruhs-uhz] caused polio. He thought that there might be a way to give people small amounts of these viruses. Then their body would build up the defenses that would keep them from getting polio.

Salk began to work on this idea in 1949. He often worked sixteen hours a day, six days a week. In 1952 our country suffered the worst outbreak of polio ever. About 57,000 people were ill, and more than 3,000 people died of this sickness.

The next year Salk was ready to test a shot that was made up of the viruses that caused polio. Salk first tested the shots on himself. What does this tell you about Salk's belief in his own work? Later the shots were tested on almost 2 million schoolchildren. The shots were found to be safe, and they worked!

Most people in our country today are protected against polio. So this sickness has almost been wiped out in the United States. Thanks is due in part to Dr. Jonas Salk—one of the leaders in the fight against polio.

3

Our country as a world leader

Uneasy peace and cold war Plans for the United Nations (UN) began even before World War II ended. The UN was to be a world peacekeeping body and to help work out worldwide problems. Over the years, the UN has helped many countries. But it has also had many troubles. Some of these troubles have been caused by differences between countries that have a Communist government and those that do not.

Such differences also troubled the United States and the Soviet Union. These two countries had become the leading world powers. These countries each had a different form of government. They each had a different kind of economy. And they each had different ideas about the rights of citizens. The United States also thought that the Soviet Union was a threat to the free world. This was because the Soviet Union helped Communists gain power in a number of countries.

The differences between the United States and the Soviet Union led to a **cold war.** A cold war is a war of ideas that is generally carried on without shooting or bloodshed. For many

The UN headquarters in New York City was finished in 1952. The flags in front of this building represent some of the countries that are members of the United Nations.

years, the two countries prepared themselves in case the cold war became a shooting war. They built powerful **nuclear weapons.** These are weapons that release energy due to changes within certain atoms. A war fought with such weapons might destroy most of the world. Why do you think the cold war led to very careful relations between the United States and the Soviet Union?

New courses of action in Europe The United States wanted to keep communism from spreading. So our country joined with other countries that felt the same way. In 1949 the United States, Canada, and ten European countries formed the North Atlantic Treaty Organization (NATO). The members of NATO agreed to aid one another in case of attack.

In 1948 the United States set up the Marshall Plan. This plan sent money to European countries that had suffered great damage during the war. United States aid helped most of western Europe become strong again. This helped keep communism from spreading in western Europe.

After the war, the United States, Britain, France, and the Soviet Union each controlled a part of Germany. Berlin, Germany's largest city, was within the Soviet part of Germany. But parts of Berlin were controlled by the United

Like other Europeans, the Germans had much rebuilding to do after World War II. The German words mit hilfe *mean "with help." What United States program supplied aid for this rebuilding?*

States, Britain, and France. The Soviets wanted to take over all of Berlin. So they closed all roads and railroads that led into Berlin. How would this make the people of Berlin depend on the Soviet Union for supplies? The United States and Britain quickly began to send goods into Berlin by plane. After almost a year, the Soviets opened the roads and railroads. Much of Berlin remained free of Soviet rule.

Working against communism in Asia Soon after World War II, trouble broke out in China. Two groups of Chinese people—the Communists and the Nationalists—fought for power. The United States sent money and weapons to the Nationalists. But the Communists won. The United States then planned to stop the spread of communism in the rest of Asia.

The United States plan was first tested in Korea. After World War II, Korea was divided into two parts. In 1950 the Communist government in North Korea sent soldiers to attack South Korea. American troops, such as those pictured on this page, and a UN army aided South Korea. The North Koreans were aided by Communists from both the Soviet Union and China. In 1953 the fighting ended without a victory. But the United States had shown that it would use force to stop Communists from trying to take over a free country.

Helicopters were widely used to carry troops and supplies during the fighting in Korea. They also took the wounded to hospitals. According to this picture, why were helicopters useful in Korea?

During the early 1950s, much of Southeast Asia belonged to France. The United States sent aid to France to help fight Communists there. In 1954 the French were defeated. The land was divided into several countries, including Vietnam. Communists ruled North Vietnam. They also tried to gain power in South Vietnam, which was not a Communist country. Throughout the rest of the 1950s, the United States sent aid to South Vietnam. Why do you think our country did this?

Our role in the Middle East and in Africa In 1956 the Egyptian government took over the Suez Canal. This canal is an important trade route from Europe to the Far East. Soldiers from Britain, France, and Israel soon attacked Egypt. The Soviet Union then threatened to send help to Egypt. President Eisenhower asked the UN to order the attacking soldiers out of Egypt. When the soldiers withdrew, some people thought this was a victory for the Soviet Union. Why do you think they felt this way?

Shortly after the trouble in Egypt, President Eisenhower promised to help any country in the Middle East fight communism. Because of this promise, the United States sent soldiers to fight in Lebanon in 1958.

During the 1950s, many colonies in Africa gained their freedom. These new countries wanted help to build up their farming, manufacturing, and business. The United States aided some of these countries, and the Soviet Union aided others. Sometimes the Soviet Union aided one side or another when groups within a country fought each other. In some cases the UN stepped in to keep order. In general, however, African countries did not allow Communists to gain power.

Relations with our American neighbors Late in the 1950s, communism grew strong close to the United States. The island of Cuba is not far from the coast of Florida. Fidel Castro led an uprising in Cuba in 1959 and set up a Communist government. Many Cubans did not like Castro or the new

Huge ships that pass through the St. Lawrence Seaway go through several locks, such as the one shown here. Locks raise or lower ships from one level of the seaway to another to bypass waterfalls or dams.

government. Thousands of these people escaped to the United States.

The United States and Canada had worked together for many years. In 1959 the two countries finished building the St. Lawrence Seaway. This inland waterway is deep enough to be used by huge, oceangoing ships. The St. Lawrence Seaway, pictured on this page, connects the Atlantic Ocean with the Great Lakes. This seaway helped improve trade for United States cities and Canadian cities on the Great Lakes. Why do you think this was so?

wrap ·up

- What led to the cold war between the United States and the Soviet Union?
- How did the United States work against the spread of communism in the late 1940s and the 1950s?
- Why did the United States become involved in dealings with many countries in the late 1940s and the 1950s?

Chapter-End Activities

The chapter-end activities may be done by writing the questions or statements and the answers on a separate sheet of paper or by writing just the answers on a separate sheet of paper, whichever your teacher desires.

Words and Terms

cold war   economy
communism   satellite
civil rights   automation

1. The ____ is the way people make, get, and use goods.
2. The use of machines to run other machines is known as ____.
3. ____ is a form of government that is generally ruled by a committee that has complete power over a country and its people.
4. ____ are a person's rights as a United States citizen.
5. A ____ is a war of ideas that is generally carried on without shooting or bloodshed.

Fact Recall

1. What caused many unions in our country to call strikes during the late 1940s and the 1950s?
2. What were some manufactured goods that became more widely used between 1945 and 1960?
3. In what way did some black Americans work to change laws that they thought were unfair?
4. What were some problems faced by poor people in our country's cities between 1945 and 1960?
5. What caused a war to break out in Korea in 1950?

Concepts and Understandings

1. How did the government of the United States take an active role in our country's economy between 1945 and 1960?
2. How did the American way of life change between 1945 and 1960?
3. Why did the United States become a world leader after World War II had ended?

CHAPTER 24

Our Country and a Time of Awareness

1. A time of great challenge and change
2. Searching for peace in an unsettled world
3. A culture of awareness

The 1960s and 1970s were a time of awakening for many Americans. People in our country began to see a need for change. They began to work for equal rights for all citizens. And they became concerned about protecting our environment. The leaders of our country continued to work for peace in the world. And poor people throughout the world began to look to the United States for help.

Recent times are often the most difficult for us to understand. Why do you think this is so? This chapter will help you understand something about our country in recent times. You will learn about some changes that took place in our country during the 1960s and 1970s. You will find out how our country became a leader in the search for world peace. And you will learn how our culture mirrored the rapid changes in our country since the 1920s.

1

A time of great challenge and change

Problems of a large population
During the 1960s and 1970s our country had to find ways to meet the needs of more and more people. Most of our country's people lived in or near cities. Some people lived in **mega-lopolises** [MEHG-uh-LAHP-uh-luhs-uhz]. These are huge stretches of cities joined to one another. One of these was along the Atlantic coast from Boston, Massachusetts, to Washington, D.C.

The pictures on this page show another problem of our large population. This was **pollution,** or the changing of the state of our air, land, and water from clean to dirty. Americans were asked to fight pollution by saving goods

The 1960s and 1970s became a time of great concern for the environment. What kinds of pollution are shown in these pictures? Why do you think people were concerned about these things?

*This house uses **solar**, or the sun's, energy. Panels on the roof collect the energy, which is stored until it is needed.*

to **recycle,** or make over into new goods. What are some other ways that people might help fight pollution?

Another problem of our large population was the need for fuel. People were rapidly using up fuels, such as oil and gas. So people began looking for new ways of producing energy. Some houses and other buildings in our country began to use energy from the sun rather than from fuel.

Our country also had to consider the needs of people in different age groups. More than half our country's people were under thirty years of age. And because of better health care, people in our country lived longer. So there was a larger number of **senior citizens,** or old people, than ever before. What needs might these people have?

Concern for the rights of many Americans Throughout our country's history certain groups of people were not given their civil rights. Blacks, Mexican Americans, Oriental Americans, American Indians, and women were among those people. The 1960s and 1970s were a time of concern for the rights of all our country's people. A number of laws were passed to protect people's rights. Two such laws were the Civil Rights Act of 1964 and the Civil Rights Act of 1968.

The Twenty-fourth Amendment and other laws were passed to protect voting rights. The Twenty-sixth Amendment lowered the voting age from twenty-one to eighteen. By the late 1970s many people were working to pass the Equal Rights Amendment. This law would give women equal rights with men.

A number of laws were passed to protect the rights of consumers. One such law stated that goods must be labeled so that people could know exactly what they were buying. Another law made sure that certain goods had safety lids so that children could not open them easily. Why do you think laws such as these are important?

In 1968 thousands of people took part in a civil-rights march on Washington, D.C. It was the largest march of its kind in our country's history. What were the goals and demands of these marchers?

A better life for more people In 1964 President Johnson began a plan called the War on Poverty. This meant that the United States government would work to help our country's poor people. The Job Corps was set up in 1964 to train people for better jobs. The Department of Housing and Urban Development was set up in 1965. One of the things it did was help to build low-cost housing for poor people.

Other government programs of the 1960s and 1970s were set up to help old people. Many old people had to use much of their income to meet the rising cost of health care. In 1965 the government set up Medicare. This plan provided money for health care to anyone over sixty-five years old.

Challenging time and space One of the challenges of the 1960s and 1970s was how to keep up with a rapidly changing world. A number of things, which were changes themselves, helped Americans keep up with other changes. Computers made it possible to store large amounts of information for use when needed. These machines could answer number problems instantly. And they could also run other machines. How do you think computers helped people keep up with their fast-moving world?

Jet airplanes, such as the 747, made it possible to go anyplace in the United States in just a few hours. People in our country began to receive television broadcasts directly from many parts of the world. They also began to know what kind of weather to expect from day to day. These things were made possible by satellites.

Perhaps the greatest challenge of the 1960s and 1970s was learning about outer space. In 1969 two United States **astronauts,** or people who journey through space, walked on the moon. In 1973 a space station called *Skylab* was tested to see if people could live in space for a long time. And in 1977 the United States tested the first **space shuttle,** or spacecraft that can be used again and again. Spaceflights cost the United States billions of dollars. Why do you think

Thousands of people watched this fireworks display in honor of our country's birthday. What important symbol of the United States is shown in this picture? How do you think it is related to this celebration?

many people thought that our government should spend that money on other things?

A special birthday In 1976 our country celebrated a very special birthday. It had been 200 years since the United States had declared its independence from Britain. Our country had come a long way in 200 years. It had grown from thirteen states to fifty states. It had stretched from the Atlantic Ocean to the Pacific Ocean. And it had become one of the most important countries in the world. What do these things show about the spirit of our country's people?

Throughout 1976 Americans honored our country in many ways. But on July 4, 1976, Americans celebrated in a very special way. Why do you think this was so? The picture on this page shows one way in which our country's birthday was honored on that day.

wrap·up

- What were some problems our country faced in dealing with its large population?
- How did our country's government help to protect the rights of its citizens and to make life better for Americans?
- How did computers, jet airplanes, and satellites help Americans keep up with their rapidly changing world?

444

A Biographical Sketch

Fighting for what you believe

Be proud of who you are, and don't be afraid to fight for what you believe. These are two things Shirley Chisholm learned early in life. She grew up in New York City during the Great Depression. So she knew what it was like to be poor. But her parents encouraged her to study hard in order to get ahead in life.

Shirley Chisholm was elected to the lawmaking body of New York State in 1964. This was a great accomplishment for a black teacher who had worked her way up through local government jobs. But it was only the beginning for Shirley Chisholm. In 1968 she became the first black woman ever chosen to serve in the United States Congress.

Chisholm believed that our country's government must serve the needs of every citizen. So she worked to provide housing, health care, and schooling for people in need.

Shirley Chisholm faced her greatest challenge in 1972. She decided to seek the vote of her political party to run for the office of President of the United States. Why do you think this took great courage? Chisholm did not win, but no other woman had ever received so many votes at a major political convention.

Shirley Chisholm still works for the things she believes. She fights to change what she thinks is wrong, even when important people do not agree with her. She has always felt it is more important to do what she thinks is right than to be well liked. Shirley Chisholm's work has given hope to others who are willing to fight for what they believe.

445

2

Searching for peace
in an unsettled world

Representatives from many countries gathered at the United Nations to view pictures of the Soviet missile bases in Cuba.

Concern over trouble spots in the world During the 1960s and 1970s the United States worked to avoid war. In 1962 the Soviet Union began sending weapons to Cuba, which is about 90 miles (140 kilometers) from the coast of Florida. The United States learned that the Soviet Union was setting up nuclear **missiles** in Cuba. These are bomblike flying weapons that are rocket powered and can hit cities that are far away. Why do you think the United States was concerned about this? President Kennedy ordered the Soviet Union to remove the missiles. He also ordered a blockade around Cuba. The leaders of the Soviet Union finally agreed to Kennedy's terms, and the weapons were removed.

Trouble developed in the Middle East from time to time throughout the 1960s and 1970s. In 1967 Israel fought a war against the Arab countries of Egypt, Jordan, and Syria. The war lasted six days and proved to be a great victory for Israel. But the peace between Israel and the Arab countries was not a lasting one. War broke out again in

1973. In the late 1970s the leaders of Israel and of Egypt tried once again to end conflict and to set up a lasting peace in the Middle East. They asked the United States to help them do this. What did this show about our country's part in helping to end conflict in the world?

The end of a long struggle   Throughout the 1960s the United States continued to send aid to South Vietnam. This was done in the hope of stopping the spread of communism in Southeast Asia. In the early 1960s some American soldiers were sent to help train the South Vietnamese Army. But the United States became more and more involved in the fighting. Our country did not declare war on North Vietnam. But in 1964 Congress gave President Johnson the power to send South Vietnam all the help that was needed. By 1966 there were more than 500,000 American soldiers in Vietnam. American soldiers were dying at the rate of more than 100 a week.

Many people in the United States were strongly against taking part in the fighting in Vietnam. Peace talks were begun in 1968, but the fighting went on. Finally in 1973 a peace agreement was signed. American soldiers began returning home. For the United States, the war was over. But neither North Vietnam nor South Vietnam followed the terms of peace. South Vietnam finally surrendered to North Vietnam in 1975. A struggle that had gone on for more than twenty years had finally ended.

Showing concern for others   During the 1960s and 1970s our country did many things to help countries in need. In 1961 President Kennedy set up a plan to help Latin American countries. This plan was called the Alliance for Progress. It provided money for building hospitals, schools, and roads in certain Latin American countries. How do you think this plan showed that the United States was interested in helping other countries?

This member of the Peace Corps is teaching English to children in the Philippines.

The Peace Corps was also set up in 1961. This plan offered a different kind of aid to countries in need. United States citizens who joined the Peace Corps offered their services as teachers and workers. They went to live and work with poor people of other countries. Their goal was to help people help themselves by teaching them new and better ways of doing things. How do you think the Peace Corps helped further the cause of peace?

Improving relations with other countries   During the 1960s and 1970s the leaders of the United States worked to improve understanding among countries. One way they did this was to work with the leaders of other countries to weaken the threat of a possible nuclear war. In 1963 the United States, Britain, and the Soviet Union agreed to outlaw aboveground and underwater testing of nuclear weapons. And in 1969 the United States and the Soviet Union began meetings called the Strategic Arms Limitation Talks (SALT). These talks generally brought good results. Both countries agreed to cut back on the number of nuclear weapons they were making.

This picture shows representatives from the United States, the Soviet Union, and Britain signing the Nuclear Test-Ban Treaty.

A sharing of information and an exchange of ideas led to understanding among countries in the 1960s and 1970s. In 1975 the United States and the Soviet Union worked together on a spaceflight. Singers and dancers from the United States performed in other countries. And our country welcomed performers from other countries. Sports teams from the United States also played against teams from many other countries. Why do you think such exchanges of ideas and culture are important?

From left to right these pictures show Mrs. Carter visiting Brazil, President Carter visiting Nigeria, and President and Mrs. Nixon visiting mainland China.

Many leaders of the United States visited other countries as a sign of friendship and peace. The pictures on this page show such visits by some of our country's Presidents and First Ladies. During the 1970s the United States government allowed people from our country to visit mainland China and Cuba. Do you think such visits by United States leaders and other citizens help bring about peace and understanding among countries? Why or why not?

wrap·up

- How did the United States help to avoid war in some places and to stop the spread of communism during the 1960s and 1970s?
- What are some things our country did to further the cause of peace?
- How did the United States work to improve understanding among countries?

3

A culture of awareness

American writers   Since 1920 the number of Americans who read newspapers and magazines has greatly increased. By the late 1970s Americans were buying nearly 62 million newspapers a day. And more magazines were printed in the United States than in any other country. How do you think this increase in the reading of newspapers and magazines helped Americans become more aware of what was going on in the world?

Americans also read many books. During the 1920s and 1930s many American authors wrote about the way of life in our country. Some of these authors found fault with the way many Americans lived. F. Scott Fitzgerald and Sinclair Lewis were two such authors. They felt that people cared too much for money and were too concerned with just having fun.

During the 1930s and 1940s some American authors wrote about problems that concerned our country. *The Grapes of Wrath* by John Steinbeck tells the story of a family searching for a better life during the Great Depression. And *For Whom the Bell Tolls* by Ernest Hemingway tells how war affects people's lives. Other authors during the 1930s and 1940s wrote about certain parts of our country or of the world. Robert Frost wrote poems about life in New England. And Pearl Buck's *The Good Earth* tells about life in China.

Many American authors during the 1950s wrote about life in our country during that time. J. D. Salinger, Norman Mailer, and Truman Capote were three such authors. And black authors such as Gwendolyn Brooks and Langston Hughes wrote about what it meant to be black. In the 1960s and 1970s many books were written about true stories. One such book was Dee Brown's *Bury My Heart at Wounded*

Knee. It tells about the history of American Indians in our country.

During the 1920s and 1930s Eugene O'Neill and Lillian Hellman were two outstanding American **playwrights,** or writers of plays. Many of their plays show people searching for a deeper meaning in their life. During the 1940s and 1950s Arthur Miller was one of our country's favorite playwrights. His play *Death of a Salesman* tells the story of a person who fails at life. During the 1960s and 1970s Neil Simon wrote many plays that show what life is really like. Such a play is *The Odd Couple.* It tells the story of two friends who try to work out their problems together. Why do you think many Americans enjoy plays such as this?

Americans painters and architects   During the 1920s and 1930s many American artists painted scenes from American history and life. In the late 1940s, though, many artists in our country began painting **abstract pictures.** These are paintings in which the artists try to create a certain feeling. Jackson Pollock, Georgia O'Keeffe, and Malvin Gray Johnson were three such artists. During the 1950s and 1960s Norman

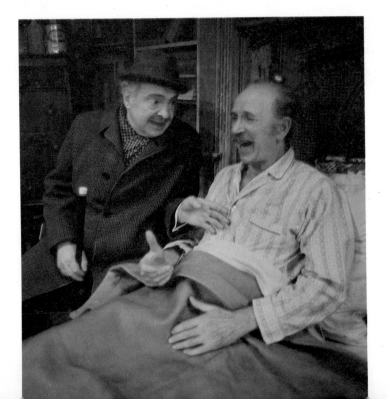

Neil Simon has written many plays that have been performed on Broadway. The picture on the right shows a scene from the Neil Simon play The Sunshine Boys. *This play is a comedy about two old-time performers who, after many years, go back on stage.*

Rockwell was a very popular American artist. Look at the picture of a Norman Rockwell painting on this page. Do you think this painting is true to life? Why or why not? In the 1960s artists began painting objects from everyday life such as soup cans. This style of art is called **pop art.**

By 1929 American architects had started using a new style. Frank Lloyd Wright had much to do with this. Wright believed a building should go with its surroundings. So he often used wood and stone as they appear in nature. Wright also believed a building should make good use of space and should be strong and safe. During the 1950s and 1960s architects such as Eliot Noyes and Minoru Yamasaki used some of Wright's ideas in the buildings they designed.

American music During the 1920s jazz was the most popular music in the United States. Louis Armstrong was one of the first great jazz stars. And jazz singers like Bessie Smith were known throughout our country. During the 1930s and 1940s songs about important happenings of the times were popular. Woodie Guthrie wrote songs about people during the Great Depression. And Irving Berlin wrote songs about World War II. Also during this time Americans listened to and danced to the music of big bands. And many

Millions of Americans are familiar with Norman Rockwell's work because of the many covers he did for The Saturday Evening Post. *Most of Rockwell's paintings show real people in real-life situations. Why do you think Rockwell called the painting above "After the Prom"?*

453

Elvis Presley was the most popular American singer in the history of rock 'n' roll music. He began performing in 1953 and soon had millions of fans throughout the world. During his career he had many hit records, and huge crowds attended his concerts.

songs from musicals such as *Oklahoma* and *South Pacific* were popular.

During the 1950s rock 'n' roll became the kind of music most teenage Americans listened to. Elvis Presley was the favorite rock 'n' roll singer of the times. Some songwriters of the 1960s wrote about things that they thought were wrong and needed to be changed in our country. Joan Baez and Bob Dylan were two such songwriters. They often wrote songs against the fighting in Vietnam. The 1970s saw a rise in the popularity of country music. This kind of music had its beginnings in the American South.

Radio, television, and movies In 1922 Americans began buying radios. Within ten years, more than 12 million families owned a radio. Radio changed the way of life for many people. It allowed Americans to be entertained right in their home. And it helped people to develop new interests. Throughout our country people listened to their favorite music or to well-known shows such as *Fibber McGee and Molly*. But radio was more than just a means of entertainment. It also was a means of learning about what was going on in the world. Why do you think this was important?

After World War II television replaced radio as the favorite pastime of the American people. By 1951 millions of Americans owned TV sets. Milton Berle became the first big TV star. And shows such as *Howdy Doody* and *I Love Lucy* were among the favorite early TV shows.

Television changed greatly over the years. By the 1970s most TV shows were in color, and TV screens were much larger than in the early days. TV also changed the way many Americans lived. Many people stayed home to watch TV instead of doing other things. And people heard about and viewed important world happenings almost as soon as they took place. Many people think that shows such as *Sesame Street* helped prepare young children for school. And people learned about important happenings of the past on TV. In the late 1970s a special show called *Roots* was presented on TV. It told the history of an American black family.

The first talking movie was made in 1927. It was called the *Jazz Singer*. Within two years the number of people in our country who attended movies nearly doubled. Even during the hard times of the 1930s people still went to movies. Many went to forget their troubles and to enjoy a few hours of entertainment. Stars such as W. C. Fields and Shirley Temple drew large crowds. In 1937 the Walt Disney film *Snow White and the Seven Dwarfs* was a big box-office hit.

The picture above shows a scene from the popular TV program Sesame Street. The picture below shows a scene from the Walt Disney movie Snow White and the Seven Dwarfs. What characters do you recognize in these two pictures?

Over the years movies changed. Sound and color were improved. Drive-in movies became popular. And the subject matter of many movies changed. More movies presented life as it really was. The film *Billy Jack* told the story of the life of American Indians during the 1970s. But other films of the 1970s were not so true to life. *Star Wars* was such a film. It told the story of what life might be like in a world totally different from the one people knew in the 1970s. Why do you think people liked such a film?

Sports and recreation Since the early 1920s the number of hours a week most Americans work has decreased. And the amount of vacation time most Americans receive has increased. Do you think these things have given Americans more free time? Why do you think so? Americans found many ways in which to spend their free time. Some enjoyed staying at

Star Wars was one of the most popular movies of the 1970s. Artoo-Detoo, shown on the left, was one of the stars of the movie.

home. Others enjoyed playing golf or tennis or going bowling or skiing. Some enjoyed fishing, boating, and camping. And during the 1950s surfing became a favorite pastime of many Americans. What kinds of things do you enjoy doing in your free time?

Many Americans enjoyed spending their free time watching sports. Throughout the years many great sports stars became favorites with the American people. There were baseball greats such as Babe Ruth, Jackie Robinson, and Hank Aaron. There were football stars such as Red Grange, Jim Brown, and Joe Namath. And there were boxers such as Jack Dempsey, Joe Louis, and Muhammad Ali. Women athletes also became favorites with sports fans. Gertrude Ederle gained fame by becoming the first woman to swim the English Channel. And Althea Gibson, Billie Jean King, and Chris Evert became well-known as three great tennis players.

Muhammad Ali, on the right in the top picture, and Billie Jean King, in the bottom picture, have both won many titles. How can you tell that watching sports is a popular pastime in our country?

wrap ·up

- How do the works of many American authors, playwrights, artists, architects, and songwriters show the American way of life?
- How did radio and television change the way of life for many Americans?
- How have many Americans spent their free time since the early 1920s?

Reading a pictograph

NUMBER OF PEOPLE TAKING PART IN OUTDOOR RECREATIONAL ACTIVITIES IN THE EARLY 1970s
(Rounded to the Nearest Million)

Camping	▲▲▲▲▲▲▲
Fishing	(fish icons, two rows)
Hiking	(hiker icons)
Bicycling	(bicycle icons)
Horseback Riding	(horseback rider icons)
Waterskiing	(waterskier icons)
Golf	(golf bag icons)
Tennis	(tennis racket icons)
Snow Skiing	(snow skier icons)

Each Figure Represents 1 Million People.

Use the pictograph to answer the following questions:

1. What does the pictograph show?

2. In which outdoor recreational activity did most people take part in the early 1970s? Which was the next-highest activity in which people took part?

3. How many more people took part in bicycling than in horseback riding in the early 1970s?

4. How many more people took part in hiking than in camping in the early 1970s?

5. How many people altogether took part in golf and tennis in the early 1970s?

6. Was the number of people who took part in waterskiing higher or was it lower than the number of people who took part in snow skiing? How much higher or lower was it?

Chapter-End Activities

The chapter-end activities may be done by writing the questions or statements and the answers on a separate sheet of paper or by writing just the answers on a separate sheet of paper, whichever your teacher desires.

Words and Terms

pop art   megalopolises
missiles   pollution
recycle   abstract pictures
playwrights   astronauts

_____ 1. Huge stretches of cities joined to one another

_____ 2. The changing of air, land, and water from clean to dirty

_____ 3. To make over into new goods

_____ 4. People who journey through space

_____ 5. Bomblike flying weapons powered by rockets

_____ 6. Writers of plays

_____ 7. Paintings in which the artists try to create a certain feeling

Fact Recall

1. What were some problems our country had to deal with during the 1960s and 1970s?

2. What helped Americans meet the challenge of a rapidly changing world?

3. What are some ways that the United States helped countries in need during the 1960s and 1970s?

4. In what ways did television change the way many Americans lived?

5. What are some of the things Americans enjoyed doing in their free time?

Concepts and Understandings

1. How did our country's government help to protect the rights of its citizens and make life better for Americans during the 1960s and 1970s?

2. How did our country's government work to improve relations with other countries during the 1960s and 1970s?

3. How have American literature and the arts since the early 1920s shown the American way of life?

Unit End

Main Ideas and Understandings

1. How did our country work for world peace during the 1920s? How did the automobile change the way of life for many Americans? What effect did the Great Depression have on the lives of many Americans? How did the New Deal help bring aid to people during the Great Depression? How did Americans help our country during World War II?

2. How did our government take an active role in our country's economy after World War II? What changes took place in American industries after World War II? How did Americans begin to fight for their civil rights in the 1950s? Why did the United States and the Soviet Union become involved in a cold war?

3. What were some ways our government worked to make life better for Americans during the 1960s and 1970s? How did the United States work to improve understanding among countries? How have American literature and the arts reflected the way of life in our country since the early 1900s?

Research Ideas

1. Equal rights for all citizens has been a major concern in our country for many years. Find out what each of the following people achieved in this regard: Marian Anderson, Jackie Robinson, Thurgood Marshall, Betty Friedan, Edward W. Brooke, Jesse Jackson, Gloria Steinem, Cesar Chavez, and Barbara Jordan. What

gains have American Indians made in their struggle for equal rights since 1920? What other groups of Americans are fighting for their equal rights?

2. Since the beginning of the space age our country has made many advances in its exploration of space. Find out how Wernher Von Braun contributed to our country's space program. Find out who the first American to orbit the earth was. What spacecraft took the first person to the moon? How have satellites changed our way of life? What are some space-age careers?

3. Many Americans have made important contributions in the fields of literature and the arts. Find out what Willa Cather, Edna St. Vincent Millay, Laura Ingalls Wilder, George Gershwin, Cole Porter, Leonard Bernstein, and Charles Schulz did. What contributions did Bobby Jones, Jesse Owens, Wilt Chamberlain, Lee Trevino, Mark Spitz, and Janet Guthrie make in the world of sports?

Activities and Projects

1. Plan a Roaring Twenties Day. Dress in the style of the 1920s, learn dances such as the Charleston, and sing songs that were popular during the 1920s. Write and perform plays showing the way of life during this time. Draw pictures of famous people who lived during the 1920s.

2. Record the number of hours a day you spend watching television and the number of hours a day you spend listening to the radio for one week. Make a chart of your findings. Compare your chart with those of your classmates.

REFERENCE MATERIALS
PRESIDENTS OF THE UNITED STATES

1.
George
Washington

5.
James
Monroe

9.
William
Henry
Harrison

2.
John
Adams

6.
John
Quincy
Adams

10.
John
Tyler

3.
Thomas
Jefferson

7.
Andrew
Jackson

11.
James K.
Polk

4.
James
Madison

8.
Martin
Van Buren

12.
Zachary
Taylor

13.
Millard
Fillmore

18.
Ulysses S.
Grant

23.
Benjamin
Harrison

14.
Franklin
Pierce

19.
Rutherford B.
Hayes

25.
William
McKinley

15.
James
Buchanan

20.
James A.
Garfield

26.
Theodore
Roosevelt

16.
Abraham
Lincoln

21.
Chester A.
Arthur

27.
William
Howard
Taft

17.
Andrew
Johnson

22. and 24.
Grover
Cleveland

28.
Woodrow
Wilson

29.
Warren G.
Harding

34.
Dwight D.
Eisenhower

39.
James E.
Carter

30.
Calvin
Coolidge

35.
John F.
Kennedy

31.
Herbert C.
Hoover

36.
Lyndon B.
Johnson

32.
Franklin D.
Roosevelt

37.
Richard M.
Nixon

33.
Harry S
Truman

38.
Gerald R.
Ford

GLOSSARY

When certain words related to the subject matter of *Understanding Our Country* are used for the first time, they are spelled in a special way to aid the reader in saying them. These words are also spelled in this special way in the glossary. The special spellings always appear in [ ]. Single-syllable words are spelled in small capital letters. When a word has two or more syllables, certain syllables are stressed more than others. In the special spelling of a word, the syllable with the heavier stress is spelled in large capital letters. The syllable with the lighter stress is spelled in small capital letters. The syllable or syllables not stressed are spelled in small letters. If there are ( ) around one or more letters within the [ ], those letters may or may not be said.

Below are the letters and letter groups used for the special spellings. Opposite each letter or letter group is a description of the way each should be said.

Letter or letter group	Say like
a	a in *hat* [HAT]
ah	a in *father* [FAHTH-ur] and o in *hot* [HAHT]
aw	a in *all* [AWL] and o in *order* [AWRD-ur]
ay	a in *face* [FAYS]
ch	*ch* in *child* [CHYLD] and in *much* [MUHCH]
ee	e in *equal* [EE-kwuhl]

Letter or letter group	Say like
eh	e in *let* [LEHT]
eye	the first i in *iris* [EYE-ruhs]
g	g in *go* [GOH]
ih	i in *hit* [HIHT]
j	j in *joke* [JOHK]
oh	o in *open* [OH-puhn]
oo	oo in *food* [FOOD] and u in *rule* [ROOL]
ow	ou in *out* [OWT]
oy	oi in *voice* [VOYS]

Letter or letter group	Say like
u	u in *put* [PUT] and oo in *foot* [FUT]
uh	u in *cup* [KUHP]
ur	er in *term* [TURM] and ir in *sir* [SUR]
y	i in *nice* [NYS]
yoo	u in *unity* [YOO-nuht-ee]
yu	u in *unite* [yu-NYT]
zh	s in *treasure* [TREHZH-ur]

Abolitionists [AB-uh-LIHSH-(uh-)nuhsts] People who worked to end slavery in the middle 1800s.

Abstract pictures Paintings in which the artists try to create a certain feeling.

Adapt To get used to something, such as a new environment.

Adobe A mixture of desert clay and straw.

Advertise To tell the public, as companies tell the public about their goods.

Almanacs Small, yearly magazines with information about many subjects. Some also have jokes, stories, and wise sayings.

Amendments Changes or additions made in a constitution or a law.

Anasazi [AH-nuh-SAH-zee] One of the early groups of Indians in North America. These people lived in the part of the present-day United States where Utah, Arizona, New Mexico, and Colorado meet.

Annexed   Added, such as land added to our country.

Anthropologists [AN(T)-thruh-PAHL-uh-juhsts] Scientists who study people, including their physical features, environmental and social relations, and culture.

Apprentices   People who worked with master craftspeople for several years to learn a job.

Archaeologists [AHR-kee-AHL-uh-juhsts] Scientists who study the remains of people who lived long ago.

Architect   A person who plans buildings.

Articles of Confederation   A set of laws setting forth the powers of both the United States government and the state governments that were in use from 1781 to 1789.

Artifacts [AHRT-uh-FAKTS]   Things that have been left behind that were made by people.

Assassinated   Suddenly murdered.

Assembly line   A way of arranging parts and workers in a line in order to made goods.

Astronauts   People who journey through space.

Astronomy   The study of the sun, the moon, and the stars.

Automation   The use of machines to run other machines.

Backcountry   The very edge of land that colonists had settled.

Bill of Rights   The first ten amendments to the United States Constitution. They list rights that cannot be taken away from the people by the government.

Black codes   Laws passed in the South during Reconstruction that said what blacks could and could not do.

Blockade   To control by the use of troops or warships what enters or leaves a place.

Border states   Southern states that decided to remain in the Union during the War Between the States. These slave states lay between other slave states and northern free states.

Boundary lines   Lines on a map that show where something begins or ends.

Boycott   To refuse to buy or use goods.

Cabinet   A group of people made up of the heads of the executive departments of government who help the President take care of the business of our country's government.

Calumet   A peace pipe smoked by certain groups of American Indians.

Canyons   Deep, narrow valleys with steep sides.

Capital   A seat of government, for a state or for a country.

Carpetbaggers   People from the North who went to the South to seek new fortunes during Reconstruction.

Cash crops   Crops that are raised to be sold.

Chart   Something that shows information in an organized way. Charts are arranged in columns and rows.

Civil rights   A person's rights as a citizen.

Climate   The kind of weather a place has over a long time. It is generally described in terms of monthly temperature and precipitation.

Cold war   A war of ideas that is generally carried on without shooting or bloodshed.

Colony   One or more settlements started by people who keep ties with the country from which they came.

Committee of Correspondence   A small group of colonists who told other colonists what the British were doing.

Communism   A form of government that is generally ruled by a committee that has complete power over a country and its people.

Communists   People who favor a form of government that is generally ruled by a committee that has complete power over a country and its people.

Compromise [KAHM-pruh-MYZ]   A plan by which each side gives up something it wants in order to gain something else.

Confederacy   The Confederate States of America. It was also known as the South during the War Between the States.

Conquerors   People who use power to overcome others.

Conservation   A means of protecting and wisely using the world around you.

Conserve   To save, such as a natural resource.

Constitution   A plan of government. The United States Constitution became the law of our country in 1788.

Construction   The business of building homes and factories.

Consumers   People who use goods and services.

Creditors   People to whom money is owed.

Culture   The way of life of a group of people.

Debtors   People who owe money.

Declaration of Independence   A paper stating that the colonies were no longer ruled by Britain but were free and independent states.

Depression   A time when many businesses fail, and many people lose their jobs.

Dictators   Leaders who have complete power over the country in which they rule.

Dig   A place where archaeologists have dug up the land to look for remains showing that a certain group of people once lived there.

Direct primary   A means of allowing people to vote to select citizens to run for office in a general election.

Disarm   To remove weapons.

Distance scale   The part of a map that shows how much of the earth's surface is represented on the map. A distance scale uses a small measure to stand for a larger measure.

Distributed   Spread throughout a certain area.

Economy   The way people make, get, and use goods and services.

Embargo   An order stopping ships or certain goods from leaving or entering a country.

Environment [ihn-VY-ruhn-muhnt]   The world around you.

Executive branch   The branch of government that carries out the laws. The President of the United States heads this branch of our country's government.

Expedition   A journey that a group of people make with a certain goal in mind.

Explorers   People who make journeys in search of new things.

Exported   Goods sent from one country to another country.

Extinct [ihk-STIHNG(K)T]   No longer existing.

Fairs   Places where people buy, sell, or trade goods. They are also places to have fun.

Fertilize   To add things to the soil that plants need to grow.

Flax   A plant from which linen cloth is made.

Fossils [FAHS-uhlz]   The hardened remains of animals and plants.

Freedmen   Those people who had been slaves during the War Between the States.

Frontier   The land on which people build new farms and settlements.

Geography [jee-AHG-ruh-fee]   The study of the earth and how people use the earth.

Governor   The head of a state government.

Graph   A drawing that uses numbers to compare certain kinds of information.

Habitants [(H)AB-ih-TAHZ]   Farmers who worked the land owned by seigneurs in New France.

Haciendas [(H)AHS-ee-EHN-duhz]   Large farms belonging to landowners in New Spain.

Hemisphere   Half of the earth. The equator divides the Northern Hemisphere and the Southern Hemisphere. The prime meridian and the 180° meridian divide the Eastern Hemisphere and the Western Hemisphere.

Hills   Raised lands that are not as high as mountains.

Historians   People concerned with the written records of people and their events over a long period of time.

Hogans   Houses that some American Indians built by covering a heavy wooden framework with a thick layer of earth.

Hohokam [HOH-hoh-KAHM]   One of the early groups of Indians in North America. These people lived in the desert where the Gila River and the Salt River meet in what is now southern Arizona.

Hopewell   One of the largest groups of Mound Builders. These early Indians lived in the Ohio River valley and in the Mississippi River valley.

House of Burgesses   The first lawmaking body in the English colonies in North America. It began in Virginia in 1619.

House of Representatives   One house of the United States Congress. The number of members from each state depends upon the number of people living in that state.

Ice Age   One of four major movements of extremely thick ice that covered millions of square miles (square kilometers) of the earth. These movements took place thousands of years ago.

Immigrants   People who come to one country from another continent or country to live.

Imported   Goods brought into one country from another country.

Indentured [ihn-DEHN-churd] **servants**   People who agreed to work for others for a certain period of time in return for their fare on a ship.

Independence   Freedom.

Initiative   A means of allowing people to vote directly for a law that they want passed.

Inn   A public place used by people for sleeping, eating, and drinking.

Installment plan   A means by which people can buy goods by making regular monthly payments over a long period of time.

Intendant [Ihn-TEHN-duhnt]   A chief officer chosen by the king of France to be the head of the government of New France.

Interchangeable   The capability of switching something, such as a part of a machine, from one item to another of the same kind.

Invented   Made for the first time, such as a new machine.

Irrigation [IHR-uh-GAY-shuhn]   The bringing of water to land by using human-made means such as ditches or sprinkling.

Islands   Bodies of land that have water on all sides.

Judicial branch   The branch of government that explains the laws. This branch of our country's government is made up of a number of different courts.

Jury   A group of people chosen to hear a court case.

Kivas [KEE-vuhz]   Underground rooms used for religious purposes by some early Indians in North America.

Land bridge   A strip of land connecting two larger pieces of land.

Landforms   Different kinds of land surfaces.

Latin America   The land south of the United States where Spanish- and Portuguese-speaking people live.

Legislative branch   The branch of government that makes the laws. This branch of our country's government is made up of the House of Representatives and the Senate.

Lines of latitude   The east-west lines on a globe or a map.

Lines of longitude   The north-south lines on a globe or a map.

Long drive   A means of getting cattle from Texas to railroads in Kansas and Nebraska during the late 1800s.

Longhouses   Large houses built by some of the Eastern Woodlands Indians in which six to ten families lived.

Loyalists   Colonists who did not want to break ties with Britain.

Mammoth [MAM-uhth]   An animal something like an elephant, only larger, that once lived in the Americas.

Manufacturing   Making raw materials into usable goods.

Map key   The part of a map that explains what the map symbols mean.

Mardi Gras [MAHRD-ee-GRAH]   A large kind of party brought to our country by the French. This party takes place in February or March and lasts for about two weeks.

Marketing   The selling of goods.

Markets   Places where people buy, sell, or trade goods.

Mass production   The making of many goods of the same kind quickly.

Meetinghouse   A building used for worship.

Megalopolises [MEHG-uh-LAHP-uh-luhs-uhz]   Huge stretches of cities joined to one another.

Merchants   People who trade with others.

Meridians [muh-RIHD-ee-uhnz]   The north-south lines of longitude on a globe or a map.

Middle colonies   New York, New Jersey, Delaware, and Pennsylvania.

Militia [muh-LIHSH-uh]   A group of citizens trained as soldiers.

Millers   People who grind grains such as corn and wheat into flour.

Minutemen   Colonists who were to be ready to fight upon very short notice.

Missiles   Bomblike flying weapons that are rocket powered and can hit cities that are far away.

Missionaries   Those who want to teach their religion to others.

Mounds   Large heaps of dirt and stone built by some groups of early American Indians living in the Ohio River valley and in the Mississippi River valley.

Mountains   Raised lands that are much higher than the land around them. Many mountains have high peaks.

Mouth   The place where a river flows into a larger body of water.

Nationalism [NASH-nuhl-IHZ-uhm]   The act of feeling love for and loyalty to one's country and of being concerned about the interests of one's country as a whole.

Naval stores   Things such as tar and pitch used by shipbuilders in making and repairing wooden ships.

Needs   Things all people must have in order to live.

New Deal   A new government program set up by President Franklin Roosevelt and his advisers to deal with the problems of the Great Depression.

New England colonies   New Hampshire, Rhode Island, Massachusetts, and Connecticut.

Nomads   People who do not settle in one place.

Nuclear weapons   Weapons that release energy due to changes within certain atoms.

Parallels [PAR-uh-LEHLZ]   The east-west lines of latitude on a globe or a map.

Patriots   Colonists who favored the American cause for freedom from Britain.

Pemmican   Dried buffalo meat mixed with berries and melted fat.

Peninsula [puh-NIHN(T)-s(uh-)luh] A large piece of land that has water on almost all sides.

Permanent Lasting, such as a settlement.

Petroleum [puh-TROH-lee-uhm] Oil.

Physical maps Maps that show how the land looks.

Pilgrims A group of people who went to Holland because they wanted to leave the Church of England. Later, they moved to America in hopes of finding religious freedom. They called the place where they settled Plymouth.

Plains Low flatlands that generally are level.

Plantations Huge farms on which people grow one or two major cash crops.

Plateaus [pla-TOHZ] Level lands that are higher than the land around them.

Playwrights Writers of plays.

Political maps Maps that show how people have divided the land.

Political parties Groups of people with certain ideas about how government should be run and who try to get their candidates elected to government offices.

Pollution The changing of the state of our air, land, and water from clean to dirty.

Pony express A means by which mail was carried across the West by riders on fast horses.

Pop art A style of art in which artists paint objects from everyday life such as soup cans.

Popular sovereignty [SAHV-(uh-)ruhn-tee] A political position that says final political power belongs to the people. During the middle 1800s it was used to let people living in new lands decide if they would allow slavery or not.

Population The number of people in a certain area.

Ports Harbor cities.

Post roads Roads built during colonial days for riders carrying mail. Such roads connected cities in New England with New York City and Philadelphia.

Potlatch A large feast at which the host gave gifts to the guests. It was the custom of the Northwest Coast Indians.

Pottery Things made of baked clay.

Precipitation Water that falls to the earth, generally as rain or snow.

Prohibition An end to the making and selling of alcohol.

Propaganda The spreading of ideas to further one's own cause or to hurt someone else's cause.

Prosperity A state of well-being. As applied to economics, it is an increase in business activity or a condition when the economy is healthy and growing.

Puritans A group of people who went to America because they did not like the Church of England. The place where they settled became known as the Massachusetts Bay Colony.

Quaker A member of the Religious Society of Friends. Many members of this group went to Pennsylvania with William Penn.

Radiocarbon dating A means of finding out the age of something that was once alive or of something made from material that once was living.

Rationed Allowed to buy only certain amounts of goods that are hard to get.

Realists People who present things as they really are.

Reapers Machines used for cutting grain.

Recall A means of allowing people to remove an elected leader from public office.

Reconstruction Rebuilding. The time in our country's history that began after the War Between the States and ended in 1877.

Recycle To make over into new goods.

Referendum   A means of allowing people to vote to get rid of a law that a state lawmaking-body has already passed.

Reform   The improving of things through change.

Represent   To speak and act for someone else. People vote for others to represent them in the government.

Republic   A kind of government in which the power to govern comes from the people, but the people choose others to represent them in the government. Our United States government is a republic.

Reservations   Government-owned lands set aside for the American Indians.

Rural   Of or belonging to the country.

Sachem [SAY-chuhm]   A North American Indian chief, especially of a group of Eastern Woodlands Indians known as the Algonquian Indians.

Sagas [SAHG-uhz]   Stories of heroic deeds and adventures, such as the Vikings told about their journeys.

Satellite   A human-made object that circles the earth.

Scalawags   People in the South who remained true to the United States and who worked with the new southern governments during Reconstruction.

Scale   The size of a map compared with what it represents. A small measure on a map stands for a larger measure on the earth.

Sea dogs   English sea captains who robbed Spanish treasure ships.

Secede   To withdraw from an organization, as some southern states did from the Union in the early 1860s.

Secret ballot   A means of allowing people to vote in a place and in a manner whereby others cannot see how they vote.

Sectionalism   The act of giving more thought to one's own part of a country than to the country as a whole.

Segregated [SEHG-rih-GAYT-uhd]   To be separated from, such as one group of people from another.

Seigneurs [sayn-YURZ]   Landowners in New France.

Selectmen   People who ran the town governments in the New England colonies.

Senate   One house of the United States Congress. Each state has two members, no matter how many people live in that state.

Senior citizens   Old people.

Settlement house   A place where people are able to form a neighborhood center to provide certain community services.

Shamans [SHAHM-uhnz]   Medicine men that some groups of American Indians believed could cure the sick.

Silent movies   Moving pictures without sound.

Skyscrapers   Many-storied buildings.

Slave states   Those states in which people could own slaves.

Slums   Parts of a city or town that are crowded, are dirty, and generally have poor housing.

Source   The place where a river begins.

Southern colonies   Virginia, Maryland, North Carolina, South Carolina, and Georgia.

Space shuttle   A spacecraft that can be used again and again.

Speaker   Leader of the United States House of Representatives.

Specialize   To do just one kind of work or to take part in just one kind of activity.

Stock   Shares in a company.

Stockade   A line of strong posts built around a settlement for defense.

Strait   A narrow body of water connecting two larger bodies of water.

Strike   A means by which workers refuse to work in order to try to gain certain things such as more pay, shorter working hours, and better working conditions.

Suburbs   Small urban communities on the outskirts of cities.

Surrender   To give up.

Surveyors   People who measure land, make maps, and mark boundary lines.

Tariff   A tax set on goods brought into one country from another country.

Telegraph   A means of sending messages by code over an electric wire.

Temperature   How hot or cold a place is.

Tenements   Cheaply and poorly built housing units.

Tepees   Cone-shaped houses usually made of buffalo skins sewn together. These houses could be taken down and moved. They were especially used by the Plains Indians of North America.

Territory   Land that is part of our country but is not yet a state.

Textiles   Cloth.

Totem poles   Tall wooden columns carved by the Northwest Coast Indians to tell a family's history.

Transcontinental railroad   A railroad going from the East coast to the West coast of our country.

Travois [truh-VOY]   A means used by the Plains Indians to move their belongings. It had two trailing poles that supported a platform or net for carrying a load.

Tributary   A river that flows into a larger river.

Tutor   A private teacher.

Underground Railroad   The secret routes and safe hiding places used by slaves who escaped from the South during part of the 1800s.

Union   The United States of America. It was also known as the North during the War Between the States.

Unions   Groups of workers who join together to gain the things they think they should have.

Urban   Of or belonging to the city.

Viceroy   A chief officer chosen by the king of Spain to be the head of the government of New Spain.

Vikings   People who lived in Norway, Sweden, or Denmark a long time ago. These people, also known as the Norse, might have come to the Americas before Columbus did.

Village green   Public land in the center of towns in the New England colonies.

Volcanoes   Hills or mountains formed of lava, or hot rock, thrown up from inside the earth.

Wagon train   A row of wagons for carrying people and supplies, often used by American settlers.

Wampum   Colored beads woven into designs by some North American Indians to help them remember certain things. The same designs always had the same meaning. Wampum strands or belts were used as money and as ornaments.

War Between the States   The war that took place in our country between 1861 and 1865. It was fought between the Union and the Confederacy.

War for Independence   The war between the colonists and Britain that took place in our country between 1776 and 1781.

Wickiups   Houses made of branches and grasses laid over a light framework of poles. These houses were built by some Southwest Indians.

Wigwams   Cone-shaped or dome-shaped houses built by covering pointed poles with strips of bark or other materials. These houses were built by some Eastern Woodlands Indians.

Wilderness   The woods or part of the land that has been changed very little by people.

INDEX

References in boldface type indicate pages on which words or terms are defined.
References marked c. refer to a chart, those marked g. refer to a graph, those marked
ill. refer to an illustration, and those marked m. refer to a map.